THE HIDDEN JO

Also by Lavinia Byrne and published by SPCK:

WOMEN BEFORE GOD:

The Search for a Way of Celebrating the
Identity and Experience of Believing Women (1988)

SHARING THE VISION:

A Creative Encounter Between
Religious and Lay Life (1989)

THE HIDDEN TRADITION:

Women's Spiritual Writings Rediscovered (editor; 1991)

THE HIDDEN JOURNEY

Missionary Heroines in Many Lands

———◆———

EDITED BY

LAVINIA BYRNE

First published in Great Britain 1993
Society for Promoting Christian Knowledge
Holy Trinity Church
Marylebone Road
London NW1 4DU

British Library Cataloguing-in-Publication Data
A catalogue record for this book is available from the British Library

ISBN 0–281–04700–6

Typeset by Action Typesetting Ltd, Gloucester
Printed in Great Britain at
The University Press, Cambridge

I am grateful to the following for permission to reproduce copyright material:

Methuen for Dorothy L. Sayers' *Creed or Chaos?*;
The Epworth Press for Dora Greenwell's *Two Lives*;
SCM Press for Kathleen Bliss' *We the People*, J. H. Oldham's *Florence Allshorn*, Olive Wyon's *Living Springs* and *On the Way*, and a member of St Julian's *Notebooks of Florence Allshorn*;
Hodder & Stoughton for Lady Hosie's *Jesus and Women* and Flora Laarson's *My Best Men Are Women*;
Lutterworth Press for Mildred Cable and Francesca French's *Wall of Spears*;
University of British Columbia Press for W. L. Morton's *God's Galloping Girl*;
James Clarke & Co. for *Women Talking*;
The Convent of St Mary the Virgin for *A Memoire of Mother Annie Louise*;
Longman's Green & Co. for Lucy Menzies' *Collected Papers of Evelyn Underhill*;
Peter Lang, New York, for Efiong Utak's *From New York to Ibadan*;
The Friends' United Press for Algie Newlin's *Charity Cook*;
Victor Gollancz for Dorothy L. Sayer's *Unpopular Opinions*;
Cargate Press for Olive Wyon's *The Altar Fire*;
Salvationist Publishing for Solveig Smith's *By Love Compelled*;
May Bounds for *Medical Mission to Mizoram*;
Pauline Webb for *Women of Our Company* and *Women of Our Time*.

For complete publication details, see the source notes and the Bibliography.
I have made every effort to trace and acknowledge copyright holders of the materials in this anthology; information on any omissions should be communicated to the publishers, who will make full acknowledgement in future editions.

*This book is dedicated to
the memory of
Mary Ward
Teresa Ball
Teresa Dease
and all the missionary heroines who have taken the
Institute of the Blessed Virgin Mary
to many lands*

CONTENTS

ACKNOWLEDGEMENTS

———

I am tempted to dedicate this book to archivists and second-hand book-dealers everywhere. Many of the books which recount the history of missionary women have survived for the very simple reason that missionary societies and church historians have so faithfully kept the records and archived their history without exercising constraint or censorship on those parts of it which relate to the experience of women; additional copies have survived because second-hand booksellers have bothered to hedge their bets. Someone, one day, was bound to turn up and ask for *Peerless Women, Missionary Heroines in Many Lands, Two Lady Missionary Women in Tibet* and the host of books which I have enjoyed collecting over the past eighteen months. I now have seven hundred of them, and the collection is growing all the time because of the generosity of friendly donors, or people who have lent me their treasured books. I can thank certain archivists and librarians by name: Rosemary Keen from the Church Missionary Society, Gordon Taylor from the Salvation Army Heritage Centre, Malcolm J. Thomas, Tabitha Driver, Rosamund Cummings and Sylvia Carlyle from the Religious Society of Friends.

I can also thank donors and lenders by name: Dr Pauline Webb, Beth Allen from the Quaker Home Service, the Religious of the Sacred Heart of Jesus in the United Kingdom, the Sisters Faithful Companions of Jesus in Canada and in Australia, Revd Flora Winfield, Revd Janet Rutherford, Margaret Quayle, Canon and Mrs Thorpe, Mr and Mrs Roberts; Leslie Orr Macdonald from the Church of Scotland kindly allowed me to read a chapter entitled 'Scottish Missionary Women' from her (as yet unpublished) doctoral thesis.

The support of second-hand book-dealers is harder to categorize. Nevertheless, I cannot let Michael Pickering from SPCK's head-quarters on the Marylebone Road in London go unnamed. He has been a real ally. The Church of Scotland's bookshop in Glasgow, Evangelical bookshops in Bath and Durham and Hull, SPCK in Winchester, an unpromising looking bookshop in west Belfast where theology and pornography sat (or rather reclined) cheek by jowl, an alphabet of booksellers from Broadstairs to Wells, Cambridge to Swansea – all have helped me by bothering to hang on to stock which even they valued by setting prices which could be met in loose change rather than megabucks.

I have been supported by fellow second-hand bookshop enthusiasts as well. The most influential of these has been John Reardon, General Secretary of the Council of Churches for Britain and Ireland. His whole-hearted support for the work of the Ecumenical Decade of Churches in Solidarity with Women has come to me as no surprise. To discover that he is a book collector as well is a bonus.

This list of acknowledgements would be quite incomplete were I not to thank Mary Houston by name. Without her secretarial help and assistance the book could never have been turned around in time. Both of us were grateful to Rachel Lidgett who provided further backup support in typing the extracts and quotations.

Finally, I must thank Judith Longman, former editorial director at SPCK. Yet again her timely comments have spurred me on; yet again I have been supported by Brendan Walsh and his other colleagues at SPCK who have played their part in ensuring that these accounts of the hidden journey of missionary women should be brought into the light. In a decade of evangelism, as well as one in which the Churches are being asked to show their solidarity with women, I have once again had demonstrable evidence that SPCK continues to stand in the best kind of missionary tradition, concerned to inform and educate and so lead to informed and educated faith. I should also add my thanks to David Mackinder for his meticulous work on the copy.

I completed this book in the week in which the General Synod of the Church of England voted to ordain women to the priesthood. I leave to the reader the excitement of making connections and drawing conclusions between what they will read here and the experience of those of us who, as ordained or lay women, whatever our Church, are still seeking to put the gospel in place in all we are and do and speak in Christ's name.

INTRODUCTION

—

This collection of writings by missionary women forms a companion volume to *The Hidden Tradition*. In collecting the texts I discovered many of the same themes and mechanisms in place. The themes gave me the form of this book by supplying the content of each chapter. For what we have here is a collection of writings which demonstrate that in the mission fields — virtually uniquely — women were called to exercise the most primitive ministries of all, those of the gospel itself. That is why I have chosen the text from Luke 4.18–19, where Jesus identifies his own ministry, as the common core around which the book's themes constellate.

Chapter 1 looks at examples of the calls which the missionary women heard, because, like Jesus, they could claim, 'The Spirit of the Lord is upon me'. The chapter title, 'Experiencing the call', is taken from the writings of a Welsh missionary, May Bounds. Her account is a sample of the many ways in which God spoke to the eighty women whose stories are recorded in this book. So who does the calling, and how? Who does the telling, and how? What the reader soon discovers is that the missionary call story is a startling witness to the power of a God who deals directly with women. What is disclosed here is a God who speaks within history and as part of that history, a God whose purpose is the freedom and empowerment of women, and who would take women to the furthest ends of the earth to demonstrate what this empowerment could look and feel like.

1

Some of these are first-hand accounts like May Bounds'; some are narrated by admiring biographers. The need to 'tell out' the story of a missionary call led to various developments. Firstly, it gave rise to a wealth of oral history. Women who told these stories in Ladies' Circles, Twilight, Sisterhood or Bright Hour groups handed on the tradition by word of mouth. Groups which met to prepare parcels or to knit for the missions became a seed-bed where this oral tradition could flourish. At its best this meant that the true heroines were celebrated in style; at its worst it meant that letters home from the missions (especially in the case of religious communities) were treated as private and not for communication beyond the magic circle.

Secondly, this need to tell out the glorious deeds of God in the lives of the missionary women led to the development of missionary writing as a distinct genre. The stories had to be told because they had become incorporated into the missionary purpose itself. They were inspirational and created a chain reaction; the example of those whom God had called served as a catalyst to fresh missionary vocations. At a time in Christian history when it is easy to complain that a sense of vocation seems absent, perhaps we might usefully ask if we have been telling enough stories to each other. And, in the case of women in particular, we might ask if one of our problems is that many of the stories which might be told nowadays are no longer about empowerment, freedom and love.

Chapter 2 picks up the theme of journey. I have called it by a somewhat esoteric name. Alice Meynell supplies us with a lovely metaphor when she uses the phrase 'I, child of process' in her poem 'I am the Way'. The way of the missionary women was the way of the gospels, a way of service and love that set them free. It was also a way that had been identified by Jesus, a way that is Jesus. Unlike the books of regular travel-writers, missionary writing has a specific quality to it. After all, what mattered was what lay at the end of the journey, not what happened *en route*. Nor would these women be inclined to complain about discomfort in their service of the Lord Jesus. And so their accounts fix on the people they met rather than the monuments they visited; the food they ate rather than the sights that they saw. Their first impressions are important to observe, because they would prove the way in for the missionary women. What first drew their attention first drew their interest, and so, inexorably, their story and that of the women they met became intertwined. But once again what we discover is a God who works within the warp and weft of their encounters, not at one remove from it.

Yet the idea of journey is also a metaphor. The missionary women's was an inward as well as an outward journey. Through exposure to *all* that they met, the missionary women had to begin to take note and to assess and to make these connections. In this sense what happened *en route* was extraordinarily important — for them certainly, but also for us, because nowadays we are inclined to use language about growth and development, about integration and wholeness, without examining if these are experienced differently by women and whether their content should not also be rather different. In these accounts we learn about how women deal with the unfamiliar, with loss, with pain, with friendship, and with God.

Any book which seeks to reclaim the history of women — whether contemporary attempts at reportage and oral history, or the work of reclamation undertaken here — runs a terrible risk. In *The Hidden Tradition* I kept my own comments and interpretation to a very minimum; the texts had their own authority, I believed, and so it was necessary for them to stand in their own right. The women who wrote them were, after all, the subjects rather than the object of their own discourse. With subtle editing I hoped to set up a conversation between them, so that they could comment on each other and initiate a conversation. The book was intended to be an aid to personal or group reflection, as well as a resource for assessing the contribution of women to Christian spirituality. A conversational approach, with little editorial comment, seemed to serve that purpose best.

At the beginning of Chapter 3 of the present volume I faced a dilemma. How does an editor responsibly hold in balance a critical understanding that has arisen from sheer exposure to the texts — and to the many thousands of alternative texts which could have been selected — with the legitimate desire for commentary on the part of the reader and the equally legitimate rights of the missionary women themselves? How can their accents most authentically be heard? How can the corporate witness of what they undertook best be critiqued, evaluated and celebrated? A golden rule would seem to me to be that any comments should not be personal. In that way they will elucidate without attacking, they will clarify without judging. In this way the missionary women are neither patronized and cheapened, nor sentimentalized by a romantic, heroic glow.

This is the note Chapter 3, in particular, seeks to strike. After all, what are in question here are the most truly authentic words and deeds of the missionary women. We catch them here at the interface of their encounter with the divine, at the place at which they sought to communicate what was most precious to them, their very identity in Christ. The theme of the chapter is the preaching ministry of women, done in thought, word and deed. The title, 'Thy prophet still', comes from the writings of one of Catherine Booth's granddaughters. For here we catch the missionary women at their most prophetic, preaching the word, and discovering what this word should be. Here we discern them struggling to understand what their access to the Scriptures could mean for those with whom they worked. How could the good news be good within the shut-in zenanas, the huts and homes, the market-places and missionary compounds to which they had brought it? How could it strike the prophetic note of the chapter title by meeting the question, 'We never heard such words. Does it mean for us women?'

Not simply the preaching but also the teaching ministry of women came into its own in the mission field. Education became a most persuasive vehicle for change. Almost single-handed, the missionary educational enterprise turned around the lives of countless women because it enabled them to inhabit a new set of experiences and call these their own. So the anonymous Indian woman's question, 'How could she learn?', is critical and gives the chapter heading. For learning challenged the established way of life, and an educated class of women were empowered to ask the question 'Why?' as well as 'How?' of structures and systems which oppressed them. So Chapter 4 looks at accounts of the missionary women as teachers.

What did they teach, and how, and why? Detailed answers to these questions are not recorded. What we do discover, however, are accounts which testify to the flexibility and imagination they brought to their task. Very quickly they latched on to the idea that in offering education they were offering something which lay at the very heart of the gospel. For not only would an educated woman be able to read, and so to read the Bible; more than that, she would be able to think with 'the mind of Christ Jesus'. Scriptural values and concepts would become her own; she would be truly converted. What they could not have anticipated was the lightning speed with which this transformation would open to the women they taught a whole new vision about accepted roles and the proper ordering of society. About what boys should do and girls should do, about who should become doctors and teachers and eventually lawyers and priests. Interestingly, those who opposed the whole educational enterprise and the teaching which the missionary women offered were more perceptive about the changes it would bring than they themselves ever were. The missionary women had a much less exalted idea of what they were doing than those who resisted them. And the verdict of history recognizes that the opponents of education for and by women were quite right; nothing would ever be the same again.

In Luke 4 Jesus stands before the crowd gathered in the synagogue at Nazareth and tells them that God's call, of necessity, is a call to freedom. The women missionaries too found themselves proclaiming a gospel of freedom. At first they did this in quite generalized ways. Yet they soon found themselves grappling with specifics, and Chapter 5 introduces us to some of these. The Misses French and Cable who contribute the chapter heading, 'Defying all prison walls', were quite clear: without the gospel there was no hope. Women would always be the losers, at the receiving end of mockery, their needs trivialized and dismissed out of hand.

Yet there are sophisticated issues at stake when one culture meets another, when Christianity applies moral sanctions which stand in judgement over other culture's norms. The women missionaries grappled with a range of issues and customs and practices which were distinctly untheoretical: drink, drugs, sex, the lot. They had a bottom line and came to apply it with a dogged sense of purpose, as though the freedom they had so recently acquired themselves gave them an unerring nose for it wherever it could be found.

Hence the energy with which they grappled with the medical agenda. Jesus declared his hand when he both spoke of healing and used a healing ministry as a sign that the kingdom of God was in place. The blind would recover their sight. Women have for centuries been agents of healing; the irony is that many have been burned at the stake or drowned for this very reason. The medicinal training or gifts they have received and practised have frequently been perceived to be part of a hidden lore, a distinctive subculture with witches and midwives and things that go bump in the night. Chapter 6 presents us with a sanitized version of all of this. The sturdy, gospel-based convictions of the missionary women meant they were all a long way way from some of the agenda of present-day alternative and holistic medicine.

This chapter is the shortest in the book because the material it relates demonstrates more clearly than any other that the missionary women arrived with the normative certainties of their generation in place.

Come what may, they would battle — in Betty Stead's stirring words — in the cause of hygiene and health. Nowadays we might lament the native cures and remedies which their ministry ruled out of order. They would be less impressed. For their campaign for health was part of a moral crusade. And yet the wonderful irony is that women nurses and doctors, by aspiring to total orthodoxy and the rule of hygiene, were eventually to spearhead medical initiatives such as the hospice movement and alternative therapies and well-women (and men) clinics. The healing ministry of Jesus took women to places where the kingdom would speak to their most intimate concerns, and all would benefit from the dialogue initiated there. The missionary women were pioneers. But they would be surprised to discover exactly what it was they pioneered.

They would be surprised too to discover that they uncovered an agenda of alarming importance. Not only did their ministry set in place a whole new spiritual, theological, historical, philosophical, educational, social and medical perception of women, it also asked a very simple and striking question about the ethical and moral codes which obtain when women's concerns are voiced.

Chapter 7 is called 'That she should be thus bound', words taken from the writings of Lucretia Mott. It reveals in precise and unsentimental detail an agenda for change which has a frighteningly contemporary note. What the missionary women discovered as they travelled to distant parts of the world was that horrendous disciplines were in place which bound women either physically, emotionally, spiritually or literally. Only a new morality could set women free. Only a new morality could challenge men to see things differently and to realize that the disciplines which they had set up were so harmful to women.

In Chapter 8 we meet the shadow side of the missionaries' venture. After all, they were colonizers and they had the mentality that went with this. So questions about their racism or their true agenda have to be addressed. The chapter title, 'Mine the mighty ordination of the pierced hands' makes an extraordinarily exalted claim about these women and their sense of purpose; it also makes a play on words. They were flawed, as hidebound by the customs and conventions of their day as the rest of us. So their language is racist, their preoccupation with cleanliness is unnerving, their attitudes to the shining glory of the Bible are quaint. Yet their achievements remain, and it is surely by these that we should judge them. It is by these that their journey should be recalled and brought from oblivion into the light.

The final chapter takes its title from a lyrical passage by Mary Warburton Booth. As she stands sweating in an Indian monsoon she revels in the natural beauty which surrounds her. We say quite glibly that travel broadens the mind. In Chapter 9 this broadening is fleshed out. We see here what the missionary women saw and what they made of it. As women began to travel in the service of the gospel they came to reflect upon the great journeys which are implicit in all adult living. So they write of transformation and glorification as they discover the amazing beauty of the outer world mirrored within.

They mirror the process identified in the gospel by the first journey ever undertaken by a Christbearing woman, the journey of Mary from the safety of Nazareth to the hill country, to 'a city of Judah'. Here is a simple account of this journey, written by one of the hidden generation, Mrs Paul Chapman:

> So she determined to make a journey into Judea and stay awhile with Elizabeth who, as the future mother of John, was, as she herself, chosen of God. Mary was possessed with a great longing to see Elizabeth and made the journey as quickly as she could, probably only stopping just long enough at the halting-places to rest her camel or her donkey. We do not know who went with her, but some one must have gone, as it would not have been safe for her to travel all that way alone. Elizabeth was very glad to see her, for God had told her that Mary was to be the mother of Jesus, and when she saw her coming she called out to her, 'Blessed art thou among women.' As for Mary, she felt words of her own would be too poor to express what she felt, and so, with the words of the song of Samuel's mother in her memory, she said, 'My soul doth magnify the Lord, and my spirit hath rejoiced in God my Saviour. For he hath looked upon the low estate of his handmaiden' – together with the rest of the psalm we know so well.
>
> Mrs Paul Chapman, *The Life of Our Lord and Saviour Jesus Christ, Simply Told for Children* (London: Henry Frowde, 1904), p. 15

What the journey of Mary triggers is a series of journeys undertaken by gospel women of every age. They range from the curious – such as those of the doughty pilgrim Etheria – to the contentious, such as those of the diplomats or the visionaries.

Between the years 398 and 400 the women Marana and Cyra, who presided over a settlement of virgins at Beroea in Syria (the present Aleppo), went on a pilgrimage to Jerusalem, whence they proceeded to Seleucia, where they saw the temple of Thecla. Their pilgrimage was described in the *Religious History of Theodoret*, their contemporary:

From him we gather that the women at Beroea usually maintained silence, and that they gave themselves up to curing the blind, the lame and the possessed.

Another visitor to Thecla's convent was an abbess, the lady Etheria, whose voyage to the East, described by herself, is dated by internal evidence to about the year 392. Starting from Tarsus, in Cilicia, she journeyed to Seleucia. The following account is from the translation of McClure and Feltoe's *The Pilgrimage of Etheria*, p. 42:

'On my arrival I went to the bishop, a truly holy man, formerly a monk, and in that city (i.e. Seleucia), I saw a very beautiful church. And as the distance thence to S. Thecla, which is situated outside the city on a low eminence, was about fifteen hundred paces, I chose rather to go there in order to make the stay that I intended. There is nothing in the holy church at that place except numberless cells (monasteria) of men and of women. I found there a very dear friend of mine, to whose manner of life all the East bore testimony, a holy deaconess named Marthana, whom I had known at Jerusalem, whither she had come for the sake of prayer; she was ruling over the cells of apotactitae and virgins.' Here apotactitae is more or less equivalent to monachi (monazontes) and parthenae (virgins).

'And when she had seen me, how can I describe the extent of her joy and of mine? But to return to the matter in hand. There are very many cells on the hill, and in the midst of it a great wall enclosing the church containing the very beautiful memorial (martyrium). The wall was built to guard the church because of the Hisauri, who are very malicious and who frequently commit acts of robbery . . . When I had arrived, the Name of God prayer was made at the memorial and the whole of the acts of Saint Thecla having been read, I gave endless thanks to Christ our Lord who designed to fulfil my desires in all things, unworthy and undeserving as I am.

'Then, after a stay of two days, when I had seen the holy monks and apotactitae who were there, I returned to Tarsus and my journey.'

Lina Eckenstein, *The Women of Early Christianity*
(London: Faith Press, 1935), pp. 86–7

St Hildegarde is the first great figure in that line of women mystics — persons of marked intelligence and unquenchable energy — who so completely refute the common accusations brought against mysticism, and so perfectly prove the thesis of St Teresa that 'the object of the spiritual marriage is work'.

Of abnormal psychic make-up, weak bodily health, but immense intellectual power, Hildegarde's personality and range of activities would be startling at any period. She founded two convents, wrote a long physical treatise in nine books, including a complete guide to the nature and properties of herbs, was skilled in medicine, deeply interested in politics, sternly denounced ecclesiastical laxity and corruption, and corresponded with and often rebuked the greatest men of her day. She was also a musician and poet, and over sixty hymns are attributed to her. In later life she travelled hundreds of miles in the course of her duties — a considerable matter for an elderly nun of the twelfth century.

Evelyn Underhill, *The Mystics of the Church*
(London: James Clarke, 1930), p. 75

When women travel, essentially they journey. The accounts collected in this book seek to bring the hidden tradition of journeying women into the light and reveal what dynamics are set up by a God who calls women to missionary activity. Kathleen Bliss made much of this in her seminal work, *The Service and Status of Women in the Churches*:

Foreign missionary work gave women their first chance of showing what services they could render to the Church, and inspite of the opening of many doors for full-time work for the Churches at home, it is still true in very many Churches that the woman with gifts, vision and a great will for service finds all her powers more fully exercised abroad than at home.

Kathleen Bliss, *The Service and Status of Women in the Churches*
(London: SCM Press, 1952), p. 104

The second daughter of Catherine and William Booth, Emma Booth-Tucker, demonstrates what this could mean:

No one could be more surprised than myself when the call came for the new work. Knitting stockings and carrying gruel to old people seemed to me, as a child, the very most I should ever dare to do! Then I began to have a great love and tenderness for the children; and when I first had twenty-five lasses in my training home I felt the responsibility was crushing! But all through, even from those early days, I have had what I may almost call a passion for woman. I saw, I felt, I grasped what a woman could do, if she only had the chance and was fitted for it. That had been in all these years my guiding thought, and in taking up this new responsibility I do not feel I am having a change of work — it is only a mighty continuation of the same.

It's curious, in looking back, to notice that India always had a special place in my heart. As a child, I could draw the map of India bigger than any other, and of all my happy training home work, the very happiest always seemed to be, when I was preparing my girls for India. My going is the clincher to all that I have ever striven to teach my lasses. I go to do what I have always taught them to do. In a letter I received a few days ago, I noticed the sentence, 'The women of India need a champion.' I yearn to inspire and lift them up, my lifework, therefore will still be to reach and serve woman.

Solveig Smith, By Love Compelled: The Story of the Salvation Army in India and Adjacent Countries (London: Salvationist Publishing, 1981), p. 37

* * *

Not only this extraordinary parallel between the gospels and the deepest aspirations of Christbearing women but also the same mechanisms I encountered when editing *The Hidden Tradition* are in place. The missionary women's story is subject to the same forms of suppression as those of the other women spiritual writers and theologians and mystics. At its best this suppression happens by accident because women's history is somehow deemed to be less important than that of men and so it fails to get told. And women themselves collude with this silence by not taking their experience sufficiently seriously, so not bothering to write it down — or worse, they keep silent out of a warped desire to avoid vainglory. At its worst an actual dynamic of suppression is operating. This means that what women were writing or talking about was not liked and so their access to the printed word was restricted. Their books were printed in small numbers by publishers whose good will alone could not guarantee their survival. They are in limited supply nowadays, curiosities in second-hand bookshops or cannon-fodder/space-fillers in charity and thrift shops. The major histories of the missions published in this century virtually ignore them. Stephen Neill's 1964 A *History of the Christian Missions* would be a case in point. But present-day histories are often just as well guarded. And so there is a reluctance to name the wives of the 'true greats' — like Livingstone (Mary, who was so frequently abandoned) or Carey (Dorothy, who died from sheer misery) or von Zinzendorf (Erdmuth, who was deceived by her husband) — just in case the truth should backfire and raise ugly questions about the extent to which a man's call should be exercised at the expense of his prior call to marriage.

Then there are questions raised by the very nature of the missionary women's ministry. When they took on the agenda of justice and began to question the cultural norms which meant that women's feet were tortured and bound in China, that widows were killed in India, that twin-children were slaughtered in Africa, that girl children were forced into prostitution and grown women into zenana harems, they challenged a world which had been established by men for the convenience and servicing of men, whatever their religious tradition. Islam, Hinduism and the African religions were judged and found wanting; but then so too was Christianity.

This was why the connections which the missionary women began to make made them a dangerous force within Christianity. The very freedom they professed to proclaim, the gospel message itself, turned round and hit them in the face and demanded that they too become accountable to the Lord of history. When they named the outrage they felt as they witnessed the violation of women's human rights, they raised difficult questions about the place of women in any society, including their own. When they called for change, they were demanding change for themselves as well. When they freed women by ensuring that they should have education, they challenged the entire social structure which, traditionally, had restricted it to men. In a most moving way the journey of the missionary women was a journey into freedom. They purported to bring a gospel of salvation; ironically, they found themselves receiving one.

Lavinia Byrne IBVM
11 November 1992

CHAPTER 1

EXPERIENCING THE CALL

'The spirit of the Lord is upon me because he has anointed me' (Luke 4.18)

The missionary call testified to in these accounts is a call which brings extra-ordinary clarity and light. God speaks to the individual, a scenario is depicted, and with the missionary woman's fiat come the fruits of the Spirit. 'I had heard of the Holy Spirit', writes the Welsh missionary May Bounds, 'and now I was myself experiencing it.'

Then very suddenly I was shown what to do. I was off duty each Friday evening and had each Saturday free. I was spending the Friday evening at the Nurses Home called Scott House. I looked through advertisements of vacant posts for Nursing Sisters in the *Nursing Mirror*. There was one asking for Sisters to go to work in India where (at the time) there was only one trained Nurse for thousands of people. The longing returned to do Medical Missionary work. I knew again that evening it was the only thing I really wanted to do with my life.

The next morning I prepared to go to Chester on the bus and as I looked out from the window of my room I had what I can only describe as a 'Spiritual Experience'. In a split moment of time, suddenly away in the distant sky, there was a dark outline of India as on a map. Then instantaneously two strong arms came, embraced me and carried me strongly and swiftly to that India. Then with the sound of a click I was back into my shoes. In a fraction of a second I had been shown what to do. I was dazed. This was broad daylight. I had no idea that such things ever happened. I went for the bus and to Chester for the day as I often did on my off duty days. The one thing that stood out clearly was that I was directed to go to India. The experience was so humbling. I could scarcely think of what had happened without a feeling of emotion. Then I thought, when I tell my family what would their reaction be, but I wasn't ready to tell them yet and the spiritual experience was so personal and so very wonderful to me that I did not, or could not, speak of it.

Two days later I was again standing at my window thinking, 'Well I am to go to India. I must make no mistake, I must go with the Church.' As I made this decision I was, as it were, filled to overflowing with a power that I had never before experienced. I had heard of the Holy Spirit and now I was myself experiencing it. I was filled with tremendous joy, difficult to describe. Such joy was coupled with deep humility. From then onwards I was able to tell people that I was applying to go to India as a Medical Missionary.

> May Bounds and Gladwys M. Evans, *Medical Mission to Mizoram*
> (Chester: Handbridge, 1986), p. 8

The theologian Dr Olive Wyon speaks of obedience to vocation and sees how such obedience brings light and truth and love to others. In this sense obedience becomes mission. Of necessity it takes peace and significance into the lives of other people and even to the darkest corners of the earth. When we are obedient we share in the life of the Trinity, which is a life of obedience. For the Creator sends the Redeemer, and the Creator and Redeemer in turn send the Sanctifier. So the work of the missionary women, of whatever church, class or age, is caught up into the life of the Trinity. Mission is God's preferred way of being, and women are invited to share and to walk in this way.

We discover the will of God in the fact of vocation. One of the tragedies of modern 'civilization' is the fact that our whole social system has travelled so far from the will of God that millions of people have no idea of vocation. But all through the centuries, since the Christian Faith has been active and creative in human life, this fact of vocation stands out as one of the most compelling forces in the life of the·

Church. From the time that Abraham set forth from Ur at the Call of God, obeying a summons but 'not knowing whither he went', countless men and women have heard the Call and have gone forth in obedience. This obedience has made heroes and saints and martyrs. This obedience has brought peace and significance into millions of lives. Through this obedience to their vocation light and truth and love have been let into the darkest corners of the earth.

Olive Wyon, *The School of Prayer* (London: SCM Press, 1943), p. 31

In a children's book about Mary Slessor, the Dundee mill-girl who went to the Calabar in Africa and became known as the White Queen of the Okoyong, there is another reference to darkest corners, only now they have become 'wildest parts'. What the author struck on this time was an image of continuity. The mill-girl goes on to weave human lives together, just as gospel fishermen became fishers of human life. Whether consciously or not, the author makes a play on words which identifies Mary Slessor's vocation as a call to a gospel ministry — that of transforming the lives of other people. In the mission field, as nowhere else, women learned that they could both receive and issue the gospel call to conversion.

Tremblingly she waited for the answer to her letter to the Mission Board of the United Presbyterian Church in Edinburgh. When it arrived she rushed to her mother.

'I'm accepted! I'm going to Calabar as a teacher.' And then, strange to say, she burst into tears.

So she who had waited so long and so patiently, working within the walls of a factory, weaving the warp and woof in the loom, was going to one of the wildest parts of Africa to weave there the lives of the people into new and beautiful patterns.

W. P. Livingstone, *The White Queen of Okoyong*
(London: Hodder & Stoughton, n.d.), pp. 20–1

Philippine Duchesne, a Roman Catholic sister, went to America at the beginning of the nineteenth century, inspired by a call to instruct 'savages'. She writes of this vocation with conviction and traces its origins to stories which she had heard told about them as a child of ten. She herself died when Mary Slessor was six. Significantly, though, both knew about the importance of storytelling. A call which remains a private experience can never inspire others. That is why the story of the missionary women must be retrieved.

Not only is it important for them, and so for an authentic narrative of the course of history; it is important for us too to recall and retell these stories of women and their vocations from God. When we listen to them, we are empowered in our turn. By writing about it, Philippine ensured that her call story, from the troubled years of post-Revolution France, would be saved. Her intention was to try to discern it with the help of the woman who would pass on God's Spirit and the spirit of her religious community's first sisters to her, and so she begins.

Dear Reverend Mother,

I have often had occasion to speak to you about my vocation to instruct 'savages' or idolaters; however, taken separately, the few traits on which I based my hopes to have God in my side, seemed very weak; only united could they gain strength to form a working whole. Therefore, after Communion I decided to leave it to you since I understood how apprehensive you must have been about entrusting this all-important work to me. A work we were to undertake at such great distance from those who had passed on their spirit to us and also too far from you for you to be able to impart your spirit to all your daughters.

But if it was God who showed me my vocation it was also God who opened the way to accomplish it and therefore I have reason to hope he will sustain his work despite the most feeble, unworthy and incapable people.

My first longing to become a missionary came from conversations with one who had been a missionary in Louisiana and told us stories about the natives. I was only about ten years old but nevertheless I considered these missionaries to be blessed. At this time I was also reading the lives of martyrs with great interest and therefore I envied them their work with little thought of the dangers involved.

Madeleine-Sophie Barat and Philippine Duchesne, *Correspondence: Second Part —*
I, North America (1818–1821), compiled by Jeanne de Charry, RSCJ,
translated by Barbara Hogg, RSCJ (Rome: RSCJ, 1989), p. 7

In convent archives, stories such as this get saved only if the sister in question achieves some status within the community. Many, many such stories have been underrated, and so lost. Interestingly, the correspondence of Philippine Duchesne and Madeleine-Sophie Barat has only recently been made available in an English translation. It marks a movement away from an obscurity which was considered desirable for the dubious reason that it helped keep the sisters humble. It also demonstrates that the Roman Catholic nuns now realize that their history is not private and particular to themselves. Convent archives form a rich source for the exploration of the hidden tradition of women's history.

The importance of the missionary story in the Protestant imagination is testified to by Mary Warburton Booth in a book she called My Testimony. What she demonstrates quite clearly here is the place of an oral tradition which was kept alive in women's meetings at centres such as the deaconesses' training home at Mildmay.

The Women's Meeting was held at 3 p.m. on Monday afternoon. I went, of course, but my body was weary and my mind full of the sorrows of the people I had left, and I was not much inclined to listen to any speaker, especially as the one appointed was a missionary. She had been a deaconess at Mildmay before going to India, and had returned to tell us what God had done for the people among whom she lived and worked in India.

No sooner had she begun her story than I forgot tiredness and everything except that the woman on the platform was one of us. She had seen marvels unknown to us, and held her audience spellbound, as she told of the Holy Spirit's working in the hearts and lives of Indian women converted from Hinduism. I sat up and listened. Here was the real thing. She told us nothing about buildings, gave us no figures to add up; she just told of one woman, and then another, and yet another, who had been convicted of sin in their Prayer Meeting. She told how they were delivered, and the joy of their salvation!

Her time was up, and she sat down, but she was recalled by the congregation. The next speaker said: 'I will stand back to listen to more about India', and she did, and we heard more, until it was time to close the meeting.

As one of us, she brought a message for us that shook the depths of our beings, and I was glad that there are some things that cannot be shaken.

Staying in the house we saw much of her. She was different, having been across the seas and seen sights unknown to us, and having faced depths we knew nothing of: and yet there, in a city given over to idolatry, she had seen how, when the door is opened, Jesus himself comes in and takes possession and the place is changed: and oh!

how I longed to be there and see it all, but I never dreamed
of going.

Every day the Conference Hall was crowded and there was a solemnity
that compelled the deepest reverence all through. It was an unforgettable experience to be in the opening meeting and to stand with that
vast congregation singing:

> Jesus stand among us
> In thy risen power.
> Let this time of worship
> Be a hallowed hour.

And when we were stilled before him we could hear his voice.

I was one of that crowd – just one – but he·spoke to me there.

It was well on in the week and my thoughts were away with the
people of the slums, wondering how they were and thinking of what
I had seen in my district. My heart was so full of gratitude to God
for saving my people, blessing them and answering their prayers, that
in spirit I was telling him that I would do anything, go anywhere for
him. 'Thou art so wonderful to me,' I said, 'I will go anywhere.' And
in the silence of my heart I heard a voice softly saying: 'Will you go
to India?' I was so sure of the voice, and so startled too, that I turned
round to see who had spoken; but there was no one behind me: I was
sitting in the back seat and I was trembling. The deaconess next to
me put her hand on mine and asked if I felt ill.

I steadied myself to listen to the voice of the preacher: he was reading
the sixth chapter of Isaiah, and Dr Pierson knew how to read the Scriptures. They were words of God. 'Whom shall I send?' like a clarion
call he read. 'Who will go for us?' Then there was a long pause as
if he searched for someone, and the silence was intense, and all my
being hearkened for the answer, and he read: 'Then said I, here I am,
send me.' That was all, but it lifted me out of the place I was in, right
into the presence of God, and the recognition of an open door to be
entered. It had never entered my head that I could be a missionary!
That high and holy calling was for others fitted from their birth to be
called to go, and I thought I had better wait until I got back into the
seclusion of my room in the Mission House in the East End – but I
had no rest in my spirit.

I knew that I was not worthy: I knew that I was not prepared: I
knew everything was against my going: and nothing for it except that

I had heard 'The Voice', and I had told him that I would go anywhere for him, but I had never dreamt of India, and the more I thought of it, the more sure I was that I was not fitted to be a missionary. 'They are all born good,' I said — how could I be a missionary? And I had many reasons to give why it was not for me, and yet — I was sure that I had heard The Voice that Calleth.

The end of the Conference came, and I returned to my district and the people I loved and cared for — but, I could *not* forget.

I was called and the voice was insistent, so I told the powers that be, but no one believed me. They were all quite sure that I was in the place God meant me to be in, and I was just as sure that I was called out and I dare not disobey. Now I prepared my heart to face what it could mean, but I did not know — who does? I had no encouragement whatsoever, and every step forward was bristling with difficulties, and I felt that I could not go through with it. It would be an easy matter to pack up and go off in the urge of my spirit, but that can't be done. There are many wheels within wheels, and a Missionary Society does not send its missionaries without asking a few questions that must be answered, and that takes time. I waited, because I had to wait, and nearly gave it up.

I was still reading my Bible consecutively, and that morning I was riveted by the words, 'If thou refuse to go forth.'

So I braced myself for the ordeal and I asked the Lord to keep me true, and one wondrous day I knew that I was accepted and would sail for India very soon. So, of course, I talked about it to my friends in the slums and their remarks were interesting and full of meaning. But why I should leave them to go to 'them foreign parts' puzzled them, and one man told me what *he* thought, and, he added: 'The Bible was written in English for English people, and it has no meaning for anybody else.' His wife, who was a member of the Mothers' Meeting, interrupted him: 'Now, Bill, you don't know what you're talking about, it says in the Bible "Go into the four corners of the earth and preach the Gospel,"' but — turning to me — 'I don't see why you should go, you are our only friend.'

Once I wavered, and he said: 'Lovest thou me more than these?' and though I loved them dearly and they had become part of my life, I knew he was first, and it was he who had given them to me to take care of for him. I could answer: 'Yes, Lord, thou knowest that I love thee,' and he claimed again his right over me.

Mary Warburton Booth, *My Testimony*
(London: Pickering & Inglis, 1947), pp. 58–61

The same blend of eagerness and a sense of unworthiness characterize what Thérèse of Lisieux had to write of her vocation to go to Hanoi. This call would never be answered because her body did indeed fail her; she died within the year. Significantly, though, Thérèse is remembered for all sorts of reasons: for her 'Little Way' of love, for her piety, her depression, her fidelity to the Carmelite vocation she had embraced as a child. Rarely is she remembered as a missionary, or for her passionate desire for priesthood.

Perhaps you are wondering what our Mother thinks of my desire to go to Tonking? She believes in my vocation (truly rather a special one is needed, not every Carmelite feels the call to go into exile); but she does not believe my vocation can ever be fulfilled: for that the scabbard would have to be as strong as the sword and perhaps (thinks our Mother) the scabbard would have to be thrown into the sea before it got to Tonking. As a matter of fact, it's no great convenience to be composed of a body and a soul! Miserable Brother Ass, as St Francis of Assisi called the body, often hinders his noble sister and prevents her from darting off where she would. Still, I won't abuse him, for all his faults; he is still good for something, he helps his companion to get to heaven, and gets there himself. I am not in the least worried about the future, I am sure the good God will do what he wills; that is the one and only grace I desire. To accomplish his work, Jesus needs no one, and if he accepted me it would be sheer kindness.

St Thérèse of Lisieux, *Collected Letters of Saint Thérèse of Lisieux*
(London: Sheed & Ward, 1949), p. 279

What Thérèse saw and others would reiterate is how essential God is to what we do. The importance of these accounts of missionary calls is that they extend across each of the religious traditions and that they belong to a fairly limited period in time. Only since the nineteenth century have women missionaries worked extensively in each of the continents. Before that time their work overseas was the exception, rather than the norm; so the rise in numbers of missionary women directly parallels women's experience in other fields. It represents a direct consequence of an increase in self-understanding on the part of women through education and training.

*   *   *

Not only have women testified to calls to work in a ministry of proclamation and direct evangelization, but they have also examined the very nature of call itself. Stories from the field are matched by an analysis provided, exceptionally, by the missionaries themselves or, more usually, by intelligent onlookers. Dorothy L. Sayers did not mince words when she described her own insight into this understanding of vocation as 'revolutionary'. She writes with a nononsense clarity of two calls which must never become exclusive, those of God and our neighbour. There is something close to deliberate irony in her final phrase.

The worker's first duty is *to serve the work*. The popular 'catch' phrase of today is that it is everybody's duty to serve the community. It is a well-sounding phrase, but there is a catch in it. It is the old catch about the two great commandments. 'Love God — and your neighbour; on those two commandments hang all the Law and the Prophets.' The catch in it, which nowadays the world has largely forgotten, is that the second commandment depends upon the first, and that without the first, it is a delusion and a snare. Much of our present trouble and disillusionment have come from putting the second commandment before the first. If we put our neighbour first, we are putting man above God, and that is what we have been doing ever since we began to worship humanity and make man the measure of things.

Dorothy L. Sayers, *Creed or Chaos?* (London: Methuen & Co., 1947), p. 61

* * *

So how are we to hear the call? Does it come from men — man the measure of all things — or from other women? What does it sound like? The missionary call which inspired the greatest of the missionary women came from God. But women shaped and explored it in theological terms in ways which were at once lyrical, analytical and practical by turns. So Frances Ridley Havergal could exhort and stir with a poem called Sisters.

Oh! for a fiery scroll, and a trumpet of thunder might,
To startle the silken dreams of English women at ease,
Circled with peace and joy, and dwelling where truth and light

Are shining fair as the stars, and free as the western breeze!
Oh! for a clarion voice to reach and stir their nest,
With the story of sister's woes gathering day by day
Over the Indian homes (sepulchres rather than rest),
Till they rouse in the strength of the Lord, and roll the stone
   away.

Sisters! Scorn not the name, for ye cannot alter the fact!
Deem ye the darker tint of the glowing South shall be
Valid excuse above for the Priest's and Levite's act,
If ye pass on the other side, and say that ye did not see?

Sisters! Yea, and they lie, not by the side of the road,
But hidden in loathsome caves, in crushed and quivering
   throngs,
Down-trodden, degraded, and dark, beneath the invisible load
Of centuries, echoing groans, black with inherited wrongs.

Made like our own strange selves, with memory, mind, and will;
Made with a heart to love, and a soul to live for ever!
Sisters! Is there no chord vibrating in musical thrill,
At the fall of that gentle word, to issue in bright endeavour?

Sisters! Ye have known the Elder Brother's love —
Ye who have sat at his feet, and leant on his gracious breast,
Whose hearts are glad with the hope of his own blest home
   above,
Will ye not seek him out, and lead them to him for rest?

Is it too great a thing? Will not *one* rise and go,
Laying her joys aside, as the Master laid them down?
Seeking his lone and lost in the veiled abodes of woe?
Winning his Indian gems to shine in his glorious crown!

Frances Ridley Havergal, *The Poetical Works*
(London: James Nisbet & Co., n.d.), pp. 527–8

Olive Wyon, meanwhile, is more concerned to find the missionary call mirrored in the call of Jesus, and so ennobled and made fruitful in the risen life of Christ. Without the work of the missionary women, however, she would never have been in a position to make this application. What is important

*too is that her list — 'parsons, missionaries, doctors and nurses' — is in no
way gender specific. It stands there as a bald statement of the fact that 'we
are all called to obedience to God's will in all things', and that obedience to
this call actually enhances the meaning of life or sense of identity of those
who hear it. Women cannot be excluded from this dynamic, nor from what
it both means and demands.*

It is not childish to think that God is concerned in our affairs. He has a
great and glorious purpose for the whole world, and within that purpose
he has a definite part for each one of us to play. It is most important to
realise that vocation applies to us all, not only to parsons, missionaries,
doctors and nurses, or teachers. We are all called to obedience to God's
will in all things, it is true, but the meaning of life is greatly enhanced
when we realise that for each of us there is also a special vocation.

This is no mere theory; this whole view of life as vocation is based
upon the deepest truth of the incarnation. All the experience of Jesus
as man, all that he learnt from the years of which we know nothing in
Nazareth, and all that he went through in Galilee and Jerusalem, were
gathered up in his final offering on the cross and brought to fruition in
his risen manhood through his resurrection. From the human point of
view much of his life here on earth must have seemed to have consisted of a great many unrelated odds and ends. Yet when God raised
him from the dead on Easter Day, he took 'these bits and pieces of a
disjointed ministry and wove from them a single garment of salvation
for the whole world'. Nothing that he had ever done or suffered upon
earth was lost or wasted. God accepted, used, and transformed it all
into the perfect pattern of redemption. So we too, united in him, are
also raised up complete in him and victorious over time and death, and
all that seems contrary to his will. For 'he must reign', and we are 'par-
takers of his resurrection'. When we realise this, when we see that each
life is ennobled by the call of God and made fruitful by Christ's risen
life, we are able to take each day as it comes.

Olive Wyon, Prayer (London: Collins, 1962), pp. 134–5

*For Kathleen Bliss the starting-point was in relationships, and notably in the
relationship God has with creation. The re-creation and endless re-creating
of the world mean that every missionary — whether working overseas or in
the home mission — is faced with the same question: Is one taking God to
other people, or finding God already there? The very fact that she could*

ask this question with such clarity is a result of the activity of the mission-
aries who went overseas in the eighteenth and nineteenth centuries. It is a
question which belongs to our times rather than to theirs, and so it becomes
a powerful reminder that the perceptions and questions of one age could not
have been anticipated by a previous age. But equally, it reminds the reader
of the interconnectedness of every part of the missionary endeavour.

It is tempting at that point to plunge into a large number of details
about the duties of the laity in their many and various worldly pro-
fessions. But if our actions are going to be theologically grounded our
thinking has to begin theologically. What, in theological terms, can be
said of this 'world'? It makes an enormous *practical* difference whether
the Christian regards the world as a place where God is already at work
and what kind of action he believes God to be taking. When he goes out
to work all day in a secular institution with non-Christian companions
does he, so to speak, take God with him or find him already there?

  The starting point of a theology of the relation of the people of God
to the world which they inter-penetrate, is the faith that this world,
here and now, is God's world. The doctrine of creation ought to mean
far more to a Christian than that God in the beginning made the universe with its light and darkness and motion, and the habitable earth
and its inhabitants. This restricts God's action as Creator to that of a
first cause — a role completed.

                    Kathleen Bliss, *We the People* (London: SCM Press, 1963), p. 102

In 1900 the American missionary Miss Thoburn had addressed the Ecumenical
Missionary Conference which brought women together in the Carnegie Hall,
long before the formal missionary societies organized their 1910 meeting in
Edinburgh. Kathleen Bliss's questions get neither a yes nor a no answer.
'Few missionaries have found the expected in the work awaiting them in
the field.' What emerges from her text is the urgency of the task, and the
particular authority which women missionaries would bring to it.

The power of educated womanhood in the world is simply the power
of skilled service. We are not in the world to be ministered unto but
to minister. The world is full of need, and every opportunity to help is
a duty. Preparation for these duties is education, whatever form it may
take and whatever service may result. The trained, which means the
educated in mind and hand, win influence and power simply because

they know how. Few missionaries have found the expected in the work awaiting them in the field. We went to tell women and children of Christ, their Saviour and Deliverer, and to teach them to read the story for themselves. But instead of willing and waiting pupils, we have found the indifferent or even the hostile, to win whom require every grace and art we know. We have found sickness and poverty to relieve, widows to protect, advice to be given in every possible difficulty or emergency, teachers and Bible women to be trained, houses to be built, horses and cattle to be bought, gardens to be planted, and accounts to be kept and rendered. We have found use for every faculty, natural and acquired, that we possessed, and have coveted all we lacked. But it is not only our power over those we go to save that we must consider. When saved they must have the power over the communities in which they live. Intemperance, divorce, degrading amusements, injurious, impure or false literature, are all serious hindrances in the mission field. Women must know how to meet them.

Helen Barrett Montgomery, *Western Women in Eastern Lands*

(New York: Macmillan, 1911), pp. 174–5

Helen Barrett Montgomery's is an important voice. She is the first missiologist to use the vocabulary and insights of the woman's movement. When she uses the word 'woman' she does so with intent, conscious that she is making a highly political point. The consciousness of other women had not been raised in quite this way. Yet, in virtue of the work they were doing, the agenda of women and women's pastoral needs forced itself into their thinking and working. No wonder, then, that Mary Warburton Booth saw that women missionaries would need to 'go and represent him' — be the life of Jesus among the 'sick and sad and baffled' — and in this way testify to truth and make real the glory of the cross. This extraordinary evangelical Christian woman quite unwittingly takes on and undermines any theological assumptions about the unique right men have to image Jesus. She even implicates women as both the recipients and, more significantly, the agents, of salvation.

> Will you? will you? are you willing
> To be true to God?
> Will you follow in his footsteps
> Walk where Jesus trod?
> See — he ever feeds the hungry,
> Folk in trouble come his way;

With the broken-hearted outcasts
He has words to say;
All the sick and sad and baffled,
All in grief or woe
Knew that he would understand them,
Sympathy would show.

Will you follow in his footsteps,
Testifying true?
Make him real to those around you
By the things you do?
Will you leave yourself behind you?
Let him have full sway?
In the preaching and the teaching
Let him have his say.
Will you be a knight of Jesus,
Counting dear thy loss,
Just to go and represent him
And the glory of his cross?

Mary Warburton Booth, 'They That Sow'
(London: Pickering & Inglis, n.d.), p. 20

What Lady Hosie, the China missionary, would add to this is the insight that the missionary vocation is in fact addressed to all who follow Christ. It is not peculiar to those who are sent overseas. All are implicated in the sending, because the Canaanite woman's question still resonates in the Christian imagination.

It is plain that no Christian can raise objections to Christian Missions. In all truth, we do but send out crumbs and morsels from our great riches of grace, to the needy ones abroad. The Churches hold meetings and sales of work, and we think well of ourselves if we manage to raise a few pounds extra this year over last; as if we spent vast sums of money for Missions, or toiled long and hard. But have we actually spent much of the country's or the Church's money this way, or sent an appreciable number of church members abroad? The mission of Christians of Great Britain, or of any other Christian country, spend far more on their own souls than on these others: the percentage from our Churches who go abroad as missionaries is an infinitesimal fraction compared with those who remain at home, to be ministered to rather than minister. That persistent Canaanitish mother's words pierce us with shame: for indeed our table is laden with good things by the Master, and we do but spare her and her children our scraps.

It is true, as some will argue, that there is plenty to do at home, 'without going abroad'. Vice and disease still call us to fight, in his name: and certainly we are called by the Master to work at home. But there are plenty to take up the fight to work in their own land, if they will. He, himself, began with Nazareth: but as certainly he bids us not to stop at that, or to leave the other work undone. We in the West have been more nurtured in Christ than other people realize: but far back of our Christian culture stand the first missionaries to our lands, which then were pagan. And further back again, is the face of Jesus bent towards a kneeling woman on a foreign shore, as she clasps her hands in anguish and cries, 'Lord, heal me'. Millions of such women, with their husbands and their children, are still waiting for us today to go over and help them, to share with them something of our knowledge of God's love. Our passport is his love for all his creatures. As Jesus told us, its citizens, whether male or female, master or slave, leper, widow, father, mother, Jew, Gentile, hungry child or gambolling puppy under the table, should share with us in God's love. For we all live upon his generous giving.

Lady Hosie, *Jesus and Women* (London: Hodder & Stoughton, 1946), pp. 110–11

What does this actually mean? The answer to this question has a surprisingly contemporary ring: fund-raising, letter-writing, singing and song-writing, making parcels and attending committee meetings, every kind of service. What Lady Hosie demonstrates is a complete absence of hierarchy. Each task is needed. Those who write letters are no better than those who make parcels. A model of interdependence means that all who work in the service of the gospel must do so in the spirit of the gospel. What she also demonstrates is that contemporary questions about debt crisis and about the relationship between the over- and the underdeveloped parts of the world are not as new as we may have unconsciously assumed. Helen Barrett Montgomery, quoting from the Panoplist, Boston 1813, provides documentary evidence of this.

DEAR SIR: Mr. M---- will deliver $177 into your hands.
The items are as follows:

From an obscure female who kept the money for many years, waiting for a proper opportunity to bestow it upon a religious object.	$100.00
From an aged woman in Barnet, Vt., being the avails of a small dairy the past year.	50.00
From the same, being the avails of two superfluous garments	10.00
From the Cent Society in this place, being half their annual subscription	11.00
My own donation being the same hitherto expended in ardent spirits in my family but now totally discontinued	5.00
From a woman in extreme indigence	1.00
	=====
	$177.00

Helen Barrett Montgomery, *Western Women in Eastern Lands,*
(New York: Macmillan, 1911), p. 20

A testimony such as this reminds us that while the rhetoric about mission may have belonged to those ordained or appointed for evangelization, the actual impetus and resourcing came very often from women. While they could not occupy pulpits or exhort from on high, they began to use what was there: for example, the Royal Mail.

Miss Agnes Weston's entire mission was as a letter-writer, 'offering interest and advice' to sailors around the globe and warning them off precisely those very 'ardent spirits' discontinued by the good folk of Boston.

The requests for these letters became so numerous that it was impossible to keep pace with them except by the regular supplementary issues of a printed one. Thus Miss Weston's invaluable 'Monthly Letter' to Seamen and Marines was started, and it proved from the outset a great success. From a circulation of 1500 copies per month in 1872, it rose to over 20,000 in fifteen years, and now is nearly 50,000. And, in addition, every year Miss Weston and her secretaries have written to thousands of men individually, but all under her personal supervision.

The pleasure which these letters give to lonely sailors all over the world, their significance to those oft-times monotonous and isolated lives, and the spiritual blessing which in innumerable cases has followed their perusal, it is impossible to estimate.

Jennie Chappell, *Agnes Weston, the Sailors' Friend*
(London: Pickering & Inglis, n.d.), p. 35

Hymns and music too would carry the gospel message from home to heathen lands, and provided an extraordinarily fertile vein for women to tap. When Frances Ridley Havergal died, one of her mourners noted:

> The Church's sweetest minstrel
> Has left her ranks today;
> The Master sent his summons
> To call her hence away:
> A summons to his presence,
> To see him face to face,
> To share with him his glory,
> In her appointed place.
>
> Thousands on earth have loved thee
> Who never saw thy face;
> In countless hearts thy teachings
> Have found abiding place.
> The truths which thou hast uttered
> In purest melody,
> Have reached the souls of numbers,
> Though all unknown to thee.

Maria V. G. Havergal, *Memorials of Frances Ridley Havergal*
(New York: Anson D. F. Randolph & Co., 1880), p. 389

The 'souls of numbers' may explain the extraordinary little 'etc.' in the title selected by the Methodist Ladies' Committee for the Amelioration of the Condition of Women in Heathen Countries, Female Education, etc.' Every eventuality has to be covered when a committee is formed.

It was to Miss Farmer of Gunnersbury that Mary Batchelor wrote and in her letter she spoke of those Wesleyan ladies who had so far been showing so much interest in the work overseas by packing parcels for missionaries, often themselves making and supplying a great deal of missionary equipment. Could they not form themselves into a Society, taking special responsibility for female education in the East, and aiming not only at equipping missionaries but also sending young women teachers out to the field?

The letter was shown to the General Committee of the Wesleyan Missionary Society who made a decision frequently made in Methodism, but not always with such dramatic results as it had then — they formed a special committee. They passed a minute which gave unqualified approval to the new enterprise for, they said, 'the subject of female education in India is regarded by this Committee with lively interest. They rejoice in the help that has been afforded by many ladies' societies in London and elsewhere, and look favourably on the project for organizing these societies more extensively for the promotion of female education in India and other parts of the mission field.'

It was on December 20, 1858, that the first Ladies' Committee met, being welcomed to the Mission House by the Secretaries, the Rev. William Arthur and the Rev. Dr. Hoole, who after commending the whole plan to the assembled ladies, tactfully withdrew. A great deal of the time of that first committee was taken up with choosing a name for themselves. The final result of their deliberations, though it sounds strange to us now, no doubt caused general satisfaction. They decided to call themselves 'The Ladies' Committee for the Amelioration of the Condition of Women in Heathen Countries, Female Education, etc.'

Pauline M. Webb, *Women of Our Company*
(London: Cargate Press, 1958), pp. 28–9

What each of these extracts describes is an offering of the widow's mite — and more. Yet it takes an independent and self-financing woman, Irene Petrie, the Kashmir missionary, to witness to anything so positive as the 'delightful consciousness' that goes with self-giving. This is not an apologetic, self-deprecating piece of writing. Her biographer, Canon Dawson, simply notes that she is 'happily situated' because she is rich enough to make this choice.

It does not fall to the lot of every woman to be able to offer her services free of charge to the directors of a missionary society. She who can do so is very happily situated; not that she is freed from any responsibility which falls more heavily upon the paid worker, nor that she is less under discipline, but that she has the delightful consciousness that against her, at least, the taunt falls barbless that she has sought the work for the sake of the pay. No doubt most of the women among who Irene Petrie spent laborious days thought that she had merely adopted a somewhat arduous method of making a livelihood. She was, however, from the first to last an 'honorary' missionary, and paid her own way wherever she went.

E. C. Dawson, *Missionary Heroines of the Cross*
(London: Seeley, Service & Co., 1930), p. 76

* * *

The missionary vocation of women does not go unopposed, however. Irene Petrie's freedom to choose to go to Kashmir illustrates what Virginia Woolf had hinted at in A Room of One's Own. *Women flourish when they have access to space and to financial independence. And missionary life brought women both into a room and into a land of their own. Inevitably, though, such independence threatened the status quo. Mary Slessor learned about this as a child:*

She was very good at make-believe, and one of her games was to sit in a corner and pretend that she was keeping school. If you had listened to her you would have found the pupils she was busy teaching and keeping in order were children with skins as black as coal. The reason was this. Her mother took a great interest in all she heard on Sundays about the dark lands beyond the seas where millions of people had never heard of Jesus. The church to which she belonged, the United Presbyterian Church, had sent out many brave men and women to various parts of the world to fight the evils of heathenism, and a new Mission had just begun amongst a savage race in a wild country called Calabar in West Africa, and every one in Scotland was talking about it and the perils and hardships of the missionaries. Mrs. Slessor used to come home with all the news about the work, and the children would gather about her knees and listen to stories of the strange cruel customs of the natives, and how they killed twin-babies, until their eyes grew big and round, and their hearts raced with fear, and they snuggled close to her side.

Mary was very sorry for these helpless bush-children, and often thought about them, and that was why she made them her play scholars. She dreamed, too, of going out some day to that terrible land and saving the lives of the twinnies, and sometimes she would look up and say:

'Mother, I want to be a missionary and go out and teach the black boys and girls — real ways.'

Then Robert would retort in the tone that boys often use with their sisters:

'But you're only a girl, and girls can't be missionaries. *I'm* going to be one and you can come out with me, and if you're good I may let you up into my pulpit beside me.'

W. P. Livingstone, *The White Queen of Okoyong*
(London: Hodder & Stoughton, n.d.), pp. 2–3

In common with many of the turn of the century missionary books, this account has no date. This is an example of how the hidden journey and tradition of missionary women has been concealed. Women were never given the prominence or recognition that could make them somehow 'real' in the public domain. That is why a more recent account, prepared in the 1950s, is so offensive. It continues to turn women and their history into a hidden underside of the human story, whose meaning and self-identity are so inexorably tied to the servicing of men that their apostolic vocation is jeopardized. This is not to denigrate domestic work; it is merely to question the rigid gender structures and stereotypes which Christianity so easily puts in place. As the seventeenth-century Englishwoman Mary Ward reminds us, 'do these things in love and freedom, or do them not at all', an insight which is a long way away from the language of oughts, standards and shoulds which dominate this piece.

The missionary wife ought to keep the home clean and in order. An aged mission executive observed in an interview, 'A missionary home kept like a pigsty is a woeful thing . . . and I have seen such'.

She will need to discipline herself to bother him as little as possible with the details of running the household so as to leave him free for his ministry.

She should serve nutritious meals as attractively as possible, always bearing in mind that his health, and that of her family, are to a great degree in her hands.

She should strive to keep his clothes in good repair — and this is quite a feat for some missionary wardrobes, especially as a term on the field nears its end.

She can plan to relieve him of the greater part of the burden of letter-writing, saving him hours upon hours of time. Most missionary wives assume this responsibility.

She should share actively in many ways in the ministry to which they have given themselves, assisting him in public or in private, but keeping always in the background. She will take over, especially, in the follow-up of women converts and children.

She should protect him, if possible, from interruption in times when he desires to be alone for study or for prayer.

A faithful missionary wife will refrain from pushing her husband into places of prominence when he does not feel the Lord is leading him to them. She will rather encourage him to fulfil to the best of his ability the type of ministry to which he feels called.

She will ask the Lord to guard her heart from the taint of jealousy, and to teach her rather the ways of trust, helpfulness, and full delight in her dear one. She will recognize his worth, and show it to him in a hundred quiet ways.

She will make every effort to be attractive for him, even out in the jungle or just 'at home'. Neatness and cleanliness and a happy spirit are irresistible companions.

She will cultivate the qualities of sympathy, perception, and courage which will enable her to strengthen him when he is in need, whatever the cause. She has every reason to do this. The word of God to a Christian is to 'be strong, and of a good courage', and the message is reiterated all through Scripture. These qualities come, however, as the work of God when a woman is in daily contact with him. As she hears God speaking to her when she reads his Word and prays, she will be able to encourage her husband because she has been encouraged. How wonderful if she can say, 'The Lord Jehovah hath given me the tongue of them that are taught, that I may strengthen with words him that is worthy: he wakeneth, morning by morning, he wakeneth mine ear to hear as they that are taught' (Isaiah 50:4).

She will learn to weigh the present in the balance with eternity, and in this fashion will counsel with her husband.

Joy Turner Tuggy, *The Missionary Wife and Her Work*
(Chicago: Moody Press, 1966), pp. 48–9

Would the Congregationalist Miss Hasseltine have been inspired by such banalities as she prepared to go east with the solemn Dr Judson, her new husband, in 1810? Her sense of duty met with a considerable challenge, both because of the unfamiliar nature of what she was about to do and because it called into question the very virtues of domesticity and cosy home-building which Mrs Turner Tuggy extols.

He made her an offer of marriage, which compelled the young lady to face the question of leaving home and kindred for the East. Her friends, with few exceptions, strongly disapproved of her purpose, but the girl of twenty resolved to go. She thus broke the ice for her sisters. 'No female has ever left America as a missionary to the heathen.' One lady expressed the general feeling. 'I hear', she said, 'that Miss Hasseltine is going to India. Why does she go?'

'Why, she thinks it her duty,' was the answer. 'Would not you go if you thought it your duty?'

'But I would not think it my duty,' was the significant rejoinder.

Miss Hasseltine had a severe struggle as she faced the dangers, trials, and hardships of a missionary's wife, but when she had reached her decision she never wavered.

John Telford, *Women in the Mission Field*
(London: Charles H. Kelly, 1895), p. 43

The Tibetan missionary Annie Taylor met an equally unworthy rebuff from John Moffat. As a single woman her duty was to herself. The year in which she completed her 1,300 mile journey from Cheshire to Tibet was 1892, ten years after the Married Woman's Property Act had allowed British women access to any kind of financial autonomy.

The call to become a missionary came to her when she was only sixteen. She was then a boarder at Clarence House School, Richmond, and with schoolfellows was taken to hear an address on mission work given by John Moffat, son of the great African missionary. The girl was deeply impressed, and her heart beat with passionate longing to walk in the steps of the devoted workers of whom the speaker told his audience. Yet she was at the same time discouraged. Mr. Moffat addressed himself entirely to young men, and strongly discountenanced the taking up of the work by women. He described in graphic terms the suffering women and children had to endure in uncivilised lands, and expressed his conviction that their presence, far from being a help to the men, did much to hinder their work.

Miss Taylor went home wishing 'for the only time in her life' that she had not been born a boy, yet not entirely convinced that there was not some work to be done in the mission field by one of her own sex. From that time she read any missionary literature she could obtain, and as she read and re-read, her first vague desire to carry the Gospel message to the heathen crystallised into a firm unalterable purpose.

Isabel S. Robson, *Two Lady Missionaries in Tibet*
(London: S. W. Partridge, n.d.), pp. 14–15

The irony, of course, is that Moffat's parents, Mary and Robert (both of whom were great African missionaries), did not see it quite like that. Their experience would have been just the inspiration Miss Taylor needed to hear.

On her return to England they once sat talking about their missionary life at the London Mission House with Mr Robinson, the Home Secretary. Mrs Moffat, with a fond look at her husband, said, 'Robert can never say that I hindered him in his work!' 'No indeed', said Moffat, 'but I can tell you she has often sent me away from house and home for months together for evangelising purposes, and in my absence has managed the station as well or better than I could have done it myself.' A grander tribute has never been paid to the wife of a missionary hero.

John Telford, *Women in the Mission Field*
(London: Charles H. Kelly, 1895), p. 22

The resistance Dorothy Jones encountered from within the bosom of her family is a stirring example of what was in fact going on. The missionary call, in her case and many others, went hand in hand with a sense of financial autonomy. It was precisely her financial independence as a painter of china which enabled her to leave home and strike out on her own. She 'longed to teach the poor blacks the way to heaven', and began by collecting money for this purpose.

She now began to visit and pray with the sick, and prevailed on some of the local preachers to hold a cottage service once a month in the village. One night when she returned home from her round as a missionary collector, her father told her that he had made up his mind. She must give up praying both in private and public, must attend no more Methodist meetings, and must no longer beg for 'those blacks'. If she would do this, she might go once on Sunday to the Methodist Chapel and twice with him to church. Then she should have all the comforts of home and share with the rest in his prosperity. If she refused to yield, she must leave the house within half an hour. The girl replied, 'Why, father, if I were to give up praying, I should lose my soul; and the means which you wish me to give up are all helps to my soul.' She reminded him of his promise to her mother, but all was unavailing. There was nothing left but to pack her things. Within half an hour she was on her way to find some shelter. She turned to the house of a widow who met in the same class, and asked for a night's lodging. When she had told her story, the good woman said: 'Now I see how it was. I was going to pay in my missionary money. I got ready, and went out, and put in the key to lock the door, but could not. I tried and tried all ways; and, at last, in forcing it, I have sprained my wrist.' The lock turned quite easily after the visitor had entered. Dorothy stayed here till the following May. She had been earning her own living for five years as a painter of china, so she was able to provide for herself.

John Telford, *Women in the Mission Field*
(London: Charles H. Kelly, 1895), pp. 78–9

The gift of God's Spirit poured out on women is a gift which empowers them and sends them out as ministers of the gospel, against all the odds. What is striking in these accounts of the missionary vocations of women is the fact that social and economic forces created the very context within which the voice of God could both speak and be heard. The God of the missionary women was not a-historical or a-contextual. Rather, what we discover when we look at their story is a God who is revealed in a common purpose: the liberation of the missionary women themselves within the very process of their telling of the gospel to others. Both the oral tradition which sustained them and the written testimonies it produced tell out the same story: God calls women and sends women on a journey by missioning them.

CHAPTER 2

─

I, CHILD OF PROCESS

'He has sent me' (Luke 4.18)

The God of the missionary women was a God who both called and sent; who called in order to send. Through leaving home and the known and the familiar for a land and a set of understandings which God would show them, they became agents of the gospel, just as Abraham and Sarah had become agents of the covenant, just as Peter and Paul became agents of the early Church. So these women were not travelling for travel's sake; their feet were light upon the mountain because they came bearing good news; good for other women, certainly, but also and ultimately good for themselves too. In this sense the missionary journey committed women to process, to a metaphorical journey in self-discovery as well as to giving up what they knew. Many were married, some were single; all were drawn into a new phenomenon in the Church's life: the visible, fully-sanctioned, fully-endorsed, public ministry of women.

In 1891 Miss Bird set sail for Persia. There is something so incredibly glamorous about the destination that somehow one assumes the same must have been true for the journey to get there. Yet the story-line in this extract compresses the narrative to give it a certain urgency and, at the same time, almost succeeds in making it sound ordinary. Immediately, then, we have an inkling as to what makes the travel writings of missionary women distinctive from those of other women travellers.

She started from England in the month of April, in company with Miss Laura Stubbs, they two being the first unmarried lady missionaries to visit Persia. The journey was a tedious one, though they experienced several modes of transit. Having crossed the Channel they proceeded by rail to Constantinople, took a French steamer across the Black Sea, then the Russian railway to Baku, a Russian steamer across the Caspian to Enzelli, thence the carriage to Resht, and finally a fortnight's ride on horseback over the mountains to Teheran and Ispahan.

Jennie Chappell, Three Brave Women: Stories of Heroism in Heathen Lands
(London: Partridge, 1920), p. 123

An account such as this highlights what was peculiar to missionary travel and what distinguishes it from the journeys of other 'wayward women' (the book title chosen by Jane Robinson for her 1990 account of women travellers). The missionary women had a vocation from God; they were travelling for God, sent by the Spirit, in the footsteps of Jesus. So they would put up with anything, and could be called to order in severe tones by one of their own. Mother Mabel Digby's admonition in California in 1898 would be a case in point.

When we heard that our Very Reverend Mother was at Maryville, the centre of the Vicariate, our expectations grew keen. We all knew by experience, however, the fatigue that, in spite of all American comfort, ensues from four days and nights consecutive railway travelling, and that she must brave snow and icy weather before penetrating as far as our delightful climate. Her conference reminded us of our duty as foundresses. 'It is Our Lord himself who has chosen each of you, and called you by name, that you might have the honour and the responsibility of this new foundation. It is you who will establish its traditions: of obedience, of poverty, and of silence. If there are fatigues and privations too be endured, you will remember his word to his apostles: when I sent you forth to preach the gospel, did you want for anything? But they answered him: Nothing.' Her last advice ran: 'Never waste time. God himself, God himself, generous and all powerful, does not give us back lost time!'

Anne Pollen, Mother Mabel Digby (London: John Murray, 1914), p. 257

In the case of the nun missionaries, it is worth remembering that until the middle years of this century the sisters wore religious habits which were better adapted to a European climate than those they would meet where they went as missionaries. *Does this explain some of the woe that has crept into a couplet of the creaky verses which describe the Faithful Companions of Jesus' twelve missionaries to Australia?*

> It was a smiling April morn, all nature seemed asleep,
> When the proud ship 'Liguria' launched out into the deep,
> And on its deck twelve maidens stood whose hearts were brave
>   and high,
> They watched old England's fading shore with many a heartful
>   sigh,
> Yet shrank they not to brave the main, the stormy wind and
>   wave,
> For on Australia's distant shore were many souls to save.
> The voice that called was a voice of love that they e'er loved
>   to hear,
> So they went with joy and bravely strove to check the rising
>   tear.

> The scene is changed. Twelve maidens are sitting on the deck.
> But who would recognize them in their state of total wreck?

There is worse to follow:

> And every time they turn their heads or move their lips to
>   speak,
> Great tears of inky blackness are flowing down each cheek!
> Their very caps are weeping and they've grown quite lean and
>   small,
> For all their under-petticoats are hung upon the wall!

> For the ship again is rolling, all their spirits bright have flown,
> And the silence deep is broken only by a sigh or moan,
> And, from time to time, some maiden, overcoming human
>   pride,
> Hangs her head, in desolation, o'er the vessel's rocking side.
>
> > Sister M. Clare O'Connor, FCJ, *The Sisters Faithful Companions of Jesus in
> > Australia* (Victoria: Faithful Companions of Jesus, 1982), pp. 16–17

A feature of this particular tale is that it gives a group experience. Character-istically, the Roman Catholic missionary women were the nuns, the religious sisters. A kind of anonymity and decorum were required of them, along with the collectivity of the habit and the homogeneous appearance it guaranteed. If ever there were a truly hidden part of the hidden journey, it is the emotions and insights of the Roman Catholic nuns. Sent in the name of Christ, they were consigned to an extraordinary sort of oblivion where only the matriarchs or visiting general superiors would make their mark. The Gladys Aylwards of the convent world would continue to serve in domestic roles in the missions, because of an institutionalized snobbism that said 'once a parlour-maid always a parlour-maid'.

*   *   *

So what did the generality of missionary women take with them, and how did they travel? The most dramatic account is that of Gladys Aylward herself, the Edmonton parlour-maid who used her practical experience to equip herself, rather than to keep herself in role. Indeed, she prided herself that she paid her own fare when she took the Trans-Siberian railway and set off for Tientsin in China.

Expedition 'Gladys Aylward' assembled on the platform at Liverpool Street Station on Saturday 18th October, 1930. It must be numbered amongst the most ill-equipped expeditions ever to leave the shores of England, possessing in currency exactly ninepence in coins and one two-pound Cook's travellers' cheque. The cheque was sewn carefully into an old corset given to the expedition by its mother, in the severe belief that even horrible foreigners would not dare to pry too closely into such an intimate, and intimidating, feminine accessory. The corset, in fact, was a treasure house. It contained, besides the travellers' cheque, her Bible, her fountain pen, her tickets and her passports.

She kissed her mother, and father, and sister, good-bye, and settled herself into the corner seat of her third-class compartment. The whistle blew, the train hissed and puffed; she waved through the window until her family were out of sight. She dried her eyes, sat back and spread out on the seat beside her the old fur coat which a friend had given her and which her mother had cut up and made into a rug. Her two suitcases were on the rack. One contained her clothes, the other an odd assortment of tins of corned beef, fish and baked beans, biscuits, soda cakes, meat cubes, coffee essence, tea and hard-boiled eggs. She also had a saucepan, a kettle and a spirit stove. The kettle and the saucepan, with a sort of gay insouciance, were tied to the handle of the suitcase with a piece of string.

Alan Burgess, *The Small Woman* (London: The Reprint Society, 1959), p. 25

Christina Forsyth, called by her biographer 'The Loneliest Woman in Africa', used the journey as an observation post. She set sail in 1879, the year that Mary Baker Eddy became pastor of the Church of Christ Scientist in Boston.

She left Southampton in the S.S. Nubian in January 1879, the month when the Zulu War opened so disastrously. The first part of the voyage was very stormy, and there was a great deal of sickness amongst the passengers, but calm came in time. The company on board was a varied one and there was much to interest and amuse the untravelled but observant and shrewd Scottish passenger who kept so quiet and tranquil amidst the petty distractions of the journey.

In her diary are brief characterisations of various persons: the Bishop who was kept busy all day escorting the numerous seasick ladies of his party on deck and who preached to a pale and listless few from the text, 'Man goeth forth to his work and to his labour till the evening'; the Curate who threw off his sanctimoniousness when he threw off his surplice; the German who was so desperate to learn English that he waylaid ladies for lessons; the bejewelled diamond-digger and gambler who said there was no proof that the Bible was true, and who, on being told to think half an hour daily, declared that if he were to think he would go mad; the children to whom she found gingerbread cake an excellent means of introduction; the lady who told her, a little spitefully, that she had seen more degraded people in Edinburgh and Glasgow than in the whole of Natal.

W. P. Livingstone, *Christina Forsyth of Fingoland*
(London: Hodder & Stoughton, n.d.), pp. 16–17

Alice Meynell's reflective poem 'I am the Way' also lingers on the process of the journey, and finds consolation in a Jesus who is way as well as goal.

Thou art the Way
Hadst thou been nothing but the goal,
I cannot say
If Thou hadst ever met my soul.

I cannot see —
I, child of process — if there lies
An end for me,
Full of repose, full of replies.

I'll not reproach
The road that winds, my feet that err.
Access, approach
Art Thou, Time, Way, and Wayfarer.

Alice Meynell, *Poems* (London: Burns & Oates, 1913), p. 84

*   *   *

These accounts identify an important area of investigation for the concerned commentator on missionary history. Is what one is reading a first-hand account? Is it a pious collage put together by the next generation? Is it written in love, in fear, in admiration, or in disbelief? Or is it simply an exploration of the timeless symbol of journeying or quest which happens to speak to the human spirit with particular insistence, especially if it is written by a woman and happens to speak to the concerns of women?

It is certainly true that a more fulsome account of the journey is often written by the next generation or by admirers. This is the case with the first companions of Julie Billiart, the Sisters of Notre Dame who went off to California, in the early 1840s.

The details of their journey form an interesting story and make one realize the magnanimity and courage demanded of those who, a century ago, 'went down to the sea in ships', and the conditions must have called for as much heroism as any the missionaries were subsequently to encounter. Not only did the food stores become so malodorous that they had to be jettisoned, not only did the rats run across the dinner table, scamper across the beds, and gnaw away the ship's timbers in places to the thickness of a sheet of paper, but the ship was chased by pirates, battered by a hurricane during the entire week, and nearly driven ashore in Patagonia. The voyagers landed in Valparaiso which welcomed them with their first earthquake. They resisted invitations to stay at Lima, crossed the Equator a second time, came to the end of their supply of food and fresh water, and on the Feast of St. Anne, July 26th, with the captain lying at death's door, escaped shipwreck as by a miracle at the mouth of the Columbia River, which they entered by the uncharted southern channel. After a few days in Vancouver they proceeded up-river to Oregon City and thence by primitive waggons to their new home at Wallamette.

Julie [Billiart] had always declared she had no use for weakling women: the Sisters sent on her foreign missions must surely have satisfied her desires. Before a year had passed these Sisters had cleared and planted an orchard of six hundred square feet, had planted barley and peas for their eighteen cows, were expecting a heavy potato crop, had discovered how to make soap by mixing grease with oak wood ashes, had sent home to Belgium scholastic exercises penned by their pupils and would have sent also samples of their needlecraft, but the eighty frocks made from the dress stuffs consigned from Europe were already on the backs of the dressmakers, and the lace surplice at which the children were working was destined for the Bishop.

All this time the Sisters had received no letters from Namur.

Sister F. de Chantal, SND, *Julie Billiart and Her Institute*
(London: Longmans, Green & Co., 1938), pp. 218–19

A first-hand and very different account is given by Hannah Kilham. Here the Quaker traveller recalls the spiritual insight that went with hardship on board and separation from loved ones — the certainty that God's will would be done. Apart from anything else, this is a wonderful account of how women can sustain emotional loss.

We went in the evening on board the ship, which lay at anchor, and waiting for the tide. As we sat down together in the cabin we were again mercifully favoured with such an overshadowing sense of heavenly love and goodness, that I could not well forbear expressing the sense I then felt, that, although 'the waves of the sea are mighty, the Lord who dwelleth on high is mightier'. Our beloved friends, R.F. and A.S., left us, and after we had watched them for a time sailing towards the shore, we retired to our cabins. It was comforting to have had these dear friends with us. I think we had been consoled together in the feeling with which it had pleased divine goodness to favour us, and believing our separation was in his will, we parted peacefully. The next morning being our first day we held our little meeting together, and were permitted to feel that we were not forsaken. I informed the captain that it was our usual practice to read the Scriptures after breakfast, and, if he did not object, we wished to continue to do so. He freely consented, and the other passengers remained with us. We came next morning opposite Deal. While we remained at anchor there the wind arose and blew strong, yet it being favourable, we again set sail. For two days the gale increased. During the night of the 31st the wind rose higher and higher, and, in the morning, a truly awful scene presented, but which I could only know by report, being too weak to go on deck. The waves broke over the vessel, and, it seemed every moment ready to go to the bottom. I had, during the awful suspense of the preceding day, been led into close searchings of heart; yet, through all the consciousness of human imperfection, and, though very humblingly sensible of my own, I could not find ground to conclude that I had been misled in this concern, either as to the cause itself or the step I had now taken in it, although fear as to the possibility of too prompt conclusions on what I had felt, would still at times present itself. I cannot say that hope of our eventual deliverance from this storm was ever quite withdrawn, and I could not but believe that should we ever be taken away at this time, the cause itself in which we had embarked would still be carried on by other agents.

Sarah Biller (ed.), *Memoir of the Late Hannah Kilham*
(London: Darton & Harvey, 1837), pp. 172–3

Christ's power over the sea inspires the reflections of Caryll Houselander. In her meditation on the sixth Station of the Cross, entitled 'Veronica wipes the face of Jesus', she writes:

The power of Christ is able to control fiercer storms than those of the wind and the sea. It is able to still the torrents of evil of the whole world in the stillness of his own heart. It is the power which enables him to command the floods of all the sorrow in the world and hold them within his peace. It is the power which can not only give life back to the dead, but can change death itself to life. It is the power of divine love.

So, for a moment, a vision more wonderful than that of Tabor is granted to the woman whose compassion drove her to discover Christ in a suffering man. Then Christ passes on, on the way of sorrows, leaving her with the veil in her hands and on it the imprint of that face of suffering that hid the beauty of God.

In Christ burying his face in that woman's veil on the Via Crucis, we are looking at the many children of today whom war has twisted and tortured out of the pattern of childhood, who are already seared and vitiated by fear, persecution, homelessness and hunger.

We see grown-up people who have been maimed or disfigured, those whom chronic illness or infirmity has embittered. We see, too, those most tragic ones among old people, those who are not loved, and are not wanted by their own, those in whom the ugliness, not the beauty of old age is visible. We see the tragic ones who are cut off from all but the very few, the Veronicas of the world, by mental illness. We see, too, many who are dying, who with Christ are coming to the end of their Via Crucis, yet sometimes without realizing that Christ is suffering for and in them.

Caryll Houselander, *The Stations of the Cross*
(London: Sheed & Ward, 1955), pp. 62–3

* * *

As Alice Meynell had hinted, though, the initial journey did not guarantee that the travellers had arrived at their goal. This goes some way to explaining the lack of curiosity with which they travelled. There was, after all, more journeying to be done, as the Australian Salvationist Gladys Calliss discovered. Her biographer notes that 'Calliss wore a shortsleeved, open-neck khaki shirt with skirt to match.' Orthodox readers will be reassured to learn that washable 'Ss' were also worn.

Not quite such a burden as the nuns' habits — and washable to boot.

We travelled 22 miles yesterday by bullock cart, at a pace of three or four miles an hour. Two boys travel with us and look after the bullocks. It is a thrill for these young people to go on tour with the Colonel. They take part in the meetings and act as translators when necessary. There are seven languages and several dialects in this division, but I have to learn Malay for the people and Dutch for the business contacts and records.

At the end of the meeting there were 12 seekers. I was particularly interested in an intelligent looking girl who appeared to be very concerned. I learnt afterwards that her father was a Moslem and her mother a spirit worshipper. This acceptance of the Christian faith in front of all

these people would be a great test for her. She had told the Captain's
wife some time previously that she wanted to accept Christianity. She
needs our prayers.

We left at seven o'clock the following morning for another village
about 10 miles away, but as the road was so rough and we had to cross
about six creeks it was 11 o'clock before we arrived there.

Frederick Coutts, *More Than One Homeland: The Story of Gladys Calliss*
(London: Salvationist Publishing, 1981), p. 31

For Irene Petrie, security came from comparison with the known and the
familiar, Loch Duich and Scottish views. It might be tempting to condemn
this as parochialism. But in a first-hand account, comparisons such as these
work rather well. They convey the mindset of a 'child of process' for whom
landmarks become rather important, giving, as they do, a sense of where the
traveller has come from as well as where the journey is going.

On May 2nd we took possession of a fleet of five boats, and starting on
a stage of the journey even more beautiful than all that had gone before,
floated up the river. Its silence contrasted strangely with the roar and
din of waters during the past week, the towing path was carpeted with
wild flowers, the mighty amphitheatre of mountains all around shone
one dazzling mass of white, save where they fell away at the point we
entered by, where the Jhelum forces a passage through to water the
hot plains of the Punjab, and loses itself at last in the Indus.

Ascension Day, May 3rd, was spent on the Wular Lake, which reflects
in its quiet waters the encircling snow-mountains, and must be in some
respects the most beautiful lake in the world. Mist and rain drew a
purple haze over the near hills at times, when the views were quite
Scottish and recalled Loch Duich.

On the sunny morning of May 4th, after breakfasting in a meadow
blue with iris, under the shade of mulberry-trees, we entered the Kashmir
capital.

So ends the first stage of the grandest journey I have ever made, in the
course of which I have walked a hundred miles. We have had no difficulty
or accident of any kind, and have enjoyed perfect weather throughout
and more congenial companionship, *Deo gratias*. It is so glorious to be
up among these dear hills, and I am in Alpine condition. Oh that all
the dear home friends were here with us now to see what we see!

Mrs Ashley Carus-Wilson, *Irene Petrie: Missionary to Kashmir*
(London: Hodder & Stoughton, 1900), p. 143

'I am in Alpine condition.' This is when first-hand accounts come into their very own, because they give a vivid turn of phrase, a judicious note of realism which makes the text come alive. At this point another distinction becomes important. Not simply the question about first- or second-hand accounts, but the question of the very narrative form itself. It would be idle to pretend that all the missionary women were equally accomplished writers, when clearly they were not. The most experienced and hardened travellers of them all were the Misses French (Evangeline and Francesca) and Miss Cable (Mildred). Not only had they got the travel bit totally worked out, but they knew how to organize men as well. More than that, they could actually write. No wonder then that my own first experience both of travel and of missionary writing came when, at the age of fourteen, I discovered their most famous book The Gobi Desert in the library of the convent school I attended. Nowadays I haunt second-hand bookshops, intent on acquiring books about women. When I go into travel bookshops I am expected to pay eight times what theological bookshops charge for the writings of French and Cable. Their writing is evocative and practical, lyrical and quizzical by turns. No wonder I've never forgotten it; no wonder it is now collected in its own right.

The nights *à la belle étoile* were delightful, the only disadvantage being that no undressing was possible, so we drew out our wadded quilts, and lay down covered with a rug, to awake at sunrise and find some ploughman with bovine eyes gazing wonderingly at us. One afternoon a storm blew up, and a woman from a poor little farm situated a quarter of a mile away came to offer us the hospitality of her home.

'I have been talking to my husband,' she said, 'and we both think that if it should rain in the night you would find this meadow turn into a swamp. I have a little second room in my house which we can clear for you. Come up and see it.'

We went with her and found a farmhouse consisting of one general room for sleeping, cooking and living purposes, but with a tiny outhouse which would be used by a man to watch the grain on the threshing-floor. This she prepared for us, and then entertained us with the best that her home could afford. Not knowing her name, we always referred to this woman as 'Lydia', in remembrance of another woman who on a former occasion offered hospitality to missionaries.

Mildred Cable and Francesca French, *Through Jade Gate and Central Asia*
(London: Hodder & Stoughton, 1927), p. 187

We divested ourselves of the familiar Chinese dress and walked out
of the cottage dressed in clothes which closely resembled those of
the Siberian peasant. We each wore a home-made skirt and jumper,
our heads were tied around with a kerchief, as we possessed no
hats, our feet were shod with sandals which a Turki shoemaker had
produced and called 'foreign' footgear, yet in spite of all we attracted
no attention, for we presented the most desirable of appearances,
that of being conformed to the style of the country in which we were
travelling.

> Mildred Cable and Francesca French, *Through Jade Gate and Central Asia*
> (London: Hodder & Stoughton, 1927), p. 295

For the whole of the next day we explored gardens and found ourselves
constantly reminded of Alice's adventures in wonderland, for each of
the enclosures was connected with others by low doors in high mud
walls, and each time we opened such a door some unexpected and beautiful scene lay before us. From an apricot enclosure we came to a peach
garden, from a walnut grove we entered an apple orchard, then on to
a vineyard or a plantation of figs, and it was impossible to know what
the next delight would be. In many of the gardens were shady pavilions
and also low, flat-roofed rooms in which the gardeners might shelter to
enjoy their midday siesta. It was quite easy to climb on to these roofs,
and when we did so our heads and shoulders were among boughs laden
with ripe mulberries. They were not easy to gather, because, as the trees
were shaken the ground was covered with berries so full of juice that it
splashed itself in all directions. Only those placed as we were can know
the full flavour of the hand-picked mulberries, some of which were black,
others honey-coloured, and some mottled in shades of delicate mauve.
When evening came the girls gathered round and performed graceful
dances, beating out the rhythm on cymbals and home-made, ass-skin
tambourines, while women came with offerings of fruit and cakes. When
darkness fell they sat in a circle and listened reverently while we sang
hymns and worshipped our God. We had many long talks with them
about God, whom they called Huda, when we told them of His love
and of His power to save. Some of the men were very hostile, but as
we were the Khan's guests they dared not say what they would have
liked, but the women listened and all of them accepted copies of the
Gospels in their Turki language, books which were given us by that
great Bible Society which was always helping us. We know that the

men would read these books in secret when there was no one at hand
to watch and report them at the Mosque.

Mildred Cable and Francesca French, *Wall of Spears*
(London: Lutterworth Press, 1951), pp. 138–9

Tomorrow morning we leave Kanchow for Suchow, seven days' cart
journey. The old 'Gobi express' which was sold in Urumchi, has been
replaced by a stylish little cart with camel-hair cover and a wadded
lining, into the curtain of which a pane of glass has been ingeniously
fixed, so that the 'Old Tai-tai' inside may see all without being seen
herself! Like so many good things, it came into our hands ready for
use, greatly to the surprise of the community which knew that we
might have great difficulty in securing exactly what we needed. A carpenter has fitted it with a pair of *ears* which stand out prominently
to either side, and hold articles of daily use as the flour bag, frying-
pan, carter's sheepskin, and parcels of tracts. The money which some
of you have entrusted to us for Central Asian evangelization has been
spent upon Christian literature and attractive posters, as well as on
necessary equipment, such as tents, lamps and paraffin oil. This latter
commodity now costs us about two shillings a pint, a heavy expense,
but an absolute necessity for evangelistic tent meetings.

We are in process of converting an honest agriculturist into a capable
cook-general. A solemn assembly was held at which he was appointed
by the Church to be our helper. A highly trained and very superior
'gentleman help', who had escorted us from Lanchow as far as Kanchow,
was entrusted with the task of initiating him into the ways of a western
household. The lesson on table-laying was given in this wise: 'Brother
Chen, the laying of a table must be done exactly in order. *If* these ladies
owned knives, forks and spoons, they would be laid thus and thus, but
seeing that they share one knife you may place it in the middle of the
table, and put the teaspoon by its side. The three pairs of chopsticks
you may lay to the right side or to the left as you will.'

Mildred Cable and Francesca French, *A Desert Journal*
(London: Hodder & Stoughton, 1934), pp. 36–7

*Francesca French and Mildred Cable wrote endlessly about their travels. They
supply practical information about food and clothes as well as transport and
money. They are the closest the missionary movement has come to professional travellers, as committed to the journey and its delights as to any arrival.*

Nothing they wrote is as funny as Rose Macauley's novel The Towers of
Trebizond, *the novel which comes closest to a parody of their writing and to
the accomplishments of missionary women, though there was certainly something of the zeal of Great Aunt Dot about them. But then Trebizond in
reality was not so funny as she had made out. Fidelia Fiske discovered this
to her cost.*

Fidelia Fiske was brought up in an intense spiritual atmosphere. She
was brought under searchings of soul at the age of thirteen, and made
a public confession before the congregation of faith in Christ when she
was only fifteen. At the age of twenty-three, means were found to send
her to Mount Holyoke Seminary. There she graduated in due course,
and became a teacher. The lady who presided over the seminary was
anxious to create a missionary spirit amongst the teachers and students,
and did not find much difficulty in impressing Miss Fiske. When a missionary from Persia visited Mount Holyoke and appealed for helpers, she
sent him the following words on a slip of paper: 'If counted worthy, I
should be willing to go'. The family at the farm were naturally reluctant
to part with her, but a prayer meeting was held at which they made up
their minds, and finally dismissed her in the name of the Lord.

She reached Trebizond, on the Black Sea, in 1842. Her station
was to be Oroomiah, where there were about a thousand Nestorians,
amongst about twenty-four thousand Mohammedans and Jews. The
condition of these people, the fringe of the ancient Church of the
East, was more unhappy and degraded. The condition of the women
was as bad as could be. Miss Fiske saw at once, with the eye of the
new-comer, that the only way to reach them would be to get them
to school.

The prospects were not encouraging. School had been tried before
with poor success. The girls did not care to learn, and their parents
were afraid that bookishness would spoil their daughters for field labour
in which most of them were employed. She, however, made a start with
one or two little girls. The first two were brought by the Nestorian
bishop, Mar Yohanan. 'They are your daughters,' he said, and left them
in her charge.

Miss Fiske had to begin from the very bottom. She had to wash her
pupils as well as teach them.

E. C. Dawson, *Missionary Heroines of the Cross*

(London: Seeley, Service & Co., 1930), pp. 170–1

A note of irony is struck more easily by a sophisticated traveller like Monica Storrs. In Canada she discover a town called Pouce Coupé (Cut thumb).

Pouce Coupé is the 'County Town' of the Peace River Block. I had plenty of time yesterday to admire it. It looks like a cross between a soldiers' permanent camp during the War, and a home for lost bathing machines. The bathing machines are apparently thrown down more or less haphazard on the waste ground, but there are two or three broad mud roads among them with raised pavements made of logs or planks. When you reach the bathing machines you find that one is a bank, another a Government Office, and another a general store, and of course there are two or three garages.

> W. L. Morton, *God's Galloping Girl: The Peace River Diaries of Monica Storrs, 1929–1931* (Vancouver: University of British Columbia Press, 1979), pp. 8–9

There was glamour and a sense of adventure, though; all was not as banal as Monica Storr intimated. The driving sense of vocation which inspired the missionary women did not totally blind them to the beauty of what they found, as another accomplished writer, Mary Warburton Booth, recalled:

The glamour of the East began at Port Said, but the real thing was arriving at Bombay by night, and driving through the lamplit streets to the Mission House where we were welcomed, and the following night we began the long train journey to the United Provinces. I spent the weekend at Benares with the friend who had brought the message to Mildmay that had stirred our depths, and on Monday she saw me off on my last day's journey to the place where I was appointed by the Society who had accepted me, and that evening I arrived in Gorakhpur.

Nothing could have been more prosaic than my arrival in the place where God has kept me all these years. There was no romance about it; it was just the plain fact of a woman arriving and another woman meeting her and taking her home: but before I had been with her an hour, I knew that I was wanted, not only needed, and that first night was full of thanksgiving, and that is how I began my life in Gorakhpur 36 years ago.

> Mary Warburton Booth, *My Testimony*
> (London: Pickering & Inglis, 1947), p. 64

And with the arrival came the opportunity to observe other apparently plain facts, about the women they found as well as the women who greeted them there. A more dense analysis would follow, especially when what looked like quaint or entertaining customs were revealed as the very stuff of the women's ministry to each other.

The Moslem women wearing the *Burkha* was one of the most engaging sights. Islam here exacts that from the age of twelve till the time of her death a woman shall not leave the precincts of her house unless she wear a dress which covers her from the crown of her head to her feet, so that she moves, as it were, wrapped in a shroud. Across her eyes one strip of open needlework forms a fine lattice through which she views the world. For her convenience there are Women's Booking Offices with women clerks, and it is significant of her illiteracy that these offices, as well as all apartments reserved for women, are so indi-cated by a picture of a veiled woman over the door.

The most farcical scenes are sometimes enacted when the woman ticket collector tries to induce Beebee (Madame) to produce the railway ticket which she has purchased and submit to have a portion of it removed with a puncher. Sometimes the altercation lasts so long that the train moves on, leaving Beebee triumphant, with a whole ticket still in her possession (that is, if she ever had one at all).

> Mildred Cable, Evangeline French and Francesca French, A *Desert Journal*
> (London: Hodder & Stoughton, 1934), p. 21

And of course there was the animal kingdom as well. It too provided a welcome and served the divine purpose by driving the missionaries back to the source of their inspiration, as Florence Allshorn discovered in Uganda.

Well what with all this loneliness, disheartening work, language, rats in your bedroom, lots of them, hyaenas, leopards and jackals in the garden, keeping you awake half the night more often than not, another seven foot black snake outside my bedroom door, ants, bites by the hundred, you've simply got to grip on to all the courage you possess and fight and fight not to get under it all. The queer thing is that I have really been happier this month than I have ever been before; you get driven back and back on God every time.

> J. H. Oldham, *Florence Allshorn and the Story of St Julian's*
> (London: SCM Press, 1951), pp. 25–6

Then there were the nationals. Joy Turner Tuggy, exemplary missionary wife and mother, has a word for us:

A MISSIONARY MINISTRY

The words seem to fit the missionary situation exactly; especially in primitive or pioneer areas. They express precisely the reason a woman need waste no tears over the hours she cannot spend doing 'missionary work'. As a wife and mother she is not *telling* people how a Christian acts at home; she is *showing* them. For this reason she must allow the Lord to be, in very truth, Lord of her life and of her home.

She dare not permit any resentment toward the people at the lack of privacy that is often her portion. She has gone to live among them in order to have contact with them to reach them with the Gospel, and while in time she *will* try tactfully to give her husband a certain amount of privacy that he can better accomplish his ministry, she must never do so by building barriers. The love of God alone will enable her to do this tactfully.

Her own chief area of contact with the nationals will be in her home, especially while her children are young. Depending on the circumstances of each case, of course, much of her actual missionary work will be done within the four walls of her home. If she is a true missionary, with a heart reaching out to minister to the needs of all about her, she will find this an ample field and a fruitful one.

> Joy Turner Tuggy, *The Missionary Wife and Her Work*
> (Chicago: Moody Press, 1966), p. 98

A much more majestical evangelical voice lays out the battle lines quite chillingly. This is the real agenda that the early missionary women faced. This is the combat to which they went. What an irony then that Isobel Kuhn uses a masculine pronoun in her second paragraph to describe an experience she herself had lived. It leaves Joy Turner Tuggy's 'she' and 'her' and appropriate roles unchallenged — like a very stronghold of Satan.

Satan has a stronghold — isolated and unchallenged for centuries — a great mountain canyon in West China. Its river takes its source in Tibet and its banks rise to the height of eleven to fifteen thousand feet. The tiers of mountain peaks, flung around chaotically on either side as far as the eye can see, are separated from each other by deep ravines and abysmal chasms. Impossible as it may seem, this canyon is inhabited by human beings, for everywhere you look the canyon sides are checked like patchwork quilt with little hamlets and villages, and these almost perpendicular mountain sides are cut up into little squares or oblongs of farmed lands. Human homes, human nests, have been built on little knolls or jutting ridges that offer a scarce foothold — even over a dizzy drop down the bank. You may see them in such precarious positions that you almost hold your breath lest, even as you watch, they slide over the edge and disappear.

Anyone coming to the canyon must be prepared to live perpendicularly as long as he stays; he must prepare to sweat and toil up and down steep mountain trails; he must prepare to live isolated from the rest of the world, from civilization with its medical, intellectual, and social comforts; he must prepare to have nature laugh at the feeble speck he is, and to have Satan hurl at him the fury of the hitherto unchallenged, unconquered lion faced in his own private lair. Surely this canyon is Satan's place of defence; here we will find his munition of rocks.

Isobel Kuhn, *Nests Above the Abyss* (London: China Inland Mission, 1949), p. 11

Gladys Aylward's assessment is more moderate, but all the more moving for that very reason.

'But surely,' I said [the narrator is her biographer Alan Burgess], 'in twenty years in China you must have had many strange experiences?'

'Oh yes,' said Gladys, 'but I'm sure people wouldn't be interested in them. Nothing very exciting happened.'

It was at least fifteen minutes before she confessed that she had once taken some children across the mountains.

The rest of the conversation went in this manner, a verbatim memory which I have never forgotten:

'Across the mountains? Where was that?'

'In Shansi in north China; we travelled from Yangcheng across the mountains to Cian.'

'I see. How long did it take you?'

'Oh, about a month.'

'Did you have any money?'

'Oh no, we didn't have any money.'

'I see. What about food? How did you get that?'

'The Mandarin gave us two basketfuls of grain, but we soon ate that up.'

'I see. How many children did you say there were?'

'Nearly a hundred.'

I became conscious that I was saying, 'I see', rather than often, and actually I was not 'seeing' anything at all, except that I was on the brink of a tremendous story.

It was not mock modesty on the part of Gladys Aylward; the stories she had been telling were, to her, the greatest in the world taken straight from the pages of the New Testament; that her own adventures might be worth setting down, she had simply not considered.

Since then, during the years she has been in England, she has been travelling around the country, lecturing and preaching at churches and schools and mission halls. She has been a second mother to scores of Chinese students from Singapore and Hong Kong arriving in England to study; and she has played a large part in helping to set up a hostel in Liverpool for Chinese nationals and Chinese seamen. As always, she has lived frugally, and simply, and from day to day.

She is one of the most remarkable women of our generation, and although one can never enter completely into the heart and mind of another human being, it is clear that she possesses that inner exaltation, that determination to go on unto death, which adversity, torture, brainwashing and hardship cannot eradicate from the human soul.

Alan Burgess, *The Small Woman* (London: The Reprint Society, 1959), pp. 254–5

Gladys Aylward was one of the stars of the missionary movement. Like Mary Slessor and French and Cable, hers is a household name. How odd, therefore, to read Stephen Neill's contribution to the Pelican History of the Church, Volume VI, entitled A History of Christian Missions *(London: Hodder & Stoughton, 1964) and find not a single reference to any of them. As a rule of thumb 'A' for Aylward and 'Z' for Zenana Missions are the two beam ends of an alphabet of women and missionary work. What lies between the two is what the women discovered once they had arrived and begun their apostolic work. By then the experience of the journey would have ensured that they were well into the missionary dynamic, at once called by God and sent by God, dancing in the dance of life we call the Blessed Trinity.*

CHAPTER 3

———

THY PROPHET STILL

'To announce good news to the poor' (Luke 4.18)

O Lord, O Lord, the fire burns –
I am thy prophet still!
Thy Word within me all pent-up
is straining at its bonds of flesh
and would burst forth in fiery speech;
but now, alas, the Spirit's thrust
too oft is stayed by man's conceit.
Ah, must thy Word be smothered still,
as womb-ed child must it be killed?
Thou mad'st me woman,
Thou mad'st me prophet,
and thou cans't not belie thyself.
That which to God is good
why should man contradict?
What then is sex but flesh and blood?
Shall God be bound by his own making?
Shall cell or gene be more than CALL
or Spirit's urge in man or woman?
Nay, God forbid!

'Tis well his right to speak through man
or ass, through child or woman —
let pride in guise of flesh, not rise
and say to God, 'What dost thou?'
I am thy prophet still,
and laugh at man's forbidding.
But now alas 'tis not by sex
alone that I am held in thrall.
The years, the years — and people say,
'Too old, you are too old.'
'Tis strange and wrong —
just when her soul
matured by knowledge and by pain
beneath thy Spirit's sway,
just when her suffering's healed,
her weakness changed to strength,
thy prophet most has strength to give and
balm to those in pain,
by circumstance of years
must hold her wealth and not impart
her given strength to those in need!
This shall not be!
As long as breath and health are mine
to serve — I must and can.
I am thy prophet still!
The 'must' is mine, the way is thine.
Have I unknowingly
betrayed my trust?
Have I, some place, some time,
side-stepped thy will?
Have I, a woman, wife and mother
allowed life's daily claims and clamor
to hush the Spirit's Voice?
If so, dear Lord, forgive —
I am thy prophet still!
Perhaps 'tis not in hallowed church
or in a public place
that now my voice must rise —
who knows thy plan?

The servant blindly follows.
Perhaps 'tis in the written word
thy Voice speaks through me —
perhaps 'tis through silence —
can it be? I do not know —
But come what e'er the years may bring,
thy will be done —
I am thy prophet still!

Victoria Booth-Demarest, 'I am thy prophet still' (1953)

This paean of praise of the prophetic and preaching ministry of women was written by Victoria Booth-Demarest when she was sixty-three years old. She produced it in the same year that Simone de Beauvoir published The Second Sex. *One of her final sermons was given when she was ninety years old at the Evangelical Women's Caucus conference held at Saratoga Springs, New York, in June 1980, the year in which Iris Murdoch's* Nuns and Soldiers *was published. Never let it be said that the history of religious women is peripheral or out of kilter with social reality. A granddaughter of Catherine Booth through her mother, the Maréchale, Victoire or Victoria had inherited the preaching gene. Not surprisingly, another eloquent testimony to the preaching ministry of women also comes from the heart of the non-conformist tradition. The ministry of this celebrated American preacher is recalled by the Quaker Rufus M. Jones. He recalled the preaching of his aunt Sybil in the Yearly Meeting of 1852, beginning with an account of how she first bared her head.*

At the first word she loosed the fastenings of her bonnet, and as she spoke handed it down to her husband with a grace indescribable. There was something very impressive in the act, as well as in the manner in which it was performed, as if she uncovered her head involuntarily in reverence to that vision of divine truth unsealed to her waiting eyes. And in her eyes it seemed to beam with a heavenly light serene, and in her to burn with holy inspiration and meekness, and to touch her lips and every gentle movement of her person with an expression eloquent, solemn, beautiful, as her words fell upon the rapt assembly from the heaven of tremulous, flute-like music with which her voice filled the building.

Like a stream welling from Mount Hermon, and winding its way to the sea, so flowed the melodious current of her message, now meandering among the unopened flowers of rhymeless poetry, now through green pastures of salvation, where the Good Shepherd was bearing in his bosom the tender lambs of his flock; next it took the force of lofty diction, and fell, as it were, in cascades of silvery eloquence, but slow, solemn and searching, adown the rocks and ravines of Sinai; then out like a sweet-rolling river of music, into the wilderness, where the Prodigal Son, with the husks of his poverty clutched in his lean hands, sat in tearful meditation upon his father's house and his father's love.

More than a thousand persons seemed to hold their breath as they listened to that meek, delicate woman whose lips appeared to be touched to an utterance almost divine. I never saw such an assembly so moved, but so subdued, into motionless meditation.

Sybil Jones came to assume a position in the Society comparable to that which had belonged at the end of the eighteenth century to Esther Tuke of York, and in the eighteen-thirties to Elizabeth Fry: that of an uncrowned Queen. She consoled Mrs. Lincoln after the President's death, admonished Harriet Beecher Stowe, silenced swearing sailors, and comforted the dying soldiers of the Union Army in the American Civil War.

John Ormerod Greenwood, *Quaker Encounters*, vol. 2:
Vines on the Mountains (York: William Sessions, 1977), p. 6

So much for Salvationists and Friends, and their particular spiritual heritage. For others there was more of an uphill climb, as Maude Royden realized.

The advance of feminism within the Church of England has already been very great. When the question of women missionaries was first raised, the great principle that women might preach was at once established. People, knowing only of the decision, and being perfectly accustomed to the idea of women missionaries, have forgotten how the battle raged, and with what earnestness and sincerity religious people pointed out that our Lord had only sent out men, chosen men apostles, and never even suggested that women could preach. St. Paul's familiar figure was at once brought forward, accompanied by St. Peter, and the author of the Epistle to St. Timothy. In fact the controversy followed lines now exquisitely familiar, and reached its cheerfully inevitable end in the defeat of the opponents of women missionaries.

More recently, women have been invited to preach to Church Congress meetings, to National Mission meetings, at conferences and in retreats. Great care was taken however, to insure that such 'preaching' was always to be called 'speaking', such sermons to be described as 'addresses', and such meetings never to be held in consecrated buildings.

Dale A. Johnson, *Women in English Religion 1700–1925*
(New York and Toronto: Edwin Mellen Press, 1983), p. 311

The point Maude Royden makes is an ambiguous one. On the one hand, it is perfectly true that the ministry of women should be named and honoured. They should have access to the same resources, training and power as their male colleagues. It is also demonstrably true that missionary work gave them access to all sorts of platforms and pulpits which simply did not exist at home for women. But, on the other hand, it is equally true that the good news the women missionaries brought was intensely practical and that they very soon developed extremely practical networks of support and evangelization which by-passed the structures of pulpit and sanctuary. In their hands — or on their lips — the ministry of preaching developed and grew and articulated something new for the Christian Churches' self-understanding as well as their own. Some examples of how this ministry was exercised remind one that the ministry of the word is a Bible-based ministry, and that the Bible can go everywhere. It does not have to be kept in church or chapel. What can usefully be examined are the ways in which women made the texts and insights of the Scriptures available to those among whom they laboured. Their practice gives us a blueprint for our own times.

This work began at home, and the statistics are awesome.

Her Bible classes had been a special feature of her work at Hertford Heath from the earliest days, especially the Ladies' Bible Reading. The fame of this had spread abroad, and from time to time my mother would be asked to give courses of six or twelve in other parishes or even in London drawing-rooms. When staying in the south of France in 1903 she delivered addresses on the Bible, in French, which she spoke like a native. It was in 1901 that she undertook to give one of these courses in the parish of St. Mary's, Leyton. It was held in the parish hall, known as the Victoria Room, and was attended by some seventy ladies. But this course did not come to an end with the number of Bible readings originally arranged for; it went on and on, enthusiasm increasing with every week's gathering. Ladies from neighbouring parishes had begun attending – from Leytonstone, Walthamstow, and even from further afield. Soon it had to be admitted that the Leyton Bible Reading, held on Friday afternoons, was a permanent institution.

My mother would prepare for it with the greatest care, and every Friday in the year (except during a few weeks in the holidays, when it was closed) would see her on the platform of the Victoria Room, open Bible in hand, full of joy and unflagging enthusiasm.

The Victoria Room would be completely packed every week, and when, in 1909, it was decided to pull down the Victoria Room and build a larger hall, the offer of the Wesleyan Lecture Hall, Leyton High Road, was gratefully accepted, and the Bible Reading re-opened there with satisfactory sense that there was now plenty of room, and that people could be encouraged to join, and friends brought, without fear of being turned away through finding a room already full to overflowing.

The membership reached 500, and there were never less than 300 to 400 present every week, wet or fine.

The Bible Reading was exclusively for ladies, but on one day in the year the members were permitted to bring their husbands, sons and brothers – namely, on Good Friday. And so, every Good Friday afternoon the great hall, with its wide galleries, would be completely packed out with over 1000 people.

One of her Daughters, *The Life of Florence L. Barclay*
(London: Putnam & Co., 1921), pp. 160–2

And in India and elsewhere the same scenario was repeated. Not only amongst the ladies of Hertford Heath, Leytonstone and Walthamstow.

It is the unspoken longing of hundreds of missionaries; it is the earnest prayer of hundreds more; it is the reason why hundreds left home and kindred, willing to lay down their lives to answer that question; and yet, it is always there, always present: how? how? how? how can it be done? How to approach that high-caste lady with the message of Salvation? She lives in seclusion; she has sent for the writer; she wants to learn to read, to write, to sew; she has never been to school; she had no opportunity to learn. A neighbour of hers is reading, and a desire has been created in her heart. Will the foreign lady teach her? The question in my letter is, 'How can I tell the story of Jesus and His love in such a way that the "High-Caste" may desire Him?'

Mary Warburton Booth, *'Them Also'* (London: Pickering & Inglis, 1934), p.2

A first necessity is to have copies of the text.

Wherever you travel in the Gobi you are sure to meet Tibetans, for their lamas are always out on long pilgrimages. An average of thirty miles a day seems a short distance for a caravan to cover, but to these people it would be an impossibly long stage, for they probably prostrate themselves all along the road. Such a pilgrim always enjoys a chat, and is sometimes a man with a real wish to find some way to gain the remission of sins. Tibetan is of course his native language, but in the course of his long pilgrimages he has had occasion to pick up some Chinese, and so he can talk with the people he meets. Every Gobi trade-route carries all these people and many more, and the missionary's problem is how to convey a message which fits every one of them. Only one book can do this, because it is the Word of God which is for every man of every nation, but it must be taken to him in his own language or it is of no use to him. This means that some-one must learn the language so well that he can translate the Bible into it. All translation is a great feat of scholarship, and among missionaries there are many fine scholars who do this work. When the translation has been done it must be printed in a script and style which is acceptable to the people for whom it is intended. This also is done by the British and Foreign Bible Society. The book must then be transported to many strange places, and again the Bible Society undertakes this work. Its distribution is done by Christian missionaries of every Society that exists. Now you understand why we wrote straight off to Bible House and asked for help when we reached Spring of Wine and saw what a big job lay before us.

Mildred Cable and Francesca French, Wall of Spears
(London: Lutterworth Press, 1951), pp. 168–9

A second necessity is to know how to pronounce and read it.

In the afternoon we met for Sunday School, one class for men, one for women, two or three for children. Then there was a short service, and questions on the lesson instead of a sermon.

  Mistakes over Scripture names arose now and then.

  'Where did Adam come from?' was the question.

'A duck laid him, of course,' was the surprising answer.

It transpired that 'Adam' in Chinese sounds very similar to 'duck's egg'. The Old Testament stories of home life were very homelike and understandable.

'Poor Hagar, of course Sarah was hard on her. They always are,' with a giggle. Jacob and Esau, too, had their counterparts in many villages.

But what never failed to hold them were the stories of the Life of Christ. Taught with the help of pictures, these appealed to all. That of Christ upon the Cross produced a silence in the women's class, till one old granny said with tears upon her wrinkled cheeks: 'And they put the nails in His hands for me?'

Edith Couche, Lighting Chinese Lanterns
(London: Church of England Zenana Missionary Society, n.d.), pp. 26–7

The wrappings of the parcels in which Bibles were delivered obviously came in handy too.

One night we were suddenly awakened by the alarming roar of a tremendous gale, shaking the boughs of the poplar-trees and stripping off every leaf that remained. This preliminary onslaught was then quickly followed by an unearthly yell as the whole force of the tempest descended upon the city, carrying with it volumes of sand that whipped and cut against our pavilion like a volley of musketry. Without a moment's interruption the gusts swept in through the fragile paper windows, deluging us with grit as we lay in our beds. No sleep was possible, and when daylight came we found our room literally buried under a thick layer of Gobi Desert dust, the shape of each one's head being defined on the pillow, while the soft earth of the floor was ripple-marked like the ribbed seashore at low tide. Experience taught us, subsequently, that the only way to smooth it down was to sprinkle the surface with water, and then spend all our spare moments stamping it flat. This process, however, was not very successful, for the powdery soil remaining loose through the winter, small articles were frequently buried in it, only reappearing at intervals when an extra watering brought them once more to the surface.

For forty-eight hours the fearful blasts persisted without one moment's pause. Not a drop of rain fell throughout, and we finally emerged with hair, eyebrows, skin and clothes heavy with the particles, and with bodies exhausted and nerves strained by the tension and magnetic quality of the storm. The danger to caravans when overtaken by such a visitation is extreme, and many instances are recorded of carts, horses and drivers, all of which having been first battered to pieces disappeared for ever under the roaring sands.

The sight of our room afterwards made us realise that something must be done to stop up the crevices and holes in the woodwork. The large sheets of brown paper used by the Bible Societies in sending their goods by post met our difficulty, and for one whole day we cut out strips, which our old retainer with the help of a basin of paste affixed to every crack through which, only too plainly, the daylight gleamed. Suchow being totally unprotected from the vast expanse of Gobi on the west, and the sands of Mongolia on the north, this last experience proved to be but the first of many, and we began to view the incoming winter, under present conditions, with a certain amount of anxiety. Seeing therefore that our life must necessarily be somewhat rigorous, we added a layer of camel's hair to our already wadded Chinese garments, and thus equipped we were subsequently enabled to meet temperatures registering fifteen degrees Fahrenheit below zero.

Mildred Cable and Francesca French, Through Jade Gate and Central Asia
(London: Hodder and Stoughton, 1927), pp. 104–5

But above all what was required was the certainty that this was a word addressed where there was need. The Persia missionary Elizabeth Thompson went straight into action.

She lost no time, but started in October 1860, intending to spend the next half-year at Beirut. She did not at that time foresee the work which lay before her, and which was to fill the remainder of her life. It was heart-breaking at Beirut. 'At first my heart,' she says, 'died within me at the squalor, noise, and misery of these people. Ignorance of the truth and deeply cherished revenge characterised the greater number of the women.' But her gentleness and sympathy soon produced some effect, and as she read to them the words of Christ they began to listen, saying, 'We never heard such words. Does it mean for us women?' She at once began to teach them to read in order that they might get to know the Scriptures, which were, to nearly all, sealed books.

E. C. Dawson, Missionary Heroines in Many Lands
(London: Seeley, Service & Co., 1912), p. 30

And because necessity is the mother of invention, underhand strategies get invented. Because it does indeed mean 'for us women', and the sheer exhilaration of Mary Warburton Booth's account, with her frank admission that 'It was a wonderful experience for me' says it all.

We decided to do more praying, and to seek a way to sow for a more bountiful harvest. Every day during that week we were persuaded that there was something intensely vital in the results of a pioneer of the Gospel. So by Saturday we had prepared for a big bazaar in the jungle, and having engaged a bullock cart, we sauntered forth. The roads had ruts knee deep, and we rocked and riddled through them.

'This is a robber infested road,' said our cartman. 'If you are out after dark, you will lose all you have.' And then with a gruesome smile he told of happenings to those he knew, and with a very decided nod of his head he said, 'We shall be back before sunset.' Then we were at the Bazaar.

'What are you going to do with those books?' he asked.

And I promptly answered, 'Sell them.' It had come at last. I was ready to sell or do anything that would help these people to know the value of the Good News we brought. So taking our stand by the cart, we began.

'Listen to this: "Come unto me all ye that are weary and heavy laden and I will give you rest,"' and a crowd gathered. 'Do you want salvation?' I asked.

'Aye verily,' was the reply.

'This book will tell you about the Giver of salvation. The price is one *pice*.'

Eager hands were stretched out, *pice* were thrust into my hands, and sharp eyes noticed that the books were not all the same colour. 'Green, green!' shouted a voice at the back. So I handed a copy of St. Luke. 'Yellow', shouted another, and St. Mark found a place. But the eagerness was lost immediately, for a man saw that his book was thinner than those of his neighbours. He thought that he had not got his money's worth. He counted the leaves. He was not satisfied, so handed it back. He preferred a thicker book for his *pice*. So a copy of St. John was passed into his hand. He came back again, this time with a friend. He was hugging his red-backed copy. He wanted to know whether the words I had read from his friend's book were in his. I opened his and read chapter 3, verse 16. He listened enthralled and then nodded approval to his friend. Very carefully he produced a rag from his pocket, spread it out on the ground, then put his purchase right in the middle and tied it up. I handed him a tract telling the way of salvation. 'It is free,' I said: 'Read it carefully with the Book.' He nodded and walked way with a triumphant step. It was a wonderful experience for me.

Mary Warburton Booth, 'They That Sow'
(London: Pickering & Inglis, n.d.), pp. 40–1

* * *

Bible work did not go unopposed, however, as the Scottish missionary Martha Croll discovered. Her strategy, to go in 'as a sister and friend', made her a moving target for those who would oppose her; totally subversive and inaccessible by turns.

The work was arduous in the extreme. The Brahmin priests were masters of the people's conscience, and bitterly resented any intrusion. They used every means short of actual violence to hinder the introduction of the Gospel among their flock. But Miss Croll was not to be denied. She went among the women as a sister and friend, and soon succeeded in winning the hearts of a few. The poor women welcomed her mingled strength and gentleness, and soon grew to regard her as a principal adviser and guide. They found in her just the refuge they needed, and which their own religion utterly refuses to women. She quickly became to these poor creatures the beloved 'Miss Sahib', whom they could trust and who alone really cared for them. The result was as might be expected, and not a few were won to accept the Gospel which their friend and counsellor so earnestly preached.

E. C. Dawson, *Missionary Heroines in Many Lands*
(London: Seely, Service & Co., 1912), p. 137

Another Scots woman, Miss Moir, had a similar experience in Africa.

Another important work Miss Moir undertook was to visit the kraals on Sunday mornings accompanied by a bodyguard of the Christian children who formed a kind of choir. In this way she came close to heathen life in its stark squalor and degradation and to the heathen mind, so curiously simple and yet so bafflingly complex.

Not always was she welcome. Some men, when they saw her coming, would slink away up the mountain — 'to look after the sheep' they said. One exclaimed in disgust, 'You are always speaking about your gods. I am sick of it.' Another muttered, 'God will be with us whether we love sin or not.' After she had spoken on the resurrection, one protested indignantly, 'I will not rise from the dead.' The only comment of a young man on an address she gave on prayer was 'Can I get what I want from God?' — then in an undertone, 'I would like a jacket.'

This materialist attitude of mind sometimes had startling manifestations. One day she was sitting in a kraal in the midst of a group of half naked men and women decked with ornaments of beads and coins. They were cooking, eating, or lounging, while lean dogs roamed around. She began to tell them the story of the Crucifixion. As she spoke the women fastened their eyes on her, their hearts touched by the pathos of the great world-tragedy. When she finished they expressed their horror at the cruelty of men who had put so gentle a Saviour to death. Then one young man, covered with beads, rose, and with dramatic posturings showed how He had hung on the Cross and suffered and died.

She never lost patience with them. Quietly, doggedly, unceasingly, she taught them the love of God and the principles of the redemptive gospel.

W. P. Livingstone, *Christina Forsyth of Fingoland*
(London: Hodder & Stoughton, n.d), pp 40–1

But the missionary women developed strategies for taking the gospel where they could not themselves go. And so native women were trained as Bible women and evangelists. This pattern of evangelism is one which repays careful study. It accords very well with the 'one-step' theory, namely the idea that the person who is one step further along the road is better able to accompany and support an enquirer or fellow pilgrim than someone who is already far over the hill and into the next valley. In this way the missionary women empowered native women and allowed the gospel to become indigenized far more quickly than if they had sought to control it and the way in which it could be told. Helen Barrett Montgomery explains:

In addition to the missionary teachers and physicians, there are women set apart for evangelistic work. With their trained Bible women they tour the villages, and visit the markets and homes of the cities. In everything but name they are preachers, and often the most effective ones. Sitting at the well-side or under some spreading trees, they gather women and children about them and tell the old, old story of Jesus and his love. Perhaps the most far-reaching work of the lay evangelists is done through the Bible women. These they gather for instruction and send them out two by two sometimes, and sometimes singly, and they talk over fully with them the experiences they meet . . .

The Bible woman has become an institution. Her work is indispensable; she multiplies the missionary's influence, goes before to prepare the way, and after to impress the truth. One of the humblest, she is at the same time one of the mightiest forces of the Cross in non-Christian lands. She is first of all an evangelist. From door to door she goes, repeating portions of the Scriptures, or reading the Bible, singing hymns, praying, telling her own personal experience of God's goodness. She may be the only Christian woman in a village. She may teach the little village school, she may nurse the sick in seasons of pestilence, she may gather together a Sunday school, she may teach needlework and reading to the shut-in women of the zenanas.

Helen Barrett Montgomery, *Western Women in Eastern Lands*,
(New York: Macmillan, 1911), pp. 114, 136

Not only were evangelists called to the service of the word, but in other ways too a variety of methods were developed, to extend this strong oral tradition. Once again the method was used at home, as well as overseas, as Miss Hope-Bell of the London Missionary Society reminds us.

In these days when there is a sincere desire that international friendship may become a reality, one of the best ways of preparing for such an ideal state among ordinary people is to encourage missionary enthusiasm wherever possible. It has been said that 'Zeal depends upon interest, and interest upon knowledge.' Those of us who are workers in women's meetings should remember that we may be the only link the women can have with God's work across the seas. Unless we plan to give them knowledge, they cannot possibly develop any interest, much less enthusiasm and a desire to help their sisters in other lands by sending them the gospel message.

The most obvious way to give knowledge is to have a regular missionary speaker. It may be possible to get 'a real live missionary' once a year in connection with the missionary anniversary at the church. On other occasions the services of local enthusiasts may be secured.

Jane Sheldon (ed.), *Women Talking: A Handbook for Women's Meetings*
(London: James Clarke & Co., 1945), p. 56

* * *

There were other ways of telling the gospel, however, and women within the missionary movement soon improvised these. Mary Warburton Booth takes up the story.

I saw her again, all eagerness now, to give something to help India to know her Saviour. She was a women working for her living, and she had an aged parent whom she helped. Her earthly possessions were not much, but love always finds a way to give. She wanted to give me a nice picture for my room, so I said I would prefer a roll of Bible pictures for my Sunday class. She ordered one at the local stationer's, and my heart was singing a song of praise, of thanksgiving; for I was counting on the things that help to make a lesson live.

The next time I visited that place, the roll of pictures, mounted on linen, was put into my hand, and I could have shouted for joy. Oh, how I had longed for one! 'Now I shall be able to explain so much more clearly when I go to Zenanas, schools, or villages,' I said to myself, and proceeded to unfold the roll. We went through them three times, they were all beautiful, but there was one missing that I wanted most of all, and I was a bit disappointed. There was no picture of Calvary, and nothing about the Cross. I wished I had asked for *that*, but we remembered that we had asked the Lord to choose the picture roll for us, it was her love gift to Jesus, for her sisters in India, and He could send the most vital picture some other way. With that we were content, and I brought the roll to India.

As I write, the temperature is 108°, and this is a humid climate, so I leave you to imagine what it is like to have a Sunday School in a tiny room, 9 feet by 12 feet, with shut doors, and windows, to keep out the furnace heat, and the hot blasts of wind. All were present, and nobody wanted to concentrate on the lesson. It was too hot to think, and too breathless to care. The hymns were flat, and the reading uninteresting. We all squatted on the floor, the girls grown so tall and attractive, but they were listless like leaves before a storm, they were nearly asleep. I went to the cupboard, and took out the picture roll, they looked up.

'This one,' I said, 'is the Lord Jesus Christ being baptised.' The statement was electric, every one sat up and took notice. Then the truth dawned on them, and I read from the Bible the peerless story, '"Suffer it to be so now: for thus it becometh us to fulfil all righteousness," and HE, the Holy One, went down into the water.' The children were astonished, they knew that baptism was something to be desired by those who were Christians, but HE, the Saviour, why should He be baptised, they questioned? And those children sat, and looked on Him there. A Holy Presence came into that little room. 'You see, first of all, He, the Holy One, was baptised, so His lovers always want to be. I have been baptised,' I said.

'I, too, will be baptised,' said one, her eyes riveted on the picture.

'I will also,' said another; and I knew the picture had done its work, it would last. Love never faileth, never, never. The saved woman in England had won two little girls in India, by her love gift to her Saviour. And I watched to see what He would do next.

Mary Warburton Booth, 'Them Also' (London: Pickering & Inglis, 1934), pp. 231–3

Texts and calendars too had their place to play. Not only the missionary but also the aspirant missionary could enjoy their access to a culture which did not judge them according to academic standards or an academic method for which they might have had no training, but rather a culture which they had developed themselves — one which enabled them to prepare messages from God.

And now, I am at Mildmay! How can I describe the place? It was a revelation to me: so many women coming in and going out, every one with something to do and busy doing it. There were no leisurely movements, and no hurry either. It was life dignified, holy, and purposeful. Yes. 'There *they* dwelt with the King for *His* work': it was not mere words, it was a fact, and I was looking on, marvelling that so many women were gathered together to go out to districts where sin and poverty were rife, to seek and to save that which was lost. The Deaconess House was built on to the Conference Hall that seated over a thousand people. There were lecture rooms, a big dining-room, a very spacious drawing-room, and many other rooms, and higher up were little bedrooms that were sanctuary for the deaconesses, and there were other houses in the compound for still more deaconesses.

There was an orphanage for girls, and a plain little building they called 'The Illumination Room,' where cards and calendars painted and illuminated by those belonging to Mildmay were printed and exhibited for sale. They went all over the world, for every card had a message from God.

Mary Warburton Booth, My Testimony
(London: Pickering & Inglis, 1947), p. 37

The contrast between this resourcefulness and the sanctification of the home envisaged by Joy Turner Tuggy requires no comment.

The home is the special pulpit of the missionary mother. In a sense it is the final proof to the world that the Gospel presented by the missionary is more than a doctrine or a concept: it is a life.

For this reason, it can be affirmed that when a missionary mother runs her home smoothly and lives in it exemplarily, she is not just serving her husband and children or satisfying her own conscience; she is giving a clear demonstration of the outworkings of the Gospel in everyday life.

A minister's wife once described life in a parsonage like being 'in a goldfish bowl'.

Joy Turner Tuggy, The Missionary Wife and Her Work
(Chicago: Moody Press, 1966), p. 97

If all your focus is inwards, of course you end up feeling like a goldfish in a bowl. How authentic, in contrast, is the spiritual anguish recalled by Amy Carmichael of the children's refuge at Dohnavur.

The woman who buys the child calls it her own daughter, and can easily get witnesses to prove the relationship. We have rarely known a temple-woman adopt only one child. Most have several; and there were thousands of temple-women in this single Presidency. It was (and it is) an overwhelming thought.

But do numbers paralyse sensation? We saw a child of six one day. She was brought to try to draw our little girl away from us. She was a gentle thing, with large, soft brown eyes and the daintiest, prettiest ways. She looked wistful — not unhappy, only wistful — and there was the aloofness of one already set apart. We stretched out our hands to her; she smiled as though across a deep ravine. We could not go to

her. She could not come to us. We never saw her again; but we heard
that she became a very noted servant of the gods.

There was another. We were not conscious of any space between us.
She sat on my knee, and looked up with smiling eyes. But she disappeared. We found her at last. And now there was a chasm. She shrank
away, her little face shadowed by horror and fear. She had been married
to the god of the temple of Joyous City, six miles from Dohnavur. They
had fastened a garland of pink flowers round her neck, and told her it
was her birthday. But under the flowers was a small gold token that
meant marriage to the god. A priest touched it in blessing, the soft
pink petals were not sweeter than the gentle little face.

It is unbearable. I know it. It feels cruel to tell of it. And yet
how can the reader cross the sea and walk in this new road with
us without at least some knowledge of the road? I do not want to
harrow for harrowing's sake, but I do earnestly desire to draw the
heart that can care for a child into fellowship, and hold it fast to
the road's end.

People, in their kindness, used to try to distract us from this that
could not be forgotten. To be with them, hearing their talk, so clear
and friendly, reading their books, looking at their pleasant things, was
like being in some clear green field full of blessed flowers. But every
now and then the face of the field would fall in and discover a vault
below; and in the vault chains and darkness and the souls of young
children.

One night – we cannot forget it because the face of the field peeled
off so suddenly, and the vault was so hatefully black – we found ourselves in the presence of one of the men who control this secret traffic.
Half animal, half demon, not man at all, he sat, a coiled mass of naked
flesh, in a huge armchair, watching us with snake-like eyes, and waiting
in silence for us to speak. The window-shutters of that upper room were
closed, though the night was hot; the room was full of sickly fumes;
a yellow flame flickered in a corner. It was an evil room. We could
not speak, but turned defeated and, climbing down the steep and slimy
stairs, escaped into the cleaner air of the street. We had heard that he
was a great sadhu, this Jeer – lately head priest of a Benares temple –
and had hoped that he might be one to whom we could appeal. Such
hopes are froth.

But words are froth too; the desolation of the children who had
no deliverer, the wrong that we could not redress, the fear, the cold

deadness of forced sin, how little of this could be shown then, can be shown now.

At last a day came when the burden grew too heavy for me; and then it was as though the tamarind trees about the house were not tamarind, but olive, and under one of those trees our Lord Jesus knelt, and He knelt alone. And I knew that this was His burden, not mine. It was He who was asking me to share it with Him, and not I who was asking Him to share it with me. And there was only one thing to do: who that saw Him kneeling there could turn away and forget? Who could have done anything but go into the garden and kneel down beside Him under the olive trees?

Amy Carmichael, Gold Cord (London: SPCK, 1932), pp. 30–1

*   *   *

All was not always so dire. Much of the work done by the missionary women is work we would associate with the ordained ministry. That is why it comes as no surprise to discover that missionary women were associated precisely with this particular ministry. Sometimes their service was recruited on a much more ad hoc basis. The women would lay their hand to whatever was needed, so that red tape was treated as a detail in the face of pastoral need. An example. Missionary women labouring in the field were called to conduct services or to give the address at a moment's notice.

Of course Mr. Neilson, whom I had twice visited about it, had not lighted the fire as promised, so Mr. Simpson lighted it when he came and the little school was still freezing. Also he had not produced any extra bench to supplement the twelve small desks. So there were about twelve kids with nothing to sit on − and out of sympathy, I suppose, or general confusion, nobody else sat down either. I mobilised two or three big boys and we went out and found a couple of planks buried in the snow, and collected four logs to put them on, and finally got everyone sitting on something. Meanwhile the little woman who was to play the harmonium suddenly struck at chants, and afterwards I wasn't sorry she had as she seemed to forget to pedal during most of the hymns! Meanwhile also Mr. Simpson implored me to give the address, so as there were over twenty children and not more than seven or eight grownups besides ourselves, I tried to talk to the children about the meaning of Christmas *and* the New Year, and fell very heavily between two stools. Altogether it was rather a melancholy little Service. The congregation [were] completely ignorant of the form of Service — or [their] way about the Prayer Book and apparently even ignorant of the four carefully chosen hymns: 'Hark the Herald,' 'Lead Kindly Light, 'Jesu Lover of My Soul,' 'Abide with Me.' They couldn't even find the hymns because they all confused the number with the *page*, owing to Mr. Simpson having given out the *page* of each part of the Prayer Book Service. Even this latter plan was not fool-proof, because a few Prayer Books were in a different size and the pages differently numbered to his own. So each time he announced for instance: 'We will now say the Creed on page 23,' I had to add in a stage whisper: 'Little books, page 34,' and rush round inspecting. Lastly, nobody knew when to stand up and sit down and Mr. Simpson was too nervous to tell them.

The culmination was probably my officiousness, and the miserable poverty of the address. Anyway these were the only elements in the general feebleness of the Service that were definitely culpable. The only part that was a tearing success (humanly speaking, of course!) was the distribution of calendars and texts at the end. Everybody wanted them and they gave quite a warm feeling at the finish such as ought to have been associated with the address or hymns.

W. L. Morton, *God's Galloping Girl: The Peace River Diaries of Monica Storrs, 1929–1931* (Vancouver: University of British Columbia Press, 1979), p. 48

'Mothering in the Lord' is the happy phrase used to describe what Gladys Calliss brought to God's service.

Under Gladys's vigorous leadership the work expanded. Meeting-halls and school buildings were erected in a number of villages, the Toradja salvationists carrying hundreds of sheets of corrugated iron on their backs for over twenty-five miles up mountain paths in order to roof their new properties. Others gathered stones and sand from the river-beds and helped in teams to drag huge logs from the forest. There was a willingness to work which cheered the heart, but when Gladys saw the people seated before her, listening intently to her teaching about Christ and the Christian faith, she felt she was really doing the work God called her to do. From the local salvationists she recommended some for training as officers to ensure future leaders.

Several years and many adventures later, Gladys Calliss was transferred to the training college in Djakarta, Java. It seemed only right that she who knew the difficulties, but also the possibilities, of field operations, should be appointed to train man and women cadets. It was work she loved. Her tall, well-built form dwarfed the tiny Indonesians, but they were not afraid of her for she gave strong evidence of her love for them.

By now Indonesian came almost more readily to her tongue than English and she had adapted in every way to her second homeland. Eighteen years had passed since the raw missionary arrived with wonder in her eyes and deep dedication in her heart. Gladys knew that she was not the same person inwardly. Her faith in God had strengthened. She had matured.

Her capacity for slogging hard work, her dependability in all circumstances, her cheerful uncomplaining spirit, led to her being appointed in 1965 to the senior position of Chief Secretary for the whole of Indonesia, with colonel's rank. Now more problems than ever came to her desk, and her journeys took her further afield; yet she revelled in the opportunities of the position. Some of the children she had enrolled as junior soldiers became cadets and officers working under her direction. She officiated at their weddings, dedicated their babies, and mothered them all in the Lord.

Flora Larsson, *My Best Men are Women*
(London: Hodder & Stoughton, 1974), pp. 90–1

But such mothering sometimes had a tragic face, and women were also needed to bury the dead.

The woman's own lamentations were pathetic. She would sit for hours singing or rather mourning out a kind of dirge over herself: 'Yesterday I was a woman, now I am a horror, a thing all people run from. Yesterday they would eat with me, now they spit on me. Yesterday they would talk to me with sweet mouth, and now they greet me only with curses and execrations. They have smashed my basin, they have torn my clothes,' and so on, and so on. There was no complaint against the people for doing these things, only a bitter sense of injury against some superhuman power that had sent this withering curse of twins down on her.

She was buried in the cemetery where so many other hapless waifs were already at rest. In her anguish Mary could not conduct the service, but sat at her window and looked out while Miss Murray bravely took her place. The people, respectful and sad, gathered round the grave — the grave of a twin! — and one woman, a leader in heathenism, praised the White Mother's God for the child, and prayed that they might all have her hope in the Beyond. 'Surely,' was Mary's comment, 'they all felt the vast difference between their burials with all their drink and madness, and ours so full of quiet hope and expectant faith.'

W. P. Livingstone, *Mary Slessor, Pioneer Missionary*
(London: Hodder & Stoughton, 1915), pp. 140–1

On a lighter note there was, of course, the ministry of song.

THE MINISTRY OF SONG

In God's great field of labour
All work is not the same;
He hath a service for each one
Who loves His holy name.
And you, to whom the secrets
Of all sweet sounds are known,
Rise up! for He hath called you
To a mission of your own.
And, rightly to fulfil it,
His grace can make you strong,
Who to your charge hath given
The Ministry of Song.

Frances Ridley Havergal, *The Poetical Works*
(London: James Nisbet & Co, n.d.), p. 29

This ministry, oral again of its very nature — and so accessible to women — led to unexpected ironies, as French and Cable discovered to their cost when visited by the local soldiery.

The General was not deceived, and in spite of the children he found a guide to the missionaries' house, and was, of course, courteously admitted.

'I hear,' he said, 'that you have the services for the children of this town, and I shall come round myself one night and see what takes place. I wonder if you teach them not to tell lies. I heard them singing a grand tune this morning, the words sounded like, "Endure hardness as a good soldier." I liked it, and want you to teach it to my men here.'

The small organ was dragged out, and the men had to stand round and learn the Christian hymn. They were then given a sheet of coloured paper on which was written in Chinese characters a verse from the book of Proverbs: 'Keep thy heart with diligence, for out of it are the issues of life.' These words went to a splendid Chinese marching tune with which they were familiar. The General had a long talk with the women, and meanwhile his men examined most of their belongings, but they had nothing to hide and were used to this kind of thing.

When the General and his escort left the garden house the Children's Band breathed more freely, though they could not understand how it was that the brigand chief had gone into a house and not ill-treated its inhabitants. It was a lesson to them that when God is the Protector it is not necessary to tell untruths even in order to shield friends from harm. Next day, to the children's delight, the brigand army marched the streets of Spring of Wine singing a Christian chorus.

Mildred Cable and Francesca French, Wall of Spears
(London: Lutterworth Press, 1951), pp. 86–7

And with hymn-singing came fellowship. Who better than a Welsh woman to tell us this?

Mizo houses, some large, some small, varied in size according to the size of the family. I well remember the times of real fellowship I have felt in them. After the first few years I was at Durtlang I spent many evenings hymn-singing in one or another of them. Sometimes it would be to celebrate a marriage, or the baptizing of a baby or an examination success. Sometimes a death in the family would be the occasion for the fellowship. The general pattern would always be the same; the house packed with relatives and friends, many of them sitting on the floor. Someone would choose a hymn, the correct note for starting would be given and everyone would sing. Sometimes there would be the accompaniment of the beating of a drum or a youth accompanying with a guitar, but more often than not just unaccompanied singing. The words of many of the hymns were known by heart.

The light would be dim, from a small paraffin lantern. The cups of tea would be served, the water would have been boiled on a fire outside. The tea would taste of smoke, but that did not matter. I often felt a sense of unreality being there as one with them.

> May Bounds and Gladwys M. Evans, *Medical Mission to Mizoram*
> (Chester: Handbridge, 1986), p. 38

*   *   *

Against the backdrop of cups of tea and Welsh hymn-singing the actual issues stand out in sharp relief. When the missionary women came, when they went into other women's homes, when they met practices which they found alien and repellant, like the compulsory killing of twins, the binding of feet, child prostitution, the self-immolation of widows, how were they to react?

Culture and religion are inextricably linked. So what the missionary women faced was a theological question. Sometimes their reactions were of outright hostility, and Islam, in particular, came in for attack. However good the teaching of the Qu'ŕan, however generous the Prophet to women, life in Muhammadan lands was oppressive to them, and so it met with a stern judgement.

The same story has come from India, Persia, Arabia, Africa and other Mohammedan lands, making evident that the condition of women under Islam is everywhere the same; and that there is no hope of effectually remedying spiritual, moral and physical ills which they suffer, except to take them the message of the Saviour; and that there is no chance of them hearing unless we give ourselves to the work.

It is in the ancient land of India that we see the deepest degradation of womanhood, a degradation that inheres in the very religious standards of the people. Enforced seclusion, child marriage, perpetual widowhood, may be said to characterize the social life of the women of India. Every one of these disabilities and evils rests on positive teaching of the most venerated scriptures. Let us take them in the order specified.

It is the custom for all those, except the poorest outcasts, to seclude their woman in the parts of the household to which no man, except those of the immediate family, is ever allowed to come. From marriage to death the most highly cultivated women of India pass their lives in jail-like seclusion. This custom of immuring their women in prison-like confinement is often laid to the outrages perpetrated by the

Mohammedan invaders; but nine hundred years before Christ, in the most sacred code of Hinduism, the code of Manu, it was enacted: 'A woman is not allowed to go out of the house without the consent of her husband; she may not laugh without a veil over her face or look out of a door or a window.'

The deepest blot upon the people of India is that all but universal custom of child marriage by which babes of a dozen years are still given in marriage to men of fifty. This custom, in all its revolting ugliness, is based upon religious sanctions of the highest authority.

Helen Barrett Montgomery, Western Women in Eastern Lands
(New York: Macmillan, 1911), pp. 56–7

Mary Slessor, meanwhile, had a more considered reaction, but her conclusions were as devastating. Women who preach the good news have, of necessity, to preach a gospel which is good news to women, which challenges structures or any set of conditions which are oppressive of women and their experience. The gospel's very authenticity is measured against the needs of women.

As she observed and assimilated, she came to hold a clearer view of the people and the problems confronting the missionaries. She realised that the raw negroes, though savage enough, were not destitute of religious beliefs: their 'Theology,' indeed, seemed somewhat too complicated for comprehension. Nor were their lives unregulated by principles and laws; they were ruled by canons and conventions as powerful as those of Europe, as merciless as the caste code of India; their social life was rooted in a tangle of relationships and customs as intricate as any in the world. The basis of the community was the House, at the head of which was a Master or Chief, independent and autocratic within his own limited domain, which consisted merely of a cluster of mud-huts in the bush. In this compound or yard, or 'town' as it was sometimes called, lived connected families. Each chief had numerous wives and slaves, over whom he exercised absolute control. The slaves enjoyed considerable freedom, many occupying good positions and paying tribute, but they could be sold or killed at the will of their master. All belonging to a House were under its protection, and once outside that protection they were pariahs, subject to no law, and at the mercy of Egbo. This secret society was composed of select and graded classes initiated according to certain rites. Its agents were Egbo-runners, supposed to represent a supernatural being in the bush, who came suddenly out, masked and dressed in fantastic garb, and with a long whip rushed about and committed excesses. At these times all women were obliged to hide, for if found they would be flogged and stripped of their clothing. Egbo, however, had a certain power for good, and was often evoked in aid of law and order. Naturally it was the divorcing of superfluous wives, and the freeing of slaves that formed the greatest difficulty for the missionaries − it meant nothing less than breaking up a social system developed and fortified by long centuries of custom. Thus early Miss Slessor came to see that it was the duty of the missionary to bring about a new set of conditions in which it would be possible for the converts to live, and the thought influenced her whole after-career.

W. P. Livingstone, *Mary Slessor, Pioneer Missionary*
(London: Hodder & Stoughton, 1915), pp. 26–7

The missionary women never found the gospel wanting; indeed, for them, eternity was 'so near', as Amy Carmichael recalls.

We turned to the people about us. They were laughing and chatting, and the women were showing each other the pretty glass bangles and necklets they had bought at the fair. Glorious sunshine filled the world, the whole bright scene sparkled with life and colour, and all about us was a 'lucid paradise of air.' But 'only as souls we saw the folk thereunder,' and our spirit was stirred within us. There is something very solemn in such a scene − something that must be experienced to be understood. The pitiful triviality, the sense of tremendous forces at work among these trivialities; the people, these crowds of people, absorbed in the interests of the moment − and Eternity so near; all this and much more presses hard upon the spirit till one understands the old Hebrew word: 'The burden which the prophet did see.'

Amy Wilson-Carmichael, *Lotus Buds* (London: Morgan & Scott, 1909), p. 47

That is the shape of the challenge. It jars when contrasted with what Mrs Turner Tuggy calls the 'spiritual burdens' of the missionary wife. What kind of a testimony does this account give of the freedom which Christianity has to offer women? This text has to be judged as severely as anything the pioneer missionary women saw. For what is bound here is not so much feet; what is bound here is the human spirit.

But the missionary mother has a special sphere of responsibility, and she must learn the secret of a steady Christian walk. Her personal testimony and her ministry in the lives of others demand that the Lord work in her a real spiritual and emotional stability. She must become in very truth 'a weaned child,' finding in her God the fulfilment of her every need and the solution to her every problem. She must steadfastly keep her eyes upon the unchanging God.

Without proper devotional life, anyone's Christian life will lack constancy and be practically devoid of power. And many a missionary is highly disturbed because it is hard for him to get time alone with the Lord. But for the missionary mother the difficulties are multiplied. If she gets up early in the morning, so do the children. If she sets aside a time after breakfast, it is hard to get the day's activities for her children or the servants under way. If she decides to have her devotions at night so she will not be interrupted, she is often too tired to pray sensibly or to benefit properly from any but the most relaxed reading of the Word.

One mother who had six children and had served many, many years on the field wrote: 'I have often envied the father the privilege of slipping away for a quiet time without family responsibilities, but perhaps I have not availed myself of the early hours when I might have done so too.'

Another mother of four (all missionaries), a veteran of well over fifty years' service on the field, said gently: 'Daddy never could understand why I couldn't drop everything and have my quiet time early in the morning as he did.'

Joy Turner Tuggy, The Missionary Wife and Her Work
(Chicago: Moody Press, 1966), pp. 20–1

Clarity is again afforded by the insightful comments of Kathleen Bliss.

Great cultures flourished centuries before Christ, embracing many millions of souls, yet remote from the whole of the Mediterranean world, let alone the particular history of the Hebrews. They raise not only the question: 'Why did God choose the Jews?' but also: 'Granted that God did choose to work in this way, what place in his purpose has all the rest of the world and its history?' It simply will not fit on to the string of beads; there is no way of breaking and rejoining the thread. This compels us to ask ourselves whether we have rightly understood the relationship of creation and redemption if we think of them as being only in a historical sequence.

Kathleen Bliss, We the People (London: SCM Press, 1963), p. 104

An equally measured voice is that of Ethel Ambrose, the pioneer medical missionary. She is prepared to go one step further, to thank God for the freedom and responsibilities which the gospel bring her. Her preaching is, as it were, consciously redirected towards herself. It draws forth a mindset like that of the Magnificat rather than the Pharisee's, 'Lord, I am not like other men.'

Sin and suffering, in many varied forms, everywhere is overwhelming. Men do not act righteously, women are burdened and down-trodden, children are brought up from babyhood in sin in' all its hideous forms. Corruption reigns inwardly although the outward appearance may be fair when looked at casually. The majority of the people are flotsam and jetsam on the sea of life, driven hither and thither by waves of ignorance, superstition, custom, doubt, having no pilot to guide them into the haven of safety and rest because they know not Him who sent His only beloved Son into the world to give Life and Light. We cannot realise their dark state — its fearfulness and terror. One has tried to imagine what it would be to be born in heathendom, to be brought up without any wholesome environment; without knowing the meaning of truth, purity, goodness; with no moral atmosphere; to grow up, with surroundings in which there are no helpful ennobling influences: one shudders at its awfulness — and then comes the greatest loss of all, to be born and brought up without the knowledge of our Saviour. Why, the first things (truth, purity, goodness, etc.) are but outcomes of the knowledge of God, the results of Christianity. We have all in God, and nothing, worse than nothing without Him. While looking at the Hindu women in their homes, or when carrying water, or working in the fields, the thought comes, 'Why am I privileged so? What if I were now one of them?' I am sincerely thankful and full of praise that it is not so, but one does yearn that these women, these people, should know our God, His wonderful salvation through Jesus Christ and His love and grace.

Mrs W. H. Hinton, Ethel Ambrose: Pioneer Medical Missionary
(London: Marshall, Morgan & Scott, n.d.), p. 98

In the same spirit, Mary Warburton Booth can write lyrically of the abandoned freedom of a Hindu crowd. Her eyes take in every sight, her senses are open to every smell. As her attention then becomes focused upon an experience common to every human being, the lighting of fire, her heart is held by the unleavened bread.

There was a covering of busy wasps and flies over the piles of sweets, and a man behind the stall boiled the sugar in a massive caldron, stirring with a big spoon that took all his strength to move. There was a very smelly smell all around that stall. It filled the air, it wrapped itself around every one near, it made an atmosphere that might be cut in slices. It was the real thing, and folk stood around and smacked their lips. These smells of India are quite different from anything else on earth. They are saturating and satiating, they are there to be taken in, and cannot be escaped from. They are a very part of this land that takes you into its secret; and yet there are so many they cannot be counted, and I believe that every smell is a kingdom in itself.

We stood there to watch the eager crowd buy and eat. There was a spring in their step as they passed on. The sweets of India are food, strength comes with the eating, and folk push on in a never ending procession.

A little group of women stand at the corner where four narrow paths meet. They have a banner, and they are singing. Two are trying to arrest the passers by, with stretched out arms they hold gaily coloured copies of the Gospel.

'One pice only! One pice each is the price!' they are saying, and some stop and look, and others buy, while prayer and praise goes up to God continually.

The cold has disappeared with the mists of the morning, but as the sun pours forth its strength, the dust rises and the heat increases, and everywhere there is the abandoned freedom of a Hindu crowd laughing, talking, pushing, jostling, and then settling down by the roadside to cook the midday meal. It is the simple life in all its naked reality.

A few sticks are gathered, a fire is lit, and the rice is put on to boil. Another fire is lit, and the flat unleaven bread is cooked.

Mary Warburton Booth, These Things Have I Seen
(London: Pickering & Inglis, n.d.), pp. 122–3

To interpret this fire and this bread, to interpret the delights of eye and ear and nose, to supply a map of meaning, such at root was the preaching ministry of the missionary women. And of course, as Jesus had noted when he compared the kingdom of heaven to a woman making bread, its influence can never be measured.

So how do they begin? Wherever there is the tiniest crack in the closed door of the Oriental high-class home, they go to teach embroidery or English, to read a book, to show some picture of strange, far-away America, to comfort a mourning mother. Whatever the errand, the little Bible goes too, and the call ends with that. Hundreds of these shut-in ladies learn to read their Bibles and to love them, whose names can never be counted in any census of native Christians. As the missionary visits, friendships are made, new ideals are formed, a big new world of thought and action is dimly seen, a breath of fresh air stirs the stagnant pool of life. Exquisite tact and sympathy must be the portion of the successful zenana worker; patience with stunted minds and sluggish wills, and the love of the Master who gave the parable of the hidden leaven.

Helen Barrett Montgomery, *Western Women in Eastern Lands*
(New York: Macmillan, 1911), p. 110

Few descriptions of what it means to form part of a hidden tradition are as picturesque as this; none points up its ironies more sharply.

CHAPTER 4

———◆———

HOW COULD SHE LEARN?

'He has sent me to announce' (Luke 4.18)

A few years ago a young widow came to see a friend who lived here. She saw for herself those that had been saved, she asked many questions, and then she asked to stay, and we accepted her in the Name of the Lord. Her child went into the class room and began to learn to read and write in his own language, but the widow scorned the idea for herself — 'how could she learn?' she asked. She was only a woman and a widow at that: and a strange smile hovered over her face. So we left her alone to think things over. 'I have never seen a woman read,' she said. 'Books are for boys and men,' and she began to help cook the food for the family, and talked very hard while she did it. 'This is a strange place,' she remarked. 'Girls learning to read and write. What is the good of it all? They are not going to be baboos (i.e., clerks).' We smiled with her, telling her that wonderful things are happening nowadays and Indian women are not only able to read and write — they go to College, like men, and some of them even become doctors.

She opened her eyes wide in astonishment. 'I've never seen one,' she remarked. 'There are none in the place where I come from.' And I thought of the villages where we go regularly, and the villages further off that can only be visited in the cold weather. Thousands live there, but there is no doctor!

She settled with us and learned to knit and it was a very serious business for her: stitches were dropped and were picked up, the width increased and decreased, and the length grew into an amazing dish-cloth which she held up to me in triumph. She had tasted the joy of creating — where would it lead her?

She continued in the knitting class until she could knit a vest, and then something stirred within her. What if she should learn to read? Another like her who had been with us longer, had learned! She could read the book of the songs they sang, she had watched her sing with others, and she opened a book when someone read at prayers. She was changing, the eyes of her understanding were opening, and one day I saw her in school, her head bent low over a little book, her body swaying in rhythm, as she repeated the characters aloud; it was her first Primer!

How I wish you could have seen her. If knitting was important, all her world moved with her change of mind, and she fought with her memory that refused to work. What she learned to-day slipped away, and every day she began again. Week after week, she was hard at it, always in the first page of the Hindu Primer!

What could be done? What was the matter? Why could she not re-member her lesson from day to day? She could remember other things. I puzzled about this and tried various ways of helping her remember those lines she went over so often every morning, but she never got beyond the first page until something happened. For two years she went into the class every day. The teacher gave a compassionate smile and said, 'She will never learn to read: what is the good of her coming to school? She has no brains.' And I wondered what the block was. She came to us with a scar on her soul. She had sinned and kept her secret: never once had she acknowledged it, and as I watched and waited and prayed, I wondered how long she would be able to go on. 'Oh, if only the Holy Spirit would convict her,' I said within myself.

'I wonder what hinders that woman from getting on. She never moves forward,' Elise remarked, and I answered: 'I think her soul is paralysed: we must get to prayer and pray her through. She has been with us over two years, she is not too old to learn to read, and there is no response to spiritual things.'

Again I asked the Lord to show me how to help her. It came very quietly and naturally in the daily contact. We were together on the back verandah: she was sorting out some things for the children and I joined her. After a bit of time, I stopped and looked into her face, questioning her of something in the past. She looked vacant for a bit, but I saw her fingers twitch and her lips tightly close. I was relying on the Holy Spirit doing His work and I kept still in the Lord.

'When He is come,' I said to myself, 'He will convict of sin,' and there I stood and closed my eyes and prayed to be so filled with the Holy Spirit that He could and would show her what was hindering her. She was in no hurry to move and I stayed with her. After a time, I said to her: 'If it would help you to tell me, I will wait, but you must tell God. There is something you must put straight or you will never get on.'

And then I saw a splash, and tears were raining down her face, so I drew her inside my room and we knelt down together.

There was no hurry, time was no object. Her sin had come to the top: it was now or never for her decision — and I waited. If you have ever knelt with a sinsick soul you will understand.

I cried unto God for her, 'Lord, save her *now*.' I said, 'Save her or she will perish,' and suddenly her cry rent the air. She never thought to be found out, but He had found her, and she was humbled in the dust.

'I did it, I did it,' she cried. 'I did it, I did it,' she repeated, and the convicting power of the Holy Spirit held her until she had confessed it all. And then I repeated the words from the Book: 'If we confess our sins, he is faithful and just to forgive us our sins and cleanse us from all unrighteousness. The blood of Jesus Christ, God's Son cleanseth us from *all* sin — cleanseth us from *all* sin, *cleanseth us* from *all sin*' — it was finished.

The change in her was tremendous, it was as if something had burst within her, and she was made free. I watched with solemn awe as I perceived how God was leading her in the paths of righteousness. She began to make the crooked things straight, she cleared her own path, and then she decided to have another try with her Primer.

The teacher greeted her with the same pitying expression, but there was new light on her face and a great hope within her. She had seen the advantage of reading and a great longing was born within her that she might so learn that she could read the Word of God for herself.

Her first new day was spent as usual, but she was awakened, and a great determination mastered her. She was going to read, and when school time was over and her work was done, she took down her one and only book to find that she really did remember what she had tried to learn in the morning. It was amazing to her, but it was true, and day by day after that time she found the impossible possible. There was nothing superficial about her, she had faced the fact of sin and felt its devastating work, and now she was saved she set out to prove it.

Mary Warburton Booth, My Testimony
(London: Pickering & Inglis, 1947), pp. 140–4

Teaching in the mission field had a distinctive thrust to it. It envisaged conversion, access to the written word of God, a personal commitment to the gospel and to the Jesus of the gospels. Inevitably, though, as Mary Warburton Booth was well aware, it brought freedom in its own right. Educated woman are empowered to make choices. The very presence of the missionary women themselves testified to this. They were a product of the Christian commitment to education and to the power of the gospel to bring about change. And education was always and inevitably about dignity — a rejoicing in 'each other's talents and capabilities' — given in the name of Jesus, 'bone of woman's bone, flesh of her flesh'.

The Christian Church always speaks of Jesus in the most exalted terms. His Divinity is its constant theme; so that He too often seems transported into starry spheres far removed from our daily lives. Yet we know He moved amidst human beings, lived in a family, toiled in a workshop, walked in farmyards and through city streets. He saw with corporeal eyes, and spoke with a human larynx.

Let us, then, for our present purposes, look at Him as very man, and leave aside this great and transcendent matter of His Divinity. Instead, let us fasten our attention on Him as the Man Christ Jesus, by which name S. Paul was right to call Him; for it is of supreme importance to discover whether He will abide our questionings in that human capacity. Obviously, moreover, if He thus lives our mortal life, we cannot separate His words and His actions into water-tight compartments; but in this book, let us try to see Him, set in the company of both women and men, as other men are, remembering that other phrase of S. Paul, that He was made of a woman — like other men.

If Jesus is, in truth, then, Very Man as well as Very God, He is bone of woman's bone, flesh of her flesh: it was a woman's heart blood which first nourished His frame, and which filled His veins. Could He, who fathomed the depths of pain and climbed the heights of joy, forget the human race, and leave Woman out of His philosophy of life, whether temporal or eternal? Could He, who quoted with approval from the Old Testament the dictum that God created the race as man and woman, omit her from His experience or purview?

Now the Man Jesus was born in a certain land, and at a certain era of the world's history. He was born a Jew, brought up in a faith which still to-day honours Man above Woman. What did He think about that attitude of life? He proved Himself a revolutionary with regard to much of the orthodox teaching of His day, and declared that Gentiles, sinners and lepers were as truly of the family of God as the righteous Pharisees: was He equally revolutionary concerning women?

What, moreover, should be the attitude of His followers in modern times to women? Conversely, how should Christian women behave to men? And what should each sex expect from the other in the matter of thought and conduct? People tell us that the foundations of a truly worthy civilization are to be found in Christ's way; but do we honestly desire such a civilization, or is it too great a strain on our human powers — whether men's or women's? It means, as we know, each ever seeking the other's true good, honouring one another in lovingkindness and forbearance; yes, and encouraging each other in the forwarding of God's purposes, so that we rejoice in the use of each other's talents and capabilities for the progress of His Kingdom; vaunting not ourselves, but each other; rejoicing in the truth, though this may mean our own humbling. Do we know of any higher standard, more fitted to be offered to the nations which, like China, have not heard of Christ until these later years?

Lady Hosie, *Jesus and Women* (London: Hodder & Stoughton, 1946), pp. 14–15

This higher standard — as Lady Hosie well knew — did not go unopposed. Opposition certainly came from those nations which sent missionary women out into the field. But it came from those to whom the good news was directed as well. This example comes from an account of the life of Grace Ovenden, a Methodist woman teacher.

Whenever the opportunity came, Grace would go into the villages herself, and as she grew more fluent in the Kimeru language, she would try to plead with the parents to let their children come to school. At the end of her first year in Meru, it was decided at Synod that she and her colleague should each spend one week a term camping in the villages round about and it was these visits which seemed to give Grace greatest joy. From the moment when she set off with camping kit piled high in the W.W. car for her first safari she felt at last she was doing the real missionary work she had always dreamed about. Soon her tent was pitched right in the midst of those mud-thatched huts she had seen in her vision so many years before — though, she admitted, at first the menfolk had tried to dissuade her from staying in the shady, grassy spot she had chosen for herself. 'You can't camp there' they said, 'Lions often come there. Go lower down.' 'I went to look,' Grace wrote home, 'but there was not grass, only fine deep brown dust. I thought of all the little sand fleas that burrow into one's fingers and toes, and pre- ferred the lions.' So she pitched her tent and from that head-quarters visited the chief and the homes of all the people trying to persuade them to send their daughters to school. But tradition dies hard. Girls were needed at home to grind corn, to carry wood, to draw water and to marry as soon as possible. Grace tried to show that if girls were such important people, then they needed to be educated.

Pauline M. Webb, *Women of Our Company*
(London: Cargate Press, 1958), p. 120.

Whether in Kenya, or among the Nestorians of Persia, the problem was the same.

The real difficulty with the women was that they had, through gen- erations of contempt, lost their self-respect. To questions as to their knowledge, they would reply, 'What do we know? we are women' — which was the equivalent of saying 'We are geese.' It took a long time to excite their interest, and then still longer patience to get them to think out any subject and learn. When once the girls were shown what they were capable of, they made rapid progress. Miss Fiske had the delight of watching a wild crew of noisy, cackling, undisciplined hoydens grow into quiet responsible and lovable Christian women. To have achieved such a change among even a few was a result worth labouring for.

E. C. Dawson, *Missionary Heroines in Many Lands*
(London: Seeley, Service & Co., 1912), pp. 50–1

The most rigorous analysis of the problems and difficulties which women missionaries met comes from the pen of Helen Barrett Montgomery.

Once in the field, with a fair start made with the language, difficulties were only beginning. Not the difficulties regarding building and equipment, those could wait. A shell did for a slate, a stretch of smooth beach or a clay floor made an admirable blackboard, a broad veranda or the shade of a tree did for a schoolroom, but to find pupils — that was a different matter. Perhaps some of those dear women in the first flush of their missionary enthusiasm thought of these millions of women and children as eager for the truth, and had visions of Madam Ethiopia stretching out her hands to God; but if so they were destined to receive a rude shock. People did not want their girls educated, didn't believe they could be educated, wouldn't even run the risk of trying it for fear that real 'womanly graces' would be sacrificed. A Chinese gentleman derisively put spectacles on his cow and suggested he send her to school; a grave Hindu quoted his sacred books, and deprecated any putting of silly notions into his child-wife's head, and the women and girls themselves giggled and smilingly refused to do any such headaching and terrible tasks as the missionary ladies set for them. Nor has this incredulity in regard to the possibility of educating girls wholly passed away even yet. I well remember a few years ago, seeing the absolute amazement of a Moslem gentleman when he learned that the sister of one of his friends, a Copt, a merchant in Luxor, kept his books. Read? Write? Cipher? Actually add, multiply, and divide? Impossible!

Helen Barrett Montgomery, *Western Women in Eastern Lands*
(New York: Macmillan, 1911), pp. 90–1

The word 'womanly' has political overtones, of course. Mary Slessor, who ruled the Okoyong with a rule of iron and lived in the heart of the jungle, wrote with no sense of irony that her pupils would be 'clean and tidy and womanly'. It is hard to imagine that her contemporaries thought her to be any of these things.

Ma's mind was as restless as her body. She was for ever planning what more she could do for Jesus. Her new dream was a beautiful one, perhaps the best of all. To understand it you must know that the women and girls in West Africa all belonged to households, and were bound, by native law, to obey the heads of these — their masters. The compounds were their only homes. If they became Christians they still had to do what their heathen master told them. When they were given orders which as true servants of Jesus they could not obey without doing wrong, they were in a fix, for if they left the compounds it was not easy for them to live, as they had no houses in which to stay and no farms where they could work and grow food. Ma had often thought of the problem, and now she made up her mind that the women and girls must be taught simple trades, so that if they had to leave the compounds they would be able to support themselves.

And this was her dream. She would start a home for women and girls where she would take in waifs and refugees and other helpless ones, and train them to do things, such as the weaving of baskets, the making of bamboo furniture, shoe-making, and so on. They could also rear fowls and goats and cows, and dig, and grow food-plants and fruit-trees. And best of all, they would learn to be clean and tidy and womanly.

W. P. Livingstone, *The White Queen of Okoyong*
(London: Hodder & Stoughton, n.d.), p. 160

This is the woman who worked as a mill-girl in Dundee, a woman to whom the missionary life gave authority, power and a range of choices which are all a long way away from the image summoned up by the words 'clean and tidy and womanly'. Would she have found her fellow Presbyterian, Christina Forsyth of Fingoland, any of these things?

On one occasion after soup and a course of fowls and vegetables a baked custard was brought to the table in a huge enamelled bedroom basin, and proved to be as delicious in quality as it was prodigious in size. She never failed to have a cup of tea ready for visitors when they arrived after the hot journey over the hills. At the annual meeting of the Women's Christian Association, of which she became President, she would kill a sheep or pig and entertain the members to a generous feast.

When alone, however, she lived sparingly. She was a good house-keeper, economical in her methods, and baked her own bread. 'That is one thing I can boast of,' she would say with a smile. 'I am a fine baker.'

She rose at six and at seven had breakfast, which consisted usually of bread and butter and eggs. Dinner was nominally at one, but as this was the best time of the day for visiting the kraals she was seldom in to eat it; the courses were soup and mealies and milk, with sometimes pudding in addition. At five she had tea with bread and scones. She partook of no supper and retired at eight, but often later.

About dress she cared little and was a law unto herself so far as fashion was concerned, her first consideration being her own comfort. There were no shops to tempt her and no critics to please, and her attire was as plain as she could well make it. Her boots, several sizes too large for her, were an eyesore to Miss Auld, who pleaded in vain for the adoption of a neater pair ...

She was never too busy to see and talk to those who called. Women came at all hours to pour out their troubles to her, or ask for assistance. One Sunday morning at five o'clock there was a knock at the door. She sprang out of bed and answered it. It was a heathen woman with a little child. 'Smoyana,' she said, 'I want a dress for my little one. I want her to go to church.' She received it. Passers-by would come and ask for water to quench their thirst, or an ash to light a pipe, and would have their request kindly granted and go away with a word or two of kindly counsel. Children brought their slates and books and left them with her to be called for the next morning on their way to school, and they never went away without a slice of bread or a handful of cooked mealies.

W. P. Livingstone, *Christina Forsyth of Fingoland*
(London: Hodder & Stoughton, n.d), pp. 174–6

Was Mary Slessor the strategist particularly womanly, for that matter?

Enlightened women frankly told Miss Slessor that they despaired of ever becoming free from the toils of tradition and custom, and that there seemed no better destiny for them than the life of the harem and the ways of sin. It was a serious outlook for those who became Christians — about whom she was most concerned — and she could not leave the matter alone. Her active mind was always moving among the conditions around her, considering them, seeing beyond them and suggesting lines of improvement and advance; and in this case she saw that she would have to show how women could be rendered independent of the ties of a House. In Calabar Christian women supported themselves by dressmaking, and much of their work was sent up-country, and she did not wish to take the bread out of their mouths. Gradually there came to her the idea of establishing a home in some populous country centre, where she could place her girls and any twin-mothers, waifs, or strays, or any Christian unable to find a livelihood outside the harem, and where they could support themselves by farm and industrial work. A girls' school could also be attached to it. Two principles were laid down as essential for such an institution: it must be based on the land, and it must be self-supporting — she did not believe in homes maintained from without. All native women understood something of cultivation and the raising of small stock, and their efforts could be easily engaged in that direction, as well as in washing and laundrying, baking, basket-making, weaving, shoemaking, and so forth. Machinery of a simple character run by water-power could be added when necessary.

In view of the uncertainty of her own future, and the opening up of the country, she wisely held back from deciding on a site until she knew more about the routes of the Government roads and the possible developments of districts. She wanted virgin land and good water-power, but she also desired what was still more important — a ready and sufficient market for products.

W. P. Livingstone, *Mary Slessor, Pioneer Missionary*
(London: Hodder & Stoughton, 1915), pp. 222–3

In 1891 the British government passed laws making it a crime to consummate marriage with a woman-child under twelve years of age. This law produced the greatest excitement, and almost caused rioting on the part of venerable Hindus whose rights were infringed so cruelly.

'Throughout India,' says Ramabai, 'widowhood is regarded as the punishment for a horrible crime or crimes committed by a woman in her former existence upon earth. Disobedience or disloyalty to the husband or murdering him in this earlier existence are the chief crimes punished in the present birth by widowhood.' On this superstitious belief rest many of the cruelties practised upon the woman or child so unfortunate as to lose her husband. Because she is accursed she is stripped of her ornaments, her hair shaved, her food restricted to one scant meal a day. Twice in the month she must go without food or water for forty-eight hours. Only one coarse white garment is allowed her, she is debarred from all the family feasts, shunned, hated, made the drudge and the slave.

Helen Barrett Montgomery, *Western Women in Eastern Lands*
(New York: Macmillan, 1911), p. 61

The woman-child under twelve years of age and the widow share the same predicament. They are not recognizably womanly and so anything could be done to them. What this might in fact mean is passed over in silence by Mary Warburton Booth's account. What she is aware of is the authority of the gospel to reach first a child and then a woman in need.

Some time after she asked: 'Is that gentleman who went to see the little girl when she was ill a relative of yours?' I couldn't remember talking to the child about a gentleman, but she enlightened me. 'You know you said she was as big as I am and He made her well. Was he a doctor? Was He a relation of yours? I told my mother and father and they said He was.' Then I remembered, and I told her a bit more about the Saviour Who loved her and wanted to save her. 'He is God's Only Son and He is the Giver of Salvation and He is always calling people saying: "Come unto Me, and I will give you rest." You must tell your mother and father about Him,' and she ran off saying she would. She often came and played around while I worked, and sometimes we had a talk about Jesus, and she always asked me to tell her more about the Kind Gentleman Who loved little girls, and I prayed she might know Him. She was a Hindu, born in a Hindu home, and before she was 12 years old she went off to a far distant village to live with her husband, and we heard no more of her for years. Suddenly, one day she appeared when we had moved into the new bungalow. She stood on the verandah, eyes flashing, and a broad grin, and picking up the punkah rope she began to pull. After a time her tongue was unloosed and a torrent of words poured forth. She was so glad to be here – she wanted to come and see how we fared. She had walked all the way – she could stay ten days – she would pull the punkah every day, and then walk back. A little chuckle, and then she repeated: 'I can stay ten days. I think much about the Kind Gentleman Who loved little girls like me, but I don't remember His Name' and she chatted away to the two women engaged for the work, and asked if they knew what she had heard those years ago? Then the conversations began in real earnest, and her descriptions were given with signs and vividly told, and my verandah lost its quietude. She came and learned a little more, and went back to tell folk in her village. Everybody liked her, she had such a good-tempered, happy nature, and was willing to do anything to help anyone. So she was very popular. The temperature was 117 in the shade and more than that where she sat pulling the punkah. She mopped her face and laughed, and I told her to let the women do the work they were paid for. She just laughed and tossed her head, saying: 'They don't love as I do,' and they laughed with her. They were simple village women engaged every hot spell to come and pull the punkahs, for which they received their wages — and Pyari was content.

She went back to her village, and for two years or more we heard nothing of her: then in the beginning of the cold weather she appeared again and we did not know her. All the shine had gone from her, her body had shrunken, she was gaunt and thin, and no smile greeted us. 'I want to stay,' she panted. 'I have walked all the way, my heart is broken, and I am too sad to live.' We opened the door and she walked in, and sat down and gave herself up to grief. Old Bua took her in, and she settled down as if she meant to stay. She chose her own work — she wanted to wash all the crockery and pots and pans — and she did it in real earnest. Everything was made spotlessly clean and she was quiet and industrious. There was no thought of going back in her mind, her heart was fixed, and she applied herself to doing all she could. Weeks and months passed by while she went into school and learnt to read, attended the Bible classes and was always at family prayers. She was drinking in the Truth and learning to know her need, till one day she asked to be baptized.

Mary Warburton Booth, My *Testimony*
(London: Pickering & Inglis, 1947), pp. 86–7

The same image of thirst and conviction that the gospel is living water is noted by the Quaker woman Sarah Grubb in 1814.

The Women's meeting was visited by Isaac Stephenson, and I was engaged to follow his testimony, which also tended to unburden my mind. Yesterday I was at their Week-day Meeting, and again engaged in a warning testimony and fervent supplication, the produce of much deep wading of spirit. We likewise appointed a public meeting for six o'clock in the evening, as I could not believe it right for me to stay from the Week-day Meeting here, eight miles from Ipswich. The evening was unusually close and warm, and the meeting very large, so that not only I, but hundreds besides, were overcome with heat; but oh! this was nothing, for the Lord was graciously pleased to overshadow the assembly with a wonderful sense of His Divine power, while I was as a channel through which the glad tidings of the Gospel were conveyed to many souls, and which proved to them as living water to the thirsty. Thus was it a blessed, heavenly meeting, ending in prayer and thanksgiving.

Sarah Grubb, *A Selection From the Letters of the Late Sarah Grubb*
(Sudbury: J. Wright, 1848), p. 141

An equally ebullient sense of the blessed, heavenly benefits of education is captured by Pauline Webb's account of its effects in Dharapuram, in India.

All this had been begun thirty years before, by a pioneer missionary, and yet now the new member of staff coming as a partner of Indian colleagues found how very much of it was in accord with modern movements in Indian education. India, like all Asian lands, is urging the importance of training people to serve not only the new cities but also the old villages of their land. And here at Dharapuram, such training was being given, and in the villages round about we were to find hundreds of women, who as presbyters' or evangelists' wives, as teachers and as mothers are carrying the love and the joy and the family life they found as girls at Dharapuram back into their own community. No wonder that to-day they gladly send their daughters to the school, no wonder that so warmly they welcomed a new member of staff, no wonder that still to-day Women's Work sees in education one of the great keys to open a whole new way of life for women the world over.

Pauline M. Webb, *Women of Our Company*
(London: Cargate Press, 1958), p. 142

This was precisely the sort of benefit envisaged by Florence Nightingale in her bid to open education to girls as well as men.

It would scarcely be too much to say that Miss Nightingale's influence is felt to-day over the whole of the British Empire in the improved sanitary conditions of every building, be it a Government establishment, public institution, or private dwelling.

And yet she has found time to help forward the cause of education, both of the child and of the woman. Her strong, active mind rebelled years ago against the emptiness of the life of the ordinary woman of leisure; she would have every such woman fit herself for something higher than a mere society butterfly, and to this end she has ever urged the broader education of our girls.

Miss Nightingale holds that if we will but educate our girls, as we do our boys, to take an intelligent interest in national matters, we shall have more sensible electors and improved parliaments, and better government will, of necessity, follow.

She even thinks the time may come when women will take an active share in the affairs of State; and there is no doubt that, could we have but a few women like Miss Nightingale in Parliament, we should be much better prepared for times of stress than is frequently the case now.

Jeanie Douglas Cochrane, *Peerless Women: A Book for Girls*
(London: Collins, n.d.), pp. 162–3

What was happening for women on the missions was prepared for by careful work on the part of women educators at home. The discussion has a surprisingly contemporary ring. Millicent Fawcett comments on the contribution of Josephine Butler.

She was one of those who in 1865 petitioned the Senate of the University of Cambridge to open their Local Examinations to girls; she herself came up to Cambridge in support of the petition, and Miss A. J. Clough, the first Principal of Newnham College, wrote of her presence and influence on this occasion: 'The charm Mrs. Butler put into all the details she gave, showing the desire of women for help in educating themselves, made the subject, which might have been considered tedious, both interesting and attractive and thus drew our cause many friends.'

Her personal influence was, as always, very powerful. She describes some of the Cambridge Dons as deeply moved; one in particular who, with tears in his eyes, said to her: 'I fear we get selfish here and forget how much there is of work and sorrow in the world outside of us.' Professor F. D. Maurice came to see her and talked very fully of the whole scheme in view, for helping forward the education of women. He said in taking leave of her: 'If there is anything else which you and your friends think Cambridge could do to be of use, I trust you will suggest it; it does us more good than it does to anyone else.'

She became President of the North of England Council for Higher Education of Women in 1867, and saw it rapidly developing in two directions; towards the University Extension movement and the foundation of Newnham College. She never for a single moment believed that what was beneficial to women could be injurious to men.

Millicent G. Fawcett and E. M. Turner, Josephine Butler
(London: The Association for Moral & Social Hygiene, 1927), pp. 26–7

How important it becomes, therefore to recall that the story of many girls' schools is the story of women's work.

Chipembi Girls' School lives up well to the motto emblazoned on its badge. Beneath an African shield, in the centre of which is an African axe, are printed the words Atuume Luteeta − Let Us Blaze The Trail. Chipembi has indeed blazed the trail in the education of African girls. From Chipembi came the first two girls in the country to become certificated teachers. Then Chipembi became the first school to start a junior secondary course. Then it became the first to progress on to Senior Secondary. Now it is the first girls' school to have a Sixth Form. Throughout Northern Rhodesia there are today African women blazing the trail as politicians, nurses, teachers, welfare workers, probation officers, women who once wore proudly the smart blue uniform of the Chipembi girls.

The story of the Chipembi Girls' School is a story of Women's Work, of the service of many women missionaries and African teachers and particularly of the first Principal of the Secondary School, Miss Helen Dugdale. At first meeting, Helen Dugdale does not look at all like most people's mental picture of a girl's school headmistress. She is short and slight in build with a soft voice and a quietly reserved manner. But one has only to read the story of all she has accomplished to know that she is no small person to deal with. She is a woman of tremendous force and determination, with a genius for organisation, whose great gifts God has used mightily at a most vital period in the history of Northern Rhodesia.

Pauline M. Webb, Women of Our Time (London: Cargate Press, 1963), p. 34

Moreover, the story of education in the mission fields is a story of the work of highly intelligent and gifted women. Gifted at languages, gardening, music, they were doubly blessed in having 'a nice cheerful religion' to impart . . .

More than once we have overheard one or other of the women, when standing in front of our book-shelves, say to an admiring visitor, 'Look at the sisters' holy books, all teach the things of God.'

And in the evenings of that first year, as a rest and refreshment after the day's doctoring and Chinese reading, I constantly sang parts of the Oratorios, to the accompaniment of my dear baby harmonium.

At such times the people would quietly wait downstairs, and remark that 'Dian-sister spent all her spare minutes in worshipping God with the wind instrument.'

But a more amusing example occurred one day, when sowing seeds in our little garden and kneeling on the ground for the purpose, a passing Christian was heard to say, 'See! our sisters pray over each seed they sow.'

There was now great excitement in the village, for a large class of women were learning to read the New Testament printed in Romanized lettering. Mrs. Bryer had lately translated it from the difficult Mandarin character into a simple form, that women, to whom the Bible had formerly been a sealed book, were enabled to master its contents intelligently in about three months.

To the missionary, this was a labour of love — to the Kien-Ning women, a gift of untold riches. They had been accustomed from childhood to hear themselves spoken of as stupid and without understanding, with neither intellect nor souls — and now, to find that they really possessed the ability to learn surprised them quite as much as it did their 'lords of creation.'

'If I learn to read, perhaps my son's father may care for me,' was a young girl's plea, when asking Miss Fleming to teach her, a remark which expressed the longing of many an un-loved wife in China.

It was beautiful to see how precious God's Word became to them.

Mrs. Eng-Nu, who was the first to learn, spent all her spare time in reading, and often came to us with a beaming face to speak of some special verse she had come across, while her sister-in-law, whose husband kept a cake-shop, was constantly seen with her Testament open on the counter, reading aloud to a group of wondering customers.

No greater benefit could have been conferred upon these Christian women. Instead of being dependent upon our faltering words, or upon other outside teaching, they were now armed for their wrestling with seen and unseen foes, with 'the Sword of the Spirit.'

Mary E. Darley, The Light of the Morning

(London: Church of England Zenana Missionary Society, 1903), pp. 40–1

Our visitors were mainly townsfolk escorting relatives and friends from the country, who had come to see the sights of town, amongst which we, our cuckoo clock, and the gramophone ranked high.

One old, white-haired lady, who came from a village six miles away, was a Christian.

'My sons don't know I have come,' she said, as she beamed upon us. 'They said I could not walk six miles, but I knew I could; and I did want to hear those English songs, the one where the birds sing in the trees' ("In a Monastery Garden"), 'and I wanted to see the bird come out of the clock, and say "Cuckoo".'

And see she did, dear old lady, and hear!

A record they always appreciated was a most infectious laughing one. No one could stand out against it for long and the company soon became hilarious.

'This is the sort of religion we need, a nice cheerful one,' one of them said one day as they wiped their eyes.

Cuckoo clocks and gramophone records were not all they heard in that room, and by and by many of them learned the true sources of Christian joy.

Edith Couche, *Lighting Chinese Lanterns*
(London: Church of England Zenana Missionary Society, n.d.), pp. 40–1

Mrs. Boardman married Dr. Judson on April 10, 1834. She now began to study Peguan that she might work among the Peguans in Moulmain and Amherst. She held female prayer meetings in her husband's church, and gathered the Burmese women into classes for Bible study and prayer. She had a serious illness, but afterwards managed to preserve her health by vigorous morning walks. Mrs. Judson set her husband free for other work by giving instruction and advice to the native Christians, and settling any little difficulties among them. She revised the standard tracts in Peguan, and translated the New Testament and a Life of Christ into that language. She sat at her study table, with two or three assistants about her, toiling at this fruitful work. George Boardman had been sent to America for education, but a little family was growing up around her. She had eight children at Moulmain, five of whom survived her. The little ones played in the verandah adjoining the room where she was busy with her Peguan translator.

John Telford, *Women in the Mission Field*
(London: Charles H. Kelly, 1895), p. 69

At its most institutionalized, that is to say in the work of the Roman Catholic and Anglican religious communities, education produced its own repertoire of 'grandes dames'. In their own way these women were like bishops as they went on tours of duty to visit their sisters overseas ...

I only saw our Mother General once, and then I was quite a small child. It was upon her return from America with Reverend Mother in 1899. We had all been counting the days; at last we stood upon the terrace waiting for the carriage. It was a perfect day, and we wore white uniform and carried flowers. However, I was put under a cloud for a minute, by my neighbour whispering to me with great joy and superiority: 'It is our coachman and our carriage that is bringing them!' Oh! how I envied her, and she had a bouquet, too! But the carriage turned in at the gates, and everything else was forgotten. We cheered and threw our flowers into the carriage and were nearly wild with joy. By the time the house was reached, Mother General was sitting in a very bower of roses; she smiled at us, and seemed so amused and happy. Then we all flocked to the church for the Te Deum. We were told that we nearly brought the roof down with our voices, and I reflected how dangerous Te Deums of that kind must be. Then Our Mother General came into the study room very slowly, smiling and looking at everything. There were beautiful tableaux, and verses that I could not understand, but at last it was over, and we waited for her to speak. She was silent for a moment or two, as if she were thinking about us, and she looked at us with her head just a little thrown back. Then she said, with that wonderful voice of hers 'Children, I have brought you back your Mother.' All eyes turned to Reverend Mother, who was sitting beside Mother General holding her bouquet; the simple phrase won all our hearts. I could not take in much else of what was said, and I was so fascinated that I did not take my eyes off her face, but watched every movement and the play of her features. Then I went up and she gave me a picture: − and that was all. Years after I wrote to the Motherhouse asking for prayers, and my correspondent replied that our Mother General remembered me quite well. The thought of this remembrance has helped me through many a bad moment.

Anne Pollen, *Mother Mabel Digby*
(London: John Murray, 1914), pp. 264−5

We settled down and waited for the train to start. This is always a very leisurely affair, trains in South Africa are never what you would call 'express'. They neither start nor arrive up to time! Suddenly, when we were almost dropping off to sleep, a voice came from Mother's bunk, saying, 'I thought trains were made to go!' Eventually we did start, and after three nights in the train, with much stopping and pottering about, we reached Irene on November 24th at 5.30 p.m. and were met by Sister Marjorie Gabriel and the car. Mother had a great and charming welcome; two of the children from the Toddlers' Home, S. Margaret's, gave her flowers on the way down to Holy Cross Home. At the gate the driver was festooned and the girls were lined up and greeted Mother with cheers. On arrival at the front door all the Sisters were gathered together on the steps to greet her. It was a perfect day with bright sunshine.

After a few days at Irene, Mother went into Pretoria to stay at the school, Hillcrest. She was not at all well while there and was unable to attend the Morning Market in Pretoria held for the Irene Homes, which she had hoped to do.

During her visit at Holy Cross, Mother saw General Smuts at his house at Irene, Doornkloof. Mother and Mother Provincial called together and General Smuts spoke to Mother about her brother Lord Templewood. Another visit was also paid to Mr. Hoffmeyer at Union Buildings in connection with business concerning the Homes. The Sisters greatly valued meditations given by Mother after Vespers during her stay.

Community of St Mary the Virgin, *A Memoir of Mother Annie Louise*
(Wantage: Convent of St Mary the Virgin, 1953), p. 63

Another grande dame, Evelyn Underhill, gives a flavour of the spirituality which underpinned their work.

Most of the children who are committed to you will grow up to busy, driven lives. They look forward to incessant work, among concrete responsibilities, anxieties and interests. They are not going to be people with special powers of spiritual devotion, able to use long periods of prayer, even if they had time for them. Hence it is very important to make them realize now that the Christian communion with God takes many different forms; that there is no outward act, no kind of work, no drudgery, joy, suffering, which cannot be turned into a means of intercourse, a virtual prayer, provided it is accepted from the hand of God

in a spirit of love; then He can and will come to them incessantly in
the tram and in the office, the shop, the factory, the home; perpetually
offering something which, faithfully accepted, will become real food for
their souls. It is your greatest privilege to teach your children to recognize
this. Teach them the fact of God's mysterious nearness, and of His constant sheltering, moulding, strengthening, feeding Presence with each
separate life.

Lucy Menzies, *Collected Papers of Evelyn Underhill*
(London: Longmans, Green & Co., 1946), p. 170

*So much for the rhetoric, beautiful though it may be. A note of caution is
added in the wry comments of Florence Allshorn. As a trainer of missionaries as well as a practitioner, she knows about the dangers which lie in wait
for the professional woman.*

We have made one great mistake in our training. We have spent much
time in educating the girl in her spiritual life and preparing her for her
work, but her emotional life we have left largely to take care of itself;
and it is in the emotional life − this queer hinterland which is in all
of us − that there huddle the anxieties, timidities, antagonisms, self-
deceptions, inferiorities, revenge attacks, superiorities and withdrawals
which somehow our spiritual life does not go deep enough to touch,
where all the fighting and friction and the wreckage begin and end. If
a woman fails to adjust her emotional life and goes on unconsciously
working with a sense of failure there, then the one spot where she can
see success is in 'the job'; but the almost inevitable result of a sense of
failure in the inner life of a woman is an urgent desire for power. I believe
that to be the chief reason why women missionaries − and indeed those
at home, too, when they get into a position of authority − so often lose
that integral quality of Christ-likeness, humility, and become so hard
and dominating and so rabid about their work.

Success must find its home on the spiritual plane above all and first
of all. If success in 'the job' comes first, then life is certain to be
foiled of its home and its peace, and if a recruit cannot cope with
the spiritual and mental tensions as well as the physical tensions of
the mission station, and cannot get help from her senior, then unless
she has an extraordinarily strong and stabilized character naturally, she
too can only follow the same losing course. Only those women who
have stabilized their own emotional lives can know what is happening

to any life in the process of stabilization, and can show a clear way through. There would be hope if we at home and those abroad could get fired with the conviction that the present situation is not good enough, that there is a forward step of understanding and a deeper way of knowing.

J. H. Oldham, *Florence Allshorn and the Story of St Julian's*
(London: SCM Press, 1951), p. 59

In another age, Fidelia Fiske had relied on a different strategy altogether: the power of prayer. These different approaches belong to two different periods of history, but also to two different Christian mindsets. There are women missionaries in both camps.

The school became so popular and so many girls wanted to attend that Miss Fiske felt strong enough to announce that only those who were entirely happy in the school and meant to take full advantage of their opportunities and keep all of the rules should remain with them. A real spirit of religious earnestness grew among the scholars. They learnt the meaning of effectual prayer. Speaking of some of them, Miss Fiske wrote: 'If they do not pray several times a day, they feel they are becoming very cold-hearted. To-day, as they were going out to walk, one of them, who, perhaps, had not prayed for three hours felt that she could not go until she should have a few moments alone. I have the whole school divided into little circles of five or six each, and have a prayer-meeting with one circle each day.'

The practical results of this consciousness of God seem to have been very marked. Stealing and lying became less frequent; gradually they became very rare. Consciences became active, and on all sides faults which were quite unsuspected would be confessed. 'The intellect of the girls seemed greatly quickened by grace in the heart. They brought better lessons, wrote better compositions, and were in all respects better scholars.'

E. C. Dawson, *Missionary Heroines of the Cross*
(London: Seeley, Service & Co., 1930), p. 172

*   *   *

*So what did the missionary women teach? Reading, certainly, as we have
seen, because it gave access to the word of God. But also industrial skills.
This education was often offered from a position of privilege. The white
woman could be accused of preparing a servant class. This charge could
certainly be laid at the feet of Mrs Thompson, the 'regenerator of Syria'!*

To understand and to act were one and the same thing with Mrs
Thompson. She began at once. The plan of an association for the
improvement of the condition of the Syrian women rapidly formed
itself in her mind. She opened a class in her hotel. She secured an
Arabic teacher. The scheme began to run. Already she saw her future
school at Beirut. It was to have a classroom for little children, an
industrial department for women and girls, a depot for obtaining work
for the unemployed, and a store-room for the supplies which she
confidently expected would flow in from England. In fact, the beautiful
and splendidly appointed school which now carried on her work at
Beirut was plain even then to the eye of her mind. She was very
fortunate in securing, at this stage, the cooperation of Mr and Mrs
Mott, who devoted themselves to carry out the same ends.

By the end of 1861 a house was secured. It was at once occupied
by some thirty Haybeyan widows. The number increased so rapidly
that within a month three schools were in active operation. Sub-
scriptions began to come in and interest in the work grew. Soon
a fourth school was started in a stable. And still the number of ap-
plicants was greater than she could receive. Yet another school was
filled with ninety little children, and a few days later a fifth school
was formed for young women. Almost anyone but Mrs Thompson
would have been overwhelmed. She writes: 'I had not the slightest
idea how large and how rapidly the work would grow; and when I
look at the schools as they now stand, I own I marvel to see what
the Lord has wrought in little more than two months and a half.
Not a single woman or child has been asked to come here but I have
had to select . . . The care of this large flock completely exhausts my
time and strength.'

Lord Shaftesbury was much interested in all that was being done, and
gave the weight of his name and influence to procure Mrs Thompson
the financial help she required. But all on the spot were quite enthu-
siastic. The officers of the fleet anchored off Beirut used to send her
all their washing to be done by her women in the laundry which she

had set up. One of the captains presented her with a mangle, and the ship's carpenters put up all the fittings.

E. C. Dawson, *Missionary Heroines in Many Lands*
(London: Seeley, Service & Co., 1912), p. 32

The work of Baroness Burdett-Coutts hints at a more prosperous outcome than might first be imagined:

For the girls who earn their living by selling flowers in the streets she established a Flower Girls' Brigade, the members of which are not only protected when carrying on their trade, but also taught the art of artificial-flower making.

The women, too — those poor misguided creatures usually considered beyond all human hope — were her next care. To her they were still God's creatures, and, as such, to be tended with even greater tenderness than others who had been born to better things.

She made a Home for them at Shepherd's Bush, where they were kindly but firmly treated, taught the different branches of household management, and afterward, should they so choose, sent to the colonies, where many of them became in time respected and prosperous.

Jeanie Douglas Cochrane, *Peerless Women: A Book for Girls*
(London: Collins, n.d.), p. 139

At an ecumenical conference held in London in 1925, an educational expert gave the game away.

Because some missionaries and colonial officers themselves did not indicate by their actions that industrial education was a societal necessity, Miss Burstall said that they should share the blame for not making industrial and technical education attractive to all Africans, not to mention African women.

In a view that may surprise some today, she did not boldly endorse all the three Rs for African women. She gave reading a strong recommendation, presumably because reading was a requirement for being a good Christian; writing received an unenthusiastic endorsement; and for arithmetic she reserved her 'extremely skeptical' view, wondering what good that will do a practical people. Against this, Miss Burstall ventured to suggest what she called the three Hs: 'hygiene, vital to the future of the race; house-craft adapted to African conditions; and handwork.' She would rather have these women cultivate their extra-ordinary gifts of music, poetry and proverbs than waste time studying 'history that means dates [and] geography that means lists.' Then, in one sentence, she, unfortunately, dismissed the idea that the African woman needs geography. For Miss Burstall, hygiene and housecraft were much more vital matters.

Efiong Utuk, From New York to Ibadan (New York: Peter Lang, 1991), p. 131

Miss Burstall was right: there was a social agenda at stake. But she was wrong in imagining that music, poetry and proverbs could not flourish alongside the three Rs and the three Hs. Her insistence on hygiene and housecraft was dangerous precisely because it fell straight into the trap she had identified — a problem 'inherently associated with the class structure and reward system in each society'.

This is a twentieth-century insight. Hannah Kilham's story is one of many, and acts as a timely reminder that the alternatives to education were dire.

P. Davis takes charge of both boys and girls, and has a lively, well-looking school of about eighty or ninety, and is well sat-isfied in her allotment. She has for house-maid one of the two poor girls who were inhumanly confined in a cask on board, to conceal them. The other girl is married. This one is the chief monitor in the school; reads agreeably, finishes her work in the bed-rooms before school-time, and then attends the whole of the school-hours.

With all the disadvantages under which the children in Sierra-Leone are taught, there are instances of great quickness. A little boy in six months learned to read the Testament, and a very little girl in Char-lotte, brought to the colony as a slave eighteen months ago, who appears now about six years old, after about fifteen months' instruction read to me the account of the man sick of the palsy, and did not misname three words.

Sarah Biller (ed.), Memoir of the Late Hannah Kilham
(London: Darton & Harvey, 1837), pp. 220–1

It helps to be reminded that as late as 1872 Mrs Carey Brock, author of the Sunday Echoes in Weekday Hours *series, could dedicate a book:*

To Schoolboys and to the
Sisters of Schoolboys
and especially to those boys whom the
Providence of God
has brought under the influence and instruction of
my own son,
this volume is inscribed.
With the prayer that it may help boys to understand the
principles of true heroism, and girls to feel that
the affection and influence of sisters
should be a blessing and a
safeguard to their
brothers.

Within a lifetime the 'principles of true heroism' would be available to girls as well as boys through the good work of publishing houses such as Pickering & Inglis. The titles included: Women Who Have Worked and Won, Women Who Ventured, Four Noble Women, The King's Daughters, Bringers of Joy *and* Missionary Heroines in Eastern Lands. *Missionary literature told of the educational work women were doing in heathen lands, and in doing so created a new literary genre which would influence the imagination of young women on the home front.*

In 1914, on the brink of the war that would change the very ordering of the social world, let alone the shape of the colonial map, Janet Erskine Stuart visited the southern hemisphere.

One thing I have heard from bishops and priests is immensely consoling, and that is the value to Australia and New Zealand of nuns. The wonderful Sisters of St. Joseph do untold good, they go by twos and threes into the neglected parishes and even into the bush, from station to station, preparing the way for the priests and keeping up the faith, hope and charity and the elements of Christian Doctrine. They devote themselves so far as to settle in places where they can most rarely have Mass and the Sacraments, in other places they make the parochial life. One Jesuit told me that he had often been 'on supply' to the parishes along the coast near Sydney for Sundays. In some, even if there was a resident priest, there would be ten or twelve at Mass and no one for Confession. But in the parishes where the Sisters are, the church would be crowded, and the confessional besieged ... and a most wonderful innocence. The nuns teach boys and girls and have a wonderful hold on the boys, even when they grow up, which confirms me in the idea that nuns are ideal teachers for little boys. The Bishop of Auckland told me that he wanted to reclaim an island called 'Barrier', where there were a number of Catholics, all lapsed. He sent a good priest to spend six or seven weeks there, and he came back without being able to effect anything. Then the Bishop thought he would try nuns, and he sent two Sisters of St. Joseph, and some time afterwards sent the priest again, and it was all alive – a harvest ready to be cut, and now he has been able to put a resident priest, and he has a steady congregation of one hundred, and Protestants creeping up more and more for instruction. These are a joy to hear of.

Maud Monahan, The Life and Letters of Janet Erskine Stuart
(London: Longmans, 1922), pp. 436–7

If there is a note of sexism in her observations, the balance is restored by Florence Young's account of a teacher named Joseph.

A young teacher, Joseph, whom I have for some years looked upon as a good, faithful teacher, and a great help in open-air meetings, suddenly, some months ago received a special anointing of power. There were conversions in the class he was teaching, and much blessing all round. One day I questioned him as to the secret of the blessing. He said:

'When I come here I found this place where I work very hard; then I begin to pray and I start school in my house. I pray for one man, and God bring him to me; then for another, and another, until my house was full; we have to build a school-house.' (There were some drunkards and gamblers amongst them.) 'Then they come to school and we have good meeting, plenty sing, and they like lesson along Bible; but one thing – I see them go out from school and they not saved. I run about along other class and preach in other place, but I not win man for Jesus. One thing spoil my blessing – my pipe. Plenty time God speak to me about this thing, but I say, "This not sin, what for I want to leave it?" When I come home at night I want to read my Bible, but then I want to smoke; when I smoke, I no more want to read my Bible.

'One night after I take meeting I go home and cry and cry along my house, "O Lord, what's the matter, I can't win these man for Jesus? Suppose my fault and something wrong with me, then You show me." And God speak to me again and show me *my pipe*. That time I throw

it away and oh, big joy and blessing come into my heart, and I no
more want to smoke!'

Florence S. H. Young, *Pearls From the Pacific*
(London: Marshall Brothers, n.d.), p. 164

Charity Cook (clean, tidy and womanly?) − exposes one final stereotype:

Charity Cook's reputation as a liberated woman grew primarily from
her long experience as a travelling minister of the gospel. Even some
of her own personal habits may support that reputation. Generally,
the course which she followed was within the limits of accepted Quaker
practice and was tolerated by society in general. There were times,
however, when she seemed to steer her course close to the border
line. One example of this was her habit of smoking a pipe in public.
Some Quaker ministers smoked pipes in the eighteenth and nineteenth
centuries, even some women, but 'when Charity Cook of Bush River,
visited London in 1797, she scandalized English Friends by strolling
around town with her pipe in her mouth.' The article softens the
shock by saying: 'But with William Logan, Thomas Lightfoot, George
Churchman and Hannah Pemberton smoking pipes she had good
company with weighty Friends.' The discipline of London Yearly
Meeting is said to have condoned smoking tobacco if done 'privately
and moderately.'

Another version of this incident gives a slightly different interpretation of it and adds an interesting sequel: 'When the two American
women (Charity Cook and Mary Swett) strolled down Melksham Street
after dinner with their pipes in their mouths they considerably astonished the natives.' And tradition adds the climax:

'It is related that (Charity) Cook dreamed that she died and presented herself for admission to the heavenly home. When she gave
her name the porter consulted the book to see if her name was
enrolled there. He reported that it was not. She insisted that it certainly was, and so he went and looked again, and returned with the
same answer. She protested that there must be some mistake about
it, for it certainly was in the Book of Life, he examined again and
reported that it was there, but so obscured by tobacco smoke that
he had not been able to see it before. This caused her to leave off
smoking.'

Though only a small percentage of the American women smoked pipes, their practice does not seem to have carried any stigma in the Society of Friends or in society in general.

Algie I. Newlin, *Charity Cook: A Liberated Woman*
(Richmond, Indiana: Friends United Press, 1981), p. 127

So what really matters, and what was the authentic gospel message the missionary women taught? Put most simply, it is revealed in a story from Fingoland:

Coming out of the 'red' huts, the children were often in an unfit state for school and a dozen at a time would be sent down to the river to be cleansed. Their quaint ways were a perpetual source of interest and amusement. A little household girl, when her turn came to repeat a verse from the Bible, thought a moment and said, 'God loves me; me loves God.' 'Where was that found?' she was asked. 'Oh,' she replied, 'me make it up; me in a hurry; not time to learn.'

W. P. Livingstone, *Christina Forsyth of Fingoland*
(London: Hodder & Stoughton, n.d), p. 38

CHAPTER 5

DEFYING ALL PRISON WALLS

'To proclaim release for prisoners' (Luke 5.18)

The conspiracy of love which says that 'God loves me; me loves God' led the missionary women into a conversation of extraordinary interest and complexity. They thought they were setting off to preach and teach but, of necessity, theirs could not be an overspiritualized version of the gospel. They found that they were part of a dialogue between Christianity and its values and those which they met on their travels. Their religious conviction led them to mediate a new understanding of freedom to the women they met. This in turn led them to experience freedom anew themselves. The experience of the Misses French and Miss Cable in Outer Mongolia is a case in point.

The poor little murderess was a pathetic figure. Her conditions were good and humane, but among her privileges was that of receiving a daily dose of opium which just sufficed to dull her senses and prevent her coming to a stark realization of her desperate position. She wept when she saw us:

'Teacher, Teacher,' she said, 'had I hearkened to your words I should not be in this cell to-day.'

The younger wardress and the two prisoners were on such pleasant terms that they stood talking to us with arms encircling each other's

shoulders. On a subsequent visit we found our two friends transferred
to a back room, a third prisoner having taken advantage of the easy-
going discipline to run away. The wardress had been given three days
in which to find her, after which she will be brought up on trial and
probably imprisoned herself. As regards the little murderess, even though
the method of her execution be such as to cause a Western tribunal to
shudder, still the girl is meanwhile treated by all as a fellow-creature
overtaken by trouble, who must be given every possible solace during
her months of prison life. Apart from the Gospel there is no word of
hope for such a woman, all else were mockery, but the Evangel pro-
claims a liberty to captives which defies all prison walls.

Mildred Cable, Evangeline French and Francesca French, A Desert Journal

(London: Hodder & Stoughton, 1934), p. 189

*The lure of opium was matched for Mary Slessor in Okoyong by the lure
of rum and gin.*

Perhaps the greatest obstacle to Christian truth and progress was not
superstition or custom, but drink. She had seen something of the traffic
in rum and gin at the coast, but she was amazed at what went on in
Okoyong. All in the community, old and young, drank, and often she
lay down to rest at night knowing that not a sober man and hardly a
sober woman was within miles of her. When the villagers came home
from a drunken bout the chief men would rouse her up and demand
why she had not risen to receive them. At all hours of the day and
night they would stagger into the hut, and lie down and fall asleep.
Her power, then, was not strong enough to prevent them — but the
time came.

The spirit came up from Calabar and was the chief article of
trade. When a supply arrived processions of girls carrying demi-
johns trooped in from all quarters, as if they were going to the
spring for water. At the funeral of one big man seven casks of
liquor were consumed, in addition to that brought in small quan-
tities by the poorer classes. A refugee of good birth and conduct
remarked to Mary once that he had been three days in the yard
and had not tasted the white man's rum. 'Three days!' she replied,
'and you think that long!' 'Ma,' he said, in evident astonishment,
'three whole days! I have never passed a day without drinking since
I was a boy.'

She fought this evil with all her energy and skill. Her persuasion so wrought on the chiefs that on several occasions they agreed to put away the drink at palavers, with the result that those who had come a distance departed, sober and in peace, to the wonderment of all around.

She saw that the people were tempted and fell because of their idleness and isolation; for they still maintained their aloofness from all their neighbours, and there was yet no free communication with Calabar. If a missionary happened to pay her a visit he would be stopped on the forest track by sentries who, after satisfying themselves as to his identity, 'cooeed' to other watchers farther on. Dr. Livingstone believed that the opening up of Central Africa to trade would help to stamp out the slave traffic, and in the same way she was convinced that more legitimate commerce and the development of wants among the people would to some extent undermine the power of drink. All the ordinary trade she had seen done so far was the sale of five shillings' worth of handkerchiefs and a sixpenny looking-glass. She urged the chiefs to take the initiative, and was never tired of showing them her possessions, in order to incite within them a desire to own similar articles. They were greatly taken with the glass windows and doors, and one determined to procure wood and 'shut himself in.' Her clock, sewing-machine, and organ were always a source of wonder, and people came from far and near to see them. The women quickly became envious of her household goods, and she could have sold her bedcovers, curtains, meat-safe, bedstead, chest of drawers, and other objects a score of times. More promising still was their desire to have clean dresses like their 'Ma,' and she spent a large portion of her time cutting out and shaping the long simple garments that served to hide their nakedness.

W. P. Livingstone, *Mary Slessor, Pioneer Missionary*
(London: Hodder & Stoughton, 1915), pp. 86–7

The verdict of history on Mary Slessor's strategy is ambiguous. On the one hand she tackled the problem of access to the down-side of white man's culture, namely cheap spirits, head on. On the other hand, was she right to encourage acquisitiveness of the up-side of white women's culture by flaunting her sewing machine, meat-safe and neat dresses? Edith Couche in China used the same technique.

The guests were drawn in at last, but refused tea. Gradually they thawed, and began to walk about, and soon found the adjoining room, my bedroom, most attractive; its twelve by eighteen-inch mirror, with comb and brush invitingly laid beside it, drew their attention; hair was combed, head-bands straightened and pleasing smiles assumed. The bed, an ancient spring one, attracted others, who sat upon it, and rose and fell like ships in a gale.

In a rash moment, thinking to add to the general cheerfulness, I opened the baby organ. Hardly had my fingers touched it when there was a general stampede.

I stopped in amazement, and asked what was the matter.

'We were so frightened.'

'Of what?'

'Of that box with the devil in it that squeals.'

Edith Couche, *Lighting Chinese Lanterns*
(London: Church of England Zenana Missionary Society, n.d.), pp. 10–11

Here for once, Helen Barrett Montgomery, writing safely from the home front about the gift of freedom which Jesus brought, sounds decidedly more theoretical.

The democracy of the New Testament got its seal and inspiration in the teaching and practice of Jesus. He took up the old teaching of the prophets, obscured by the prejudices of centuries, brushed aside the dishonouring conventions which the rabbis built up, and associated with women in the plane of a beautiful, free human relationship. He sat wearied by the well conversing with a woman to the scandalizing of his disciples who thought this quite beneath him as a holy man and rabbi. To women he reared the lovely memorial of his praise, and at the faith of women he marvelled. Women followed him and ministered to him. He alone among religious teachers had a word of hope for the harlot, and to a woman he gave the first resurrection commission.

Helen Barrett Montgomery, *Western Women in Eastern Lands*
(New York: Macmillan, 1911), p. 72

In the mission field women discovered their own freedom. They stood in a place where they could influence the making of laws and their practical administration. Of necessity they became decision-makers, women who would apply the insights of the gospel to whatever they met. This place was identified by Millicent Fawcett in her biography of Josephine Butler.

The contrast between prisons, hospitals, work-houses, etc., as they exist to-day and as they existed in the time of Dickens is sufficient evidence of the practical value of women's share in the administration of the laws. Much of what Mrs. Butler foresaw fifty years ago has now actually taken place and is still taking place under our very eyes; women are more and more taking their place as the mothers of the race in influencing not only the making of the laws but their practical administration.

Millicent G. Fawcett and E. M. Turner, *Josephine Butler*
(London: The Association for Moral & Social Hygiene, 1927), p. 28

Christina Forsyth's biographer makes a cultural judgement when he generalizes about the 'bright and intelligent aspect of Christian womanhood'. But his exploration of how she came to locate the exact place of confrontation and dialogue is compelling.

In her going in and out amongst the people she came more closely in contact with the conditions of primitive native life than she had hitherto done. Outwardly she found them picturesque enough.

The majority of the Fingoes were not black but dark brown in skin, and their bodies, shining under the fat and red ochre or clay rubbed upon it, looked like polished bronze. The blanket was the sole article of clothing of the men, and even this was often thrown aside in warm weather. It was greased and coloured in the same way as their skin and embroidered with blue and white beads. The dress of the women was a skirt fastened round the waist, with sometimes a shawl wound over the upper part of the body and a coloured handkerchief or fillet round the head. Both men and women decorated themselves with necklets and armlets of beads, shells, copper, ivory and wild beasts' teeth, and the men usually carried a knobkerry or stick.

The women drew out her sympathies in a special degree. There was much simple dignity about them. As she met them with their babies tucked into a fold of their blankets on their backs, or carrying head loads of wood or green maize and other produce, she admired their symmetry and grace. But they were practically little better than chattels, being acquired in marriage by the highest bidder of stock. This is a custom which, on account of some advantages it possesses in existing circumstances, is not altogether condemned, but is bound to disappear under the continued impact of Christian ideals. The wives were the real workers in the native hive, being not only domestic drudges but all-day toilers in the fields, while their husbands only performed some perfunctory tasks and lounged and smoked. Often cheerful enough, their faces had that look which one usually sees in non-Christian lands — the patient but lustreless expression as of an unawakened soul, which contrasts so notably with the bright and intelligent aspect of Christian womanhood.

Involuntarily, however, she penetrated deeper beneath the surface of native life, and saw heathenism in all its naked effrontery, and then she began more fully to realise the tremendous difficulty of the task she had undertaken. It was the rites and practices of centuries she was challenging.

The system of religion she did not fear; it was merely a superstitious belief in goblins, demons, and ancestral spirits, which, potent enough in its practical effect on their lives, would gradually disappear before the light of the truth.

Nor did she dread the witch-doctors, men often of great cunning and ability, always a powerful influence for evil, who played on the weakness and follies of native nature, and terrorised young and old.

What she did fear was the terrible hold which the tribal customs had over their bodies and souls.

W. P. Livingstone, *Christina Forsyth of Fingoland*
(London: Hodder & Stoughton, n.d.), pp. 71–3

Compared with that account, cultural difference such as that perceived by the Welsh missionaries in Mualvawm loses some of its threat.

The previous night they had killed a goat in my honour, but were too shy to eat with me, saying they couldn't eat with a white person, it was not their custom. I asked them what they would say if I couldn't open their chapel because they were not white, and explained that we were all the same, and as God's children all members of one family. They smiled and came and sat on the floor beside me, and when I ate with my fingers as they did, they were quite happy. They have small baskets with flat bottoms, turned upside down to form a table or altar as they call it. Over this they spread a plantain leaf and the rice is served on that. After the meal the leaves are just thrown away.

Their houses are large and they have plenty of floor space. There is one large baked mud hearth for cooking for the whole family, the son's family sits around a separate fire of burning bamboo on a raised mound of earth. Each family also sits around a separate up-turned basket or altar at meal times.

The babies are seldom nursed which is a contrast with the Mizo women, who are rarely without a baby on their backs. The babies are put into cots slung from the rafters of the roof. The mother while cooking or weaving can rock the baby if necessary by means of a piece of rope fastened to her big toe with the rope attached to the cot.

The service in the chapel on Saturday evening was unforgettable. Forty-five men, women and children were baptised. They came forward in families and twenty three were received into full church membership. Many in the chapel that night were not really well enough to be out of bed, but if they could manage to walk they came. Several who were to be baptised were unable to leave their beds, so early Sunday morning the pastor and I went to their homes and they were baptised in bed.

The Communion Service on Sunday afternoon was most impressive. The little chapel was full for the three services, and between services the people gathered together to sing hymns. How I wished that events of that weekend could have been televised for the people in Wales to see. In the same way as God had blessed the work of the missionaries from Wales amongst the Mizos, so He was blessing the work of the Mizos as they went out to preach the Gospel of Salvation to those living in spiritual darkness around them.

May Bounds and Gladwys Evans, Medical Mission to Mizoram
(Chester: Handbridge, 1986), p. 70

Indeed missionary women became adept at operating cultural practice to their advantage, as French and Cable demonstrated in a train from Bombay to Rawalpindi.

On the third day we started on the long railway journey to Rawalpindi. We three occupied a 'purdah' compartment, but for the first twenty-four hours we were alone, and so were able to invite Mr. Mather to leave his bachelor carriage next door, to share the contents of a special food basket prepared for us at Bombay. At Delhi, an elderly Hindu lady joined us, and Mr. Mather had henceforth to receive his portion through the railway carriage window and devour it in solitude elsewhere.

Mildred Cable, Evangeline French and Francesca French, A Desert Journal
(London: Hodder & Stoughton, 1934), p. 189.

Occasionally this facility deserted a missionary woman when what she saw filled her with horror. Gladys Aylward told her story to Alan Burgess, her biographer. This account is her own.

She halted in mid-thought when she saw the woman sitting on the pavement with her feet in the roadway. The woman was swarthy, coarse, dirty. Heavy silver ear-rings dangled from her ear-lobes. Silver and jade pins were stuck in her hair; she wore a silver necklace and embossed bracelets; her baggy trousers were secured at the ankle by bright green puttees. The puttees first attracted Gladys's attention. Although they were a normal part of Shansi dress, she had never seen them of that colour before; she thought at once that the woman must come from a village which she had never visited, that she had not even heard about. Gladys walked towards her intending to find the answer to these questions. As she approached she saw that a child leant against the woman's knee; an appalling, sickly scrap of a child, clad in a dirty bit of loincloth; it had legs like stalks, a swollen belly which told of malnutrition, and its head and body were covered with running sores. Gladys was horrified. Its condition made it impossible even to tell its sex. The pleasantries stopped in her throat.

Alan Burgess, *The Small Woman* (London: The Reprint Society, 1959), p. 97

No wonder that horror and despair could be overwhelming. From the very heart of China Jessie Payne wrote.

One day, coming home alone from one of our regular services at the church, I remember feeling very happy. The women in the meeting had visibly enjoyed the message. There was a lovely spirit of fellowship abroad, that I felt sure meant steady growth in grace, and my heart was singing with joy.

I was in a quiet lane, with Chinese walled houses on either side. The cart-gates were all closed and everyone busy inside. There was no one in sight, as far as I remember, and I was walking down the middle of the sunlit road. A strange place and hour for what was to happen!

A shadow darkened the air, and immediately a voice loud and stern, and cold with infinite contempt, addressed me, filling me with fear and indescribable horror. 'You deluded fool! Why pretend you are doing work that is permanent and real? You are like a child building

with sand. Do you imagine for a moment that you and a handful of
sin-eaten and ignorant women can make any change in this ancient
land of deep-rooted vice and corruption? The time-honoured customs
of China have irresistible power and will sweep down and obliterate
for ever your puny efforts.'

Trembling I stood, chilled through and through, and shaken by a
malignity such as I had never dreamed of. My gladness was gone. I
could not see where I was nor guess what time had passed. I was
utterly shaken, and could make no reply to this onslaught even in
my thoughts.

'Am I self-deceived? Is this the bitter truth in a moment of keen
insight mercilessly revealed? Have I mistaken the will of God?' My
mind for a time groped helplessly, and then threw out a despairing
cry: 'Lord, Lord! Is this a message from Thee? Is this Thy voice? In
pity, Saviour, tell me!'

Swift came the answer down, but how can I describe it? Where are
the words to tell of heavenly things? Waves of light and ecstasy thrilled
around me, bearing tenderness and comfort so sweet that it seemed
like music in my heart. Fragrance and love came to me, passing and
repassing through me. Sweetest reassurances chased away my fears. The
air of heaven itself filled all my being. A presence came near, but behind
and above me, that nearly broke my heart with joy. A glad and glorious
fact was told me. God was not displeased. He approved our tiny scrap
of service and wished it to go on. As the rapture grew more intense I
learned that with us, even so unworthy us, He was 'well pleased.'

I have tried to tell what can never be told in words. I cannot
explain it. It is one more proof of the occupation of God with 'the
least of these' His children. Nothing could shake my belief in that
message. Nothing could make me fear God or death. The gate that
leads to Him will always be beautiful and fair to me. The path to
the God who came to me that day can only be a door of hope and
beauty.

Was it a vision? Well, what did Peter and Paul base on visions? I
am sure of this for ever, that whether we in our wisdom do missionary
work or not, God does it, and will do it. If we care about Him and
His desires, after that message it must be done. No, say not it must
be done! Infinite and eternal honour and glory it is to us that we are
permitted to do it.

Jessie Payne, *The Very Heart of China* (London: The Carey Press, n.d.), pp. 36–9

*A dramatic account such as this contrasts well with Mr Simpson's blues in
the Canadian Peace Mission.*

Tommy then drove Mrs. Devlin and me, in good time, to the school
where we were joined by Mr. Simpson. He brought in a nice little plain
white wooden cross which he had got a friend to make for him, and I
contributed a special new blue tablecloth and picture of the Nativity.
For about half an hour after the service was due to start we only had
a funny farouche little boy called George C. At about 3.00 the first
sleigh arrived bringing a bunch of mothers and children; about 3.30 the
second, and a little later, a third. We began the Service after the first
sleigh, and finally there rolled up twenty-three people, chiefly mothers
and boys except for two men.

 Mr. Simpson took shortened Evensong. We read the Christmas psalm
and sang three Christmas hymns. He managed to give a tiny address
on the value of coming together, and altogether I admired his spirit
immensely. I really think that the women at least enjoyed it. They
warmed up a lot at the end, forced a collection of $2.60 (about 11/-)
upon us, and asked us to arrange another Service as soon as possible.
So I was very much encouraged, though Mr. Simpson had the blues
about his incompetence and the absence of men. I bucked him up
all I could, and agreed to aim at the same Service next Sunday at
Fort St. John.

W. L. Morton, *God's Galloping Girl: The Peace River Diaries of Monica Storrs,
1929–1931* (Vancouver: University of British Columbia Press, 1979), pp. 32–3

*The absence of men was less of a problem to the women missionaries.
Indeed Mrs Fry tried actively to substitute women for men on the convict
ships.*

Meanwhile Mrs. Fry had, with the assistance of another lady, Mrs. Pryor,
continued her work on the transports, and their efforts met with the
happiest results. Just as she had secured female attendants for female
prisoners in the jails, so now she obtained the appointment of matrons
on board the convict-ships, being greatly helped in this, as in all other
of her good works, by a guild of women known as the 'British Ladies'
Society.'

Jeanie Douglas Cochrane, *Peerless Women: A Book for Girls*
(London: Collins, n.d.), p. 179

No wonder Mary Sumner had such an exalted theology of the place of women.

Rank, education, riches, different spheres of life, are outside the human sympathy which exists in Mothers one to the other, for their anxieties and sufferings, hopes and fears, are the same from the Queen to the peasant; and the need of a high standard of life is equally necessary for every one who bears the honoured name of Mother, and who would bring up her children well.

A good Mother, be she rich or poor, shines like a bright light in this dark world. She receives the flame straight from Christ Himself — she reflects His Image. Husband, children and neighbours rise up and call her blessed. She sheds a benignant influence on all around. This may sound a high ideal, but should it not be our aim? There are many who have wasted their lives and neglected their duties, and are now conscious of it. They are stretching out their hands to God, yearning to retrieve mistakes, and bring back the children who, through their fault in part it may be, have wandered away into the 'far country' and given up their principles and their prayers. Let no one despair — let no one doubt the power of God. The tares may become wheat; the prodigal may return; and even this union of Mothers may be the means, not only of awakening many a careless Mother to her high vocation, but it may also, by the strength of united prayer, bring back many a wandering son and daughter to the Bosom of our Saviour.

Dale A. Johnson, *Women in English Religion 1700–1925* (New York and Toronto: Edwin Mellen Press, 1983), p. 204

No wonder Lady Hosie, writing thirty years later, could identify the need women have to develop. This is the source of their God-sanctioned freedom.

He, once a Carpenter living with His Mother in a workman's home, knew as well as any man that a home needs constant care and thought and skill from its mistress. Yet He said that the arts of kitchen and household are not all that the Kingdom of Heaven requires of its women. *Kinder* and *Kuche* were not for Him the be-all and end-all of woman's activities: they are Nazi and Fascist ideas.

It is strange, but it is true, that John Stuart Mill could not have written in Queen Victoria's day of The Emancipation of Women, had

it not been for this Carpenter of thirty, who told Martha, and no doubt
certain listening disciples, that Mary had many gifts which must be given
freedom to develop. The intellectual woman of every sort of to-day, university graduate, writer, artist, musician, social worker, world traveller,
may feel she goes forward in her work with the approval of Jesus Christ;
that He looks for her part as a thoughtful citizen of His Kingdom, and
would miss it, were she not to use her talents. He sat down gratefully
to Martha's good meal; He also took joy in Mary's acceptance of His
wisdom. His Courtesy to Woman includes the liberty of the whole of
the personality, the use of all the gifts with which God has endowed
her. The Parable of the Talents is for her equally with man.

Lady Hosie, *Jesus and Women* (London: Hodder & Stoughton, 1946), pp. 195–6

*The young Chinese woman who sits by a broken gateway, at the intersection
of two cultures — one of which no longer works for her — envies the single
missionary woman who has 'no man to rule her down'. Mary Darley's story
is simply told.*

Passing through a very unfriendly village one day I noticed a young girl
sitting by a broken gateway. She looked at me eagerly; so I, hoping for
an opportunity, went up and sat beside her. She was not afraid, but
said almost immediately, 'I am waiting for you, from my house I often
see you pass, I long to speak to you, my relations prevent me. Your
face looks exceedingly happy; your happiness, what is it?'

'Have you never heard?' I asked.

'Yes,' she answered; 'they tell me you are not married, you have no
man to rule you down, to govern you.'

What sadness lay behind these words! A life of bondage surrounded by
superstition, neglect, and ignorance, in which happiness was unknown,
and all longings had to remain unsatisfied.

We had only a few minutes together, and then she slipped away,
dreading the consequences which might follow were it known she had
been talking to me.

Mary E. Darley, *The Light of the Morning*
(London: Church of England Zenana Missionary Society, 1903), p. 81

*   *   *

In all fairness, it should be noted that this elevated sense of self and of the gift-edness in freedom of women was not shared by all the missionary women.

At this time, as throughout her life, Miss Taylor's wonderful gift for inspiring others with her own faith and enthusiasm won for her all she asked. She appealed for twelve missionaries, six of whom if possible were to be medical men, to go back with her to Tibet. The number was not to include women. Miss Taylor felt that few of her own sex could withstand the hardships and privations inseparable from pioneer work in that inhospitable country, and Tibet must be opened up to the missionary more completely before women began to work there.

Isabel S. Robson, *Two Lady Missionaries in Tibet*
(London: S. W. Partridge, n.d.), p. 80

In their account of the story of the early Church, entitled The Story of Christ's First Missionaries, *Miss Penstone and Mrs Hughes, eminent Sunday school teachers, are equally dismissive. The only 'woman' in their book is Diana of Ephesus. The women who helped spread the good news of Christ are dispensed with; in their place we have a figure of fear and of ridicule.*

The Temple. The great centre of all this revelry, the place to which the processions were constantly moving, was the famous Temple of Diana, which was counted among the seven wonders of the world. The sun, it was said, saw nothing more magnificent between his rising and setting. The Temple was situated at the head of the crowded harbour, and had every beauty that care and wealth could lavish on it. The columns, sixty feet high, were over a hundred in number, and each one the gift of a king; the great doors were of wonderfully carved cypress wood; and the roof of the inner temple was of cedar-wood supported by columns of jasper, on which hung priceless gifts from grateful worshippers. Behind the great altar were the folds of an enormous purple curtain, hiding a sacred shrine.

Diana. What was in this shrine? Surely some wonderful figure in gold or ivory, like the Athene at Athens? No. A hideous idol, roughly carved in the form of a woman, and terminating in a shapeless block. It was in fact an old lump of wood, so old that no one knew its origin. Like several other ancient idols, it was supposed to have fallen from heaven (Acts xix. 35). Its very ugliness and mysteriousness added to the awe

with which it was regarded, and a vast army of priests and priestesses
with their attendant slaves spent their lives in the services and the
care of this temple and image.

Diana and Magic. Closely connected with the worship of Diana was
the practice of magic. On the crown and girdle of the figure of the
goddess there were mysterious letters and words. If pronounced, they
were supposed to have power over evil spirits, and to keep away disease
and misfortune. Quite an elaborate science had grown up round them,
many books had been written about them, and professors of magic made
a living by their use.

Diana and Criminals. One more point should be noted in connection
with the worship of Diana. A certain area all round the temple was
permitted to be a place of refuge, so that murderers, thieves, cheats,
debtors, or any kind of criminal could live there free from punishment.
On this account Ephesus contained as it were the scum of all the cities
within easy reach.

Miss M. M. Penstone and Mrs M. V. Hughes, The Story of Christ's First Missioners
(London: National Society's Depository, n.d.), pp. 226–7

*   *   *

*How persuasive, therefore, the argument of the Chinese women whose
message was conveyed by the Reverend David Abeel to women gathered
in a London drawing-room. The year was 1834, when the two-wheeled,
one-horse Hansom cab was introduced — a mode of transportation which
would go far to introduce freedom and mobility to women in the British
capital. Aloysius Hansom's aunt Martha, cook at the Bar Convent in
York, would have approved. The appeal from China, meanwhile, though
couched in quaint language, demonstrates that within the missionary enterprise both those who were sent and those to whom they were sent were
engaged in an exploration of freedom. Both stretched out helping hands to
their sisters.*

After a half century of skirmishing, during which a new generation,
trained to pray and give by their missionary mothers, had come upon
the stage, the main body of the woman's missionary army had come
rapidly into the field to begin its organized campaign for oppressed
womanhood and childhood in non-Christian lands. Before considering
the organization of these societies in our own land, it is necessary to

glance at the beginnings in England, ante-dating ours by many years, and inspired by the same appeal.

In the summer of 1834 an American missionary in China, Rev. David Abeel, was on his way home to recruit his shattered health — the regular route at that time being by way of England. While in London Mr Abeel was invited to address a little company of ladies gathered in a private drawing-room, in what was destined to be perhaps the most important afternoon tea in history. The missionary was fresh from his work, burning with a great conviction. The helplessness and misery of the women of the Orient had profoundly touched him, and he had seen also the hopelessness of attempting to dislodge heathenism while its main citadel, 'the home,' was unreached, and unreachable by the agencies then employed. Thinking long and deeply over the problem, he had come to hold the then revolutionary doctrine that it was absolutely necessary to bring into the field unmarried women to reach and teach the women and children. Men were shut out from ministry by the iron bars of custom that imprisoned women in zenanas, secluding them from all contact with the world. The missionary wife at best could give only a fragment of her strength and time to do the work; then why not send out women to minister to the uncounted millions of women in non-Christian lands? The hearts of the sheltered women were stirred as he told them of the degradation which his own eyes had witnessed in India, and delivered the message of some Chinese women, 'Are there no *female* men who can come to *teach* us?' He pictured to them the tremendous power for good locked up in these millions untaught, untrained; and now thrown on the side of superstition and evil custom. Would they not, he asked, stretch out a helping hand to their sisters?

Helen Barrett Montgomery, Western Women in Eastern Lands
(New York: Macmillan, 1911), pp. 21–2

The literary snapshots which convey this most compellingly come from the spinsters French and Cable. Their freedom was inextricably intertwined with that of the women for whom and with whom they worked.

One afternoon a very tall woman, upright, with fine aquiline features and deep-set eyes, whose grey hair was braided in three plaits reaching the knees, came to us with a request that we visit the Princess. We followed our guide through the large portal, across the outer court where peacocks paraded their gem-like plumage, to a large, richly carpeted apartment where the Princess, dressed in emerald silk nearly as gay as the peacocks' feathers, received us. A table was immediately spread by the attendant slaves with dried fruits and tea, and during the next two hours we strayed through the rooms of the various Princesses who were all dressed in green, all pale, vacant and decadent. The pall of listlessness was on the whole household. High vaulted corridors led to twisted passages to the back of which were always more handsome rooms, lit by high lattices. A few of the Princesses nursed quiet, solemn-eyed babies, but mostly they were childless and the only time when interest lit up their immobile faces was when they enquired:

'Among your foreign drugs is there one which will help me bear a child?'

Mildred Cable, Evangeline French and Francesca French, A Desert Journal
(London: Hodder & Stoughton, 1934), p. 189

In the mutual ministry of the mission field, Lucretia Mott's dream was realized.

The usurpations of the church and clergy, by which woman has been so debased, so crushed, her powers of mind, her very being brought low, and a low estimate set upon these, are coming to be seen in their true light. But woman must avail herself of the increasing means of intelligence, education and knowledge. She must rise also in a higher sphere of spiritual existence and suffer her moral nature to be developed, her mind to be made right in the sight of God. Then will the time speedily come when the influence of the clergy shall be taken off of women, when the monopoly of the pulpit shall no more oppress her, when marriage shall not be a means of rendering her noble nature subsidiary to man, when there shall be no assumed authority on the one part nor admitted inferiority or subjection on the other. One of the abuses of the Bible (for Apostolic opinion has been taken and no doubt false opinion, for there have been abundant quotations and some mistranslations in order to make the Apostle say what the priests declare he did say) has been to bind silence upon woman in the churches, fasten upon her that kind of degrading obedience in the marriage relation which has led to countless evils in society and indeed has enervated, and produced for us a feeble race. Oh my friends, these subjects are subjects of religious interest and of vast importance. I would that there were successors coming forth in this great field of reform. The Almighty is calling upon both man and woman to open their mouths and judge righteously, to plead the cause of the poor and needy and many are thus emphatically called to lift-up the voice and declare the truth of God and this will give evidence of the divinity of their mission just as Jesus did. The Spirit of the highest is upon me; The Spirit of the Lord is upon me, because he hath anointed me to preach the gospel, because he hath anointed me to bind up the broken-hearted to preach deliverance to the captive, the opening of the prison to them that are bound, and so preach the acceptable year of the Lord. May they then not be afraid, may they not be ashamed to lift up their voices for the right so let the sound be heard far and wide and let it go forth to the ends of the earth; The Spirit of the Lord is come upon them and they are called to go forth on this mission. A blessing will be to them for they will acknowledge that the highest has been of the Lord that whereas they were a few and feeble but that they have been made strong and mighty in him who is ever with his children. Whoever giveth them mouth and wisdom, tongue, and utterance to speak that which he commandeth.

Dana Greene (ed.), *Lucretia Mott: Her Complete Speeches and Sermons* (New York and Toronto: The Edwin Mellen Press, 1980), pp. 132–3

CHAPTER 6

———

BATTLING IN THE CAUSE OF
HYGIENE AND HEALTH

'Recovery of sight for the blind' (Luke 4.18)

Missionary women had an especially powerful ministry of release in their work with the sick. Jesus himself, when ministering his gospel, demonstrated the authenticity of his claim to be sent by God through his work for the halt, the lame, the deaf, the blind and the dumb. So in turn the missionary women undertook a ministry of healing. Just as they had gained access to medical training, so the sick in many lands could benefit. In the sphere of medical care, possibly more than most others, the integrity of missionary work as a work of healing and restoration has been recognized. As Ethel Ambrose put it,

Medical work is privileged to be a means whereby the Gospel is spread in the heathen lands. The medical missionary tries to win souls through healing bodies. People who would not sit and listen to the Gospel in an ordinary way, will willingly listen to the Story of Salvation, even if only to pass the time while waiting for a surgical dressing or a bottle of medicine, and at a time when hearts are softened through suffering the Gospel brings its message of comfort.

The scene of our labours is Pandharpur in the Bombay Presidency, one of the sacred cities of India, sometimes called the Benares of Western India. A stronghold of Brahmanism, a centre of Vishnu worship, yet Christianity is knocking at the door, and entrenched and fortified as it is in its strong places, Christ had laid His claims upon a few in Pandharpur. Tens of thousands have listened to His call in the streets trodden through the ages with countless feet, and there are those who having come to seek the favour of the no-gods, have returned home with their hearts satisfied by the salvation that is through Christ alone.

There is an eager, restless throng of women in those streets. Happy, careless matrons, mothers of sons, and therefore bringers of good-fortune to their home; proud, well-satisfied elderly women rejoicing in a little flock of grandchildren; high caste widows condemned by custom, by their relations, and by themselves, to privation and cruelty, pass along those roads with averted faces, carrying offerings to placate the gods which they have so hopelessly offended. Little girl-wives, oft-times with miserable faces, move along in tow of mother-in-law, to whom is regulated so much authority in India. In the marriage processions which pass our dispensary door, so frequently the bride is a little girl led by her mother's hand, or even seated on her father's shoulder. These are the women whom we try to help in our out-patient work, and even more definitely hope to influence through our hospital. Their needs are great. Sin, vice abound. Jealousy, ill-treatment work their ravages. The women are often crippled with physical ills, and the fact that they are frequently mothers when just entering their teens or younger, is a crime which can only be laid at the door of the general viciousness which is allowed to prevail in the dark places of the earth. Most missionaries can tell of wives being murdered for nothing more than insubordination, the husband could not bend her to his will, or perhaps he wanted to get her out of his way because another woman had won his heart. There are young wives who commit suicide to escape the daily misery of living, being driven thereto by cruelty on the part of husband or mother-in-law, or both. We hear, on the other hand, of the young wife putting poison into the food of her tormentors, and so bringing down upon herself the rigorous treatment of the law. I remember once being called upon to examine the body and give evidence before a native judge, in a native state, in the case of a young woman (well known to our lady missionaries) whose body was one morning found floating in a disused well in the village. Her husband had often used her cruelly, strung her up and beaten her. On this night her cries had been heard by passers-by, but none had interfered, and she was beaten to death, then the body was taken out and placed in the well. No inquest would have been held had not the missionaries made a stir, then a so-called legal enquiry took place, but, as was expected, officials and witnesses alike were bribed by the murderer and nothing resulted.

> Mrs W. H. Hinton, *Ethel Ambrose: Pioneer Medical Missionary*
> (London: Marshall, Morgan & Scott, n.d.), pp. 152–3

This Indian account is matched by one from China. Here, though, it is the missionary herself who is murdered, even as she attempts to bind one final wound.

Trouble rose at the mission over some misunderstanding during a religious festival. The mob seized the mission and drove out and murdered the missionaries. Two of them were a young husband and his wife who had reached their new station only the day before.

When the mob brought Dr Chestnut down the temple steps to the foot of a large tree, and she sat down upon a mound at the side, waiting her death, a little boy in the crowd had an ugly gash in his head which she noticed. She called him to her, tore off the hem of her dress, and bound up his wound with skilled, kind fingers that did not tremble. Then they struck her and threw her into the river, where she lay as if asleep. After stabbing the poor body, they brought it ashore.

Thus one of the choice spirits of American womanhood laid down her life for the redemption of China.

> Helen Barrett Montgomery, *Western Women in Eastern Lands*
> (New York: Macmillan, 1911), pp. 198–9

Helen Barrett Montgomery adds another insight when she writes of the ministry of Isabella Bishop in India. The point being that the missionary women soon discovered that there is a specific health agenda for women.

Isabella Bird Bishop probably saw more of the home life of the Orient in many lands than any other European woman. Her testimony in regard to the need of medical missions and the suffering of women is positive and unimpeachable:

'In the case of women, and especially of the secluded women, the barbarities inflicted by those who profess to attend them in sickness cannot be related in such an audience. It is enough to say that native midwifery abounds in ignorant and brutal customs which in thousands of cases produce life-long suffering and, in many, fatal results. It is not unusual in polygamous households for discarded or uncared-for wives to bribe the midwife to inflict such an injury upon the favourite wife as shall render her incapable for further child-bearing.

'In Farther India, and even in India, it is usual for midwives to jump on the abdomen of the mother in her agony, or to put a plank across it and jump on the ends of the plank in order to accelerate the processes of nature; and in one of your own mission hospitals in northern India which I visited I saw, among nine patients, five who were suffering from severe abscesses and internal injuries produced by fracture of one or more of the false ribs under this barbarous treatment. And thus, in aggravated agony, the curse of Eden is fulfilled upon the child-mothers of the East. It is customary in many parts to place a mother after childbirth without clothing in front of a hot fire until the skin of the abdomen is covered with severe blisters, after which she is plunged into cold water.'

Helen Barrett Montgomery, Western Women in Eastern Lands
(New York: Macmillan, 1911), pp. 123–4

In Africa too, Mary Slessor had met with the medical agenda created by cultural practice.

For many weeks she was an inmate of the harem, a witness of its degraded intimacies, enduring the pollution of its moral and physical atmosphere, with no other support than hallowed memories and the companionship of her Bible. Her room was next that of the chief and his head wife; the quarters of five lesser wives were close by; other wives whose work and huts were at the farms shared the yard with the slaves, visitors, and children; two cows – small native animals that do not produce milk – occupied the apartment on the other side of the partition; goats, fowls, cats, rats, cockroaches, and centipedes were everywhere. In her own room the three boys slept behind an erection of boxes and furniture, and the two girls shared her portion. Every night her belongings had to be taken outside in order to provide sufficient accommodation for them all, and as it was the wet season they had usually to undergo a process of drying in the sun each day before being replaced.

There was a ceaseless coming and going in the yard, a perpetual chattering of raucous voices. The wives were always bickering and scolding, the tongue of one of them going day and night, her chief butt being a naked and sickly slave, who was for ever being flogged. There was no sleep for Mary when this woman had any grievance, real or imaginary, on her mind.

Both wives and visitors conceived it their duty to sit and entertain their white guest. To an African woman the idea of loneliness is terrible, and good manners made it incumbent that as large a gathering as possible should keep a stranger company. All that is implied in the word 'home,' its sacredness and freedom, its privacy, lies outside the knowledge and experience of polygamists. Kind and neighbourly as the women were, they could not understand the desire of Mary to be sometimes by herself. She needed silence and solitude; her spirit craved for communion with her Father, and she longed for a place in which to pour out her heart aloud to Him. As often as politeness permitted, she fled to the ground reserved for her, but they followed her there, and in desperation she would take a machete and hack at the bush, praying the while, so that her voice was lost in the noise she made.

One woman of mark was Eme Ete — Ma Eme as she was usually called — a sister of the master, the same who had attracted her attention on the previous visit. She was the widow of a big chief, and had just returned from the ceremonies in connection with her husband's death, where she had undergone a terrible ordeal. All his wives lay under suspicion, and each brought to the place of trial a white fowl, and from the way in which it fluttered after its head was cut off the judgement was pronounced. The strain was such that when the witch-doctor announced Ma Eme free from guilt she fainted. Big-boned and big-featured, she had been fattened to immensity. One day Mary pointed to some marks on her arms and said, 'White people have marks like these,' showing the vaccination cicatrice on her own arm. Ma Eme simply said, 'These are the marks of the teeth of my husband.' In that land a man could do as he liked with his free-born wife — bite her, beat her, kill her, and nobody cared. When consorting with the others Ma Eme had the coarse tone common to all, but as she spoke to Mary or the children her voice softened and her instincts and manners were refined and gentle. A mother to everyone, she scolded, encouraged, and advised in turn, and when the chief was drunk or peevish she was always between him and his wives as intercessor and peacemaker. She watched over Mary, brought her food, looked after her comfort, and helped her in every way, and did it with the delicacy and reserve of a well-bred lady.

W. P. Livingstone, *Mary Slessor, Pioneer Missionary*

(London: Hodder & Stoughton, 1915), pp. 70–1

The Scriptures offered more than companionship, however, they actually sanctioned the kind of judgements Miss Slessor could make. They offered a frame of reference which made everything possible because they offered moral authority, as Christina Forsyth discovered.

Taking her Bible, she turned over its pages thoughtfully and read in Ezekiel:

> The heathen that are left round about you shall know that I the Lord build the ruined places, and plant that that was desolate: I the Lord have spoken it, and I will do it.

And then there came into her mind a vision of Xolobe won for Christ, and from that moment she never faltered.

A lover of nature, she was helped by the beauty of her environment. The mission reserve was situated on a lip of land surrounded by majestic precipices and steep hill-sides covered here and there with patches of woodland or bush, and was almost completely isolated by a couple of streams which, after a series of minor falls, met and flowed on to join the Great Kei River. Down the valley her eye rested upon high hills faced with rugged rock, clustering kraals, fertile fields, and herds of cattle and flocks of sheep and goats tended by native boys. The scarlet aloe relieved the sombre greens by its splashes of brilliant colour. As the fleeting changes of light and shadow settled into the soft tones of evening the fierce and naked fronts were lit with glory . . .

At sunset the women returned from their 'gardens' or fields, where they had been at work since daybreak, and set about making the evening meal — Kafir corn, pounded and boiled, served with amasi or sour milk. This was the hour of gossip, and the man who did not know God kept the company shaking with laughter by retailing the scandal of the day. Smoyana, however, created her opportunity, and spoke to them of deeper things. After prayer she was glad to retire to a hut where the women, the children, and a couple of kids were her companions. She slept on a mat with her clothes on. At dawn she left for another long journey to attend some sick children.

W. P. Livingstone, *Christina Forsyth of Fingoland*

(London: Hodder & Stoughton, n.d.), pp. 63 and 68

Attending to their own children's needs could also be turned to apostolic advantage, as Jessie Payne's account from China reveals.

In the midst of a dense crowd we climbed the steep little street. At the top was the house we were to stay in. The crowd, all uninvited, went in with us, filling the courtyard and then the room. I sat down by the table with my baby on my knee, and confessed I should like a cup of tea. Water boiled. I unpacked cups, tea and teapot, and made tea, the crowd staring fixedly at every movement. These massed batteries of dark eyes that we have to endure make one feel almost hysterical sometimes. The people had never seen foreigners before. They were frightfully excited and interested in us, and not a little suspicious. I poured out tea and then took out a tin of condensed milk to make a drink for the baby, who, pale and fair in her little white dress, sat placid in the dark room and cheerfully contemplated the crowd. The bright tin of milk attracted attention.

'What's that?' someone asked.

'Milk,' said my husband.

'Milk!' They laughed incredulously. They had never seen solid milk that shone like silver, and wouldn't believe that.

We opened it and took out a spoonful to show them, but they were not convinced. My husband took the spoon and handed it to our old host. He knew nothing about tinned milk either, and was as timid as the rest, but he was our host. He put out his hand, took the spoon, and ate all the milk.

'Very good,' he replied, with a bow, as he gave it back, to the visible relief of the crowd.

Now we could proceed, but before her food I asked the child to 'say grace.' She spoke only Chinese then and so they all could understand.

'Thank you, Heavenly Father, for this nice food,' she said, clearly, her hands together and her fair head bowed.

'There!' exclaimed the old lady who was standing by. 'Never let me hear another word against these foreigners! If they were bad people would they teach their child to worship Heaven? Is that a bad thing that is done?' And she was won straight off.

Jessie Payne, *The Very Heart of China*
(London: The Carey Press, n.d.), pp. 30–1

This ad hoc *ministry, where caring for children — whether sick or well —
was part and parcel of the missionary presence, was soon matched by the
active work of the professionals.*

*Here too, though, a moral agenda was necessary. And this time it was
European influence which stood judged and condemned, as Grace Ovenden
discovered.*

Grace began to see some of the worst effects of European influence
in Kenya. One morning as she came out of her bungalow she caught
such a glorious glimpse of the sunrise through the banana trees that
she walked out beyond the compound to get a clearer view of the
sun rising behind the mountains. There she nearly fell over a little
brown bundle, which she discovered to be a woman, so emaciated and
deformed that she looked like a leper. Grace fetched for the woman
some rice on a banana leaf, and then went to plead for someone to
take her to hospital. Meanwhile she herself put pads of dressing on
the woman's feet. The toes had completely gone from the one foot
and she could not take the rags off the other — they were filthy and
the wounds were green. But she put clean bandages on them and then
wrapping the woman in clean calico, carried her to the mission car.
When they arrived at the hospital the doctor diagnosed not leprosy
but venereal disease, and it transpired that a white man was morally
responsible for her condition, and so she had come to the white women
hoping for help from them.

Pauline M. Webb, *Women of Our Company*
(London: Cargate Press, 1958), p. 122

*Disease so graphically described demands the kind of response Helen Barrett
Montgomery had witnessed.*

To men and women alike it comes with a shock of surprise to see beautiful
hospitals and dispensaries built just for women. For ages the women have
been so used to taking the left-over bits of life that they cannot understand such consideration. But in their own eyes and in that of their male
relatives they assume a new importance. To see a young mother tenderly
cared for in a clean white bed, is revolutionary in countries where childbirth has been regarded as unclean. To see a woman physician, strong,
capable, wise, able to direct even my lord the husband and secure his
respectful compliance with her orders, wakens dangerous thoughts in

the dullest feminine brain. 'The world was made for women also,' said a Hindu woman after a month's stay in a hospital where she had seen all women, caste or outcaste, treated with respect as human beings.

Helen Barrett Montgomery, *Western Women in Eastern Lands*
(New York: Macmillan, 1911), pp. 132–3

It also meant the diversification of medical care, as May Bounds discovered when she arrived in Mizo.

I lacked experience in so many things and could only trust in God that all would be well. Miss Gladwys Evans told me how she had been praying for a Sister to come out from Wales to relieve her of her Hospital duties so that she could start up new Health Centres in isolated areas. Her plans to do so had already progressed quite a lot.

May Bounds and Gladwys M. Evans, *Medical Mission to Mizoram*
(Chester: Handbridge, 1986), p. 16

If getting to these isolated areas took its toll on the women missionaries' own health, they were empowered by the very experience of wide spaces, lofty mountains and the freedom these represented.

When we did find a road, the ruts were so deep and wedged the cart wheels until the axles writhed with pain that found an echo in our bones. We struggled out and walked. Our feet sunk into sand or trod on hard sun-burned mud that cut our shoes. Hour after hour we went on, and at sunset we camped for the night. There was no village by the wayside, but wherever there was a clump of trees there were a group of mud huts huddled together, and nearby a pond to help out with water, and there was always a well — these are the villages of India. The people plough the land and sow their crops, and then wait for harvest. The damp mists rise when the sun goes down, and out in the country all is silence. Wide spaces, lofty mountains, freedom to go where you will, and a people always ready with patience to listen to Good News. Could anything be more attractive to a missionary?

The silent awe of the dawn when the sun rises over the highest mountains in the world, seen from the plains of India, brings something into the soul that nothing else can. Alone with God, in space ineffable and untellable, the soul is stilled. Those mountains are the messengers to remind us that though they seem secure and unmovable, they may be removed. But there is something more than they, it is the Word of God.

Who are we that such a Treasure should be entrusted to us?

Mary Warburton Booth, 'They That Sow'
(London: Pickering & Inglis, n.d.), pp. 22–3

This treasure came with a cost, though, as Betty Stead discovered.

Very early on, before there was any hospital for her to work in, she had assumed sole responsibility for the medical work in the area. Much of this was undertaken on her long journeys trekking out to the villages where, in many a skirmish with local midwives and unscrupulous witch doctors, she did battle in the cause of hygiene and health. On more than one occasion, she speedily nipped in and literally snatched her patient away to safety before even the relatives could realise what was happening. That was how she came to save the lives of her first twins — babies whose arrival caused pandemonium among the demented relatives, who at that time were terrified of twin births. By the time Betty arrived on the scene on the back of the minister's motorbike, matchettes were being flourished by men dancing wildly round the new mother, threatening to destroy her and her babies. Before anyone could realise what was happening the little white nurse had darted in among them, snatched up the babies, pushed the mother into the side car and sped them all away to safety!

Having assisted at birth, Betty soon found that she was expected to assist at death too, and very early on in her missionary career, when Mr. Groves was away on tour, she found herself having to conduct a funeral. It must have been an eerie experience, surrounded by black faces she could hardly see in the darkness of the night, taking only a hurricane lamp as they processed through the bush in the ghostly African moonlight, leading the crowds as they sang their Christian hymns and then trying to find some message of comfort for the stricken relatives. As the bearers lowered the coffin into the grave they turned to Betty for instruction as to how they should place it. Instinctively the little nurse quoted a hymn she had learned in her days at Guy's hospital —

'For awhile the tired body lies
With feet towards the morn.'

So there, in an African cemetery, she spoke of an Eastern sunrise and its message of resurrection hope — and felt her fears vanish in the confidence which came from the memory of Christian companions supporting her with their prayers.

That confidence was perhaps the secret of this little woman who became in Africa one of God's giant personalities. Her great time of testing came eight years after her arrival in Nigeria when she was sent to open a hospital in the Oron District. She was told originally that this was just to be a centre for out patient work and midwifery, but the men of the district were determined that they should have the benefit of medical aid near at hand, and that if the new nurse refused to treat them, then they would not allow their wives to be treated either. While the committee was still discussing this scheme, the matter was settled for Betty when, as soon as the first beds were put up, a man was brought in at midnight having been mauled by a crocodile. He had already been carried five miles. It was impossible to send him away. So Betty set to and stitched him up and thus her men's ward came into being, a ward which later grew extensively through the generous gifts of the men of the Oron Town Council. For Betty Stead soon had the men of Oron Town Council just where she wanted them — wrapped right round that little finger so tightly that when she beckoned, they could not help coming to her aid! Even a member of the Medical Committee admitted that she always got what she wanted in the end, a fact she stoutly denied, saying that she had not yet asked for half the things she really did want!

What she wanted most was an adequate staff, but that remained a dream throughout her whole career in Africa. Most of the time she was without any doctor at Oron and had to rely on visits from the doctors stationed at Ituk Mbang, twenty miles away. She also had to train her own nurses. So her duties included those of surgeon, matron, tutor and ward-sister. Perhaps the only responsibility she did not enjoy was that of business manager, for Betty never had been able to wrestle with figures. She sympathised with one of her first nurses, a boy called William who, commenting on the rise in his fortunes which came through the years, said, 'When I earned £1 a month I thought I was the richest man alive. Now I have £12 a month I just can't make do!'

Nevertheless, William was the proud owner of a bicycle and it was on the back of this bicycle that Sister Betty made most of her famous journeys, often setting out in the middle of the night to answer an emergency call. One such typical journey is described by her colleague Dr. Howard Souster, who used to visit Oron from the Ituk Mbang hospital and who, many years later, at a Medical Meeting in London spoke of Sister Betty as one of the great saints it had been his privilege to know:

'One morning I arrived at Oron Hospital as usual about 8.30 a.m. and asked Sister Betty whether she had had an undisturbed night. "No," she said, "I was called out to Ebukhu in the night." Ebukhu was one of the maternity homes in the bush, associated with her hospital, about ten miles away. It was in the charge of a trained African midwife who could deal with all the straight-forward cases that came her way, but for any-thing complicated she had to send for the experienced Ma Stead.

'So it was on this night that Ma had gone to bed and was awakened at midnight by a knocking on her door. Three cyclists had come for her from Ebukhu with the message that Nurse Atim was in difficulties with a woman in labour. Would Ma Stead go at once? Ma Stead would. She dressed quickly, called her steward boy and told him to prepare a thermos flask of tea and some sandwiches. He would come with her, as her only means of transport would be his bicycle; she would sit on the carrier at the back.

'Soon they were on their way; four bicycles returning to Ebukhu. Three cyclists came in the first place because the road through the forest to Ebukhu was known as the leopard path; no person would travel that way alone at night. Now four made the return journey. Ma Stead was so short that she could only mount the carrier by standing on a block on the ground. Once on, she drew up the block by a rope and held it next to her until she had to dismount. This she had to do on several occasions, as the road to Ebukhu was crossed by wide and deep streams which were spanned by a single tree-trunk, over which all travellers must cross. The cyclists sang Methodist hymns at the top of their voices to frighten away the leopards. No noise could be more effective than this!

'After an arduous journey Ma Stead arrived at the little maternity home at 3.00 a.m. Within those walls two women attempted to conceal from the other their desperate anxiety. The midwife had done all she could, to no avail. The only person now who could deal with the situation was Ma Stead. She had been sent for; would she get here in time? The woman knew that the nurse had done her best, but that now there was only one person in the whole district who could save her life and that of her baby. And now the door opened and in came Ma Stead, cheerful and confident. All the weight of responsibility was at once transferred from the midwife on to the frail but capable shoulders of Ma.

'She went up to the patient, whose relief at seeing her could not be disguised, and told her that she was not nearly so ill as she thought she was; ordered the midwife to boil up a syringe and some instruments, and in no time at all had given the woman an injection to relieve her pain. Then she set to work, and in half-an-hour or so there was a baby. Sister held it up upside down, gripping the ankles between her fingers and smacking its little buttocks, and then laid it down in a cot, wagging an admonishing finger at it and telling it not to cry as its mother lay very exhausted on her bed nearby. As if it understood perfectly, it went gently to sleep.

'Then Sister Betty turned her attention to the mother again and, using all her skill and experience, slowly brought back her strength and made her comfortable. When all was done and cleaned up, she and the midwife, by now greatly fatigued, sat down at the little wooden table in the middle of the room, ate the sandwiches and drank the tea which Sister had brought with her.'

Pauline M. Webb, *Women of Our Time* (London: Cargate Press, 1963), pp. 16–21

Accounts such as these smack of derring-do; a more measured account of what medical practice might achieve is offered by this account of the establishment of St Catherine's Hospital in Cawnpore.

The more savage acts of the Mutiny made those who understand what lies at the root of all cruelty the more desirous to conquer evil with good.

No better way of doing this could have been devised than to establish at Cawnpore a hospital for Indian women, staffed and supported by women of that race which Cawnpore would fain have destroyed.

St. Catherine's Hospital at Cawnpore was established in 1899, in connection with the S.P.G. It was officered wholly by women. Doctors, nurses, dispensers, and attendants were all women. It was intended for the use of native women who are shut away by custom and who cannot receive the attendance of medical men. To this hospital Alice Marval was sent out as junior doctor, and was supported as 'our own missionary' by the Girls' Friendly Society.

E. C. Dawson, *Missionary Heroines of the Cross*
(London: Seeley, Service & Co., 1930), p. 89

This account hints at a dialogue between what was happening on the mission front and what was happening for women at home. A mocking voice from home is that of Dorothy L. Sayers.

It is necessary, from time to time, to speak plainly, and perhaps even brutally, to the Church.

The first thing that strikes the careless observer is that women are unlike men. They are 'the opposite sex' — (though why 'opposite' I do not know; what is the 'neighbouring sex'?). But the fundamental thing is that women are more like men than anything else in the world. They are human beings. *Vir* is male and *Femina* is female: but *Homo* is male and female.

This is the equality claimed and the fact that is persistently evaded and denied. No matter what arguments are used, the discussion is vitiated from the start, because Man is always dealt with as both *Homo* and *Vir*, but woman only as *Femina*.

I have seen it solemnly stated in a newspaper that the seats on the near side of a bus are always filled before those on the off side, because, 'men find them more comfortable on account of the camber of the road, and women find they get a better view of the shop windows.' As though the camber of the road did not affect male and female bodies equally. Men, you observe, are given a *Homo* reason; but Women, a *Femina* reason, because they are not fully human.

Probably no man has ever troubled to imagine how strange his life would appear to himself if it were unrelentingly assessed in terms of his maleness; if everything he wore, said, or did had to be justified by reference to female approval; if he were compelled to regard himself, day in day out, not as a member of society, but merely (*salva reverentia*) as a virile member of society. If the centre of his dress-consciousness were the cod-piece, his education directed to making him a spirited lover and meek paterfamilias; his interests held to be natural only in so far as they were sexual. If from school and lecture-room, press and pulpit, he heard the persistent out-pouring of a shrill and scolding voice, bidding him remember his biological function. If he were vexed by continual advice how to add a rough male touch to his typing, how to be learned without losing his masculine appeal, how to combine chemical research with seduction, how to play bridge without incurring the suspicion of impotence. If, instead of allowing with a smile that 'women prefer cavemen,' he felt the unrelenting pressure of a whole social structure forcing him to order all his goings in conformity with that pronouncement.

Dorothy L. Sayers, *Unpopular Opinions*
(London: Victor Gollancz, 1946), pp. 117–18

What a contrast between this authoritative irony and the preoccupations of Joy Turner Tuggy.

Sometimes a woman will become conscious of a nagging worry that is inexplicably sapping her energy. It is wise to stop and ferret it out. Sometimes it is just the way her fellow missionary spoke to her, or her own sense of shame and sorrow at having failed to live Christ before one of the nationals or before her children. Such nagging thoughts can be turned over immediately to the Lord, asking Him for forgiveness or expressing willingness to freely forgive. However, what is bothering the missionary is often much more simple: a garbage can that needs scrubbing out, a dresser drawer that has been in disorder for weeks, a pile of trousers that has waited 6 months for mending. It is amazing what emotional relief a woman experiences when she takes time out to do that little thing which has been nagging her conscience. The half hour (or half day) it requires is better than a shot of Vitamin B12.

Joy Turner Tuggy, *The Missionary Wife and Her Work*
(Chicago: Moody Press, 1966), p. 116

When parcels had arrived in the Okoyong one hundred years earlier, Mary Slessor's mind was a million miles away from worrying about the state of the garbage can or mending men's trousers.

What a delight it was to Ma to open the packages! What cries of rapture came from the children and the people looking on as they saw all the things that were to them so wonderful and beautiful.

There were print garments by the dozens, woollen articles, caps, scarves, handkerchiefs, towels, ribbons and braids, thimbles, needles and pins, beads, buttons, reels, spoons, knives, scrap-books, picture-books and cards, texts, pens, and a host of other things. It was almost with awe that the women touched the pretty baby-clothes, and the men clapped their hands as Ma held up a blue or scarlet gown or jacket.

The dolls were looked upon as gods, and Ma would not give them away in case they were worshipped: she kept the prettily dressed ones to teach the women and girls how clothes were made and how they were worn. Some common things, which children at home would not value, they treasured. When Janie was handed a penwiper, 'Oh, Ma,' she said reproachfully, 'wipe a dirty pen with that? No, no.' And she out it up on the wall as an ornament!

One old woman was given a copy of the picture 'The Light of the World.' 'Oh,' she cried in joy, 'I shall never be lonely any more!'

If you had watched Ma closely when she was opening the packages, you would have seen that she was seeking for something with a quick and impatient eye. When at last she found what she wanted she gave a shout of triumph. Tins of home-made toffee and chocolate! They were always there, for every one knew she liked sweets. When at home she used to ask that these might be sent out, because the bush bairns were fond of them, but her friends just laughed in her face. 'Miss Slessor,' they would say, 'you can eat as many as the bairns!' 'Of course I can,' she confessed.

After the children had looked at all the gifts Ma would tell them where they came from, and would kneel down and thank Jesus for putting it into the hearts of the givers in Scotland to care for His forlorn black folk in Africa.

Ma did not give all the things away. A brilliant gown might go to the chief as a gift – and he would sit proudly in Court with it and be admired and envied by all – or a flannelette garment to some poor and aged woman to keep her warm during the shivery fog season; but as a rule Ma liked the people to work for what they got, or to pay something for them. Thus she taught them to want clothes and other things, and showed them how to get them, and in this way she was a real Empire builder. She used to say that there was no truer or more successful Empire maker than the missionary.

W. P. Livingstone, *The White Queen of Okoyong*
(London: Hodder & Stoughton, n.d.), pp. 102–4

The medical missionaries not only brought expertise, they brought conviction. For this reason they mirrored a sane mental map to those for whom they worked and were unambiguous about wanting to be 'real', 'true' and 'successful' in their battle for hygiene and health. An altogether sounder formula than any amount of Vitamin B12.

CHAPTER 7

THAT SHE SHOULD BE THUS BOUND

'To let the broken victims go free' (Luke 4.18)

My itinerating companion was to be a woman known by name to many – our dear Gaing-Seng – with whom love for her Master and earnest seeking for souls form the ruling passions of a most self-sacrificing life.

Her father was a native of Ku-Cheng – a literary man, who, growing fond of his little daughter, actually taught her to read.

She had a happy disposition, and knew little of pain until her tenth birthday, when she entered upon a year of torture. For then her mother commenced binding the poor child's feet, drawing the bandages more tightly each morning, bruising, crushing, breaking bones, but ever with increasing satisfaction, as she fashioned her daughter's feet to the required size, and felt how thoroughly the girl's welfare was being attended to.

Under such treatment Gaing-Seng grew thin and weak. Often at night-time, when the pain was very bad, she just put her head under the wadded quilt and cried. Then the kind-hearted father, distressed at what he only thought of as the inevitable suffering of girlhood, would occasionally whisper, 'Daughter loosen the bandages, your mother is asleep'; thus relieving her sufficiently to allow a few hours' rest.

By the time she was eleven years old, her feet measured exactly two and a half inches in length.

Soon after this, a marriage was arranged for her, and she was sent off to live in her husband's distant village. Here she was only one of several daughters-in-law living in the same house, over whom the mother-in-law reigned supreme.

For a while Gaing-Seng was happy enough, and the days passed quickly, as she helped in the household duties and learnt to embroider beautifully.

But soon one sorrow followed another in rapid succession. First, her husband became ill with consumption, and was quite unable to work. Then year after year passed away, during which time no child came to gladden them, and the poor little wife was in bitterness of soul.

When a baby boy was bought for her, she loved him almost as if he had been her own son, but one day he fell sick and died, leaving her with empty arms and a desolate heart.

From earliest childhood she had been conscious of sin, and this she thought must be the cause of all her trouble.

More and more earnestly she prayed to the idols for deliverance, and made constant offerings to those that were possessed of a reputation for power.

'They cannot save me, they cannot save me!' was her cry in times of great anguish. Then, morning and evening, she went outside the house and, looking up to the sky, burned a few sticks of incense to the Sun-god, and to a Being greater than he, Whom in her inmost heart she believed to exist.

Thus, feeling after, she at length found the One Who never fails those who seek Him.

One night she had a dream, in which some one with a beautiful face and dressed in long, white, shining garments called her, saying, 'Gaing-Seng, Gaing-Seng, to-morrow morning you will hear of a Saviour.'

Awakening full of joy, she quickly finished the necessary work of the house, and waited. Before long a shadow fell across the threshold. Her dream had become a reality for, looking up, she saw a man quite unknown to her standing in the doorway.

He greeted her, while she quickly invited him in, handed the customary tea, and said: 'Have you not come to tell me of a Saviour, Who can save me from my sins?'

How eagerly she listened to his answer, and as she listened she believed.

Her visitor was a Christian teacher, belonging to the American Church Mission, and the task given him by his Master that morning, was one the angels might well have envied.

Gaing-Seng at once passed on the 'glad tidings of great joy' to her husband, who accepted the truth as naturally as a child; and a few months later, when entering the Home Land, he assured her they would one day meet again.

And now a great hatred of idols arose in her heart. One by one she burnt and destroyed them all, taking delight in the deed, as she thought of the many tears, prayers, and offerings vainly presented before them in her times of utter desolation.

This stirred up no little opposition. 'How dare she — a woman — presume so to treat the gods of her ancestors?' exclaimed her eldest brother-in-law one day, as he cruelly beat her with the leg of a broken table.

Gaing-Seng, shewing no anger, only prayed that 'likeness to Jesus might appear in (her) body,' and that forenoon she took special care to prepare him a dinner of his favourite vegetables.

Bringing in bowl after bowl to set before him, she saw his face becoming 'red hot,' but he neither looked towards, nor spoke to her.

Soon after this she returned to her former home in the neighbourhood of Ku-Cheng city, and thus was brought within reach of Christian services and teaching.

Sunday after Sunday, in spite of weariness and pain, she joyfully walked five miles to church on her tiny bound feet.

Then she was taken into the women's school, and her happiness was complete. 'Like Heaven the same' were those days in which God's wonderful plan of salvation became clearly revealed to her mind, making her rejoice and expand, much as a flower does in the sunlight.

Verse by verse she learnt Miss Havergal's hymn:

> Take my life and let it be
> Consecrated, Lord, to thee!

praying over every clause, until she came to the fifth verse:

> Take my feet and let them be
> Swift and beautiful for Thee,

which decidedly puzzled her, for how could poor crushed feet be 'swift and beautiful'?

Mary E. Darley, *The Light of the Morning*
(London: Church of England Zenana Missionary Society, 1903), pp. 88–91

Texts such as Mary Darley's about foot-binding in China serve as a reminder that a gospel of healing of necessity becomes a gospel of liberation, and one which women were well suited to proclaim. And so theirs became a healing word as well as a healing touch. It sought out and found the world's most unimaginable and invisible victims; it offered freedom to those most truly broken. The authority of this word came from the ministry of Jesus, whose own word, of its very essence, was a transforming one. This insight is well illustrated by Lady Hosie's analysis of the special needs of widows.

It was not on the youth lying sightless and motionless on the bier that the Master had compassion; it was upon the mother, the widow, the lonely woman, the mourner.

She is not the only widow we meet in the Gospels. Jesus seems to have let His eyes often linger upon them, and always in chivalry and under-standing. Perhaps in His own home He had known what that particular variety of bereavement means, and the trials that beset widowhood. An aged widow, Anna, had praised God for His birth, though she could not have foreseen in what exact way He would bring redemption for His nation. According to tradition, S. Joseph, that man of tender heart, was elderly when he married Mary, and had died before Jesus came to manhood; so it might well have been the first duty of Jesus as Eldest Son to provide for His mother. One wonders if His mother, or some other widow in Nazareth, had been cheated by some doctor of the law; for later, Jesus fiercely denounces those of the priestly class who 'devour widows' houses.' And in a parable He speaks of a widow clamouring at an unjust judge's gates for her rights.

Another widow, a working-woman, one day threw into the Temple collecting-box, which stood in the Women's Court, a couple of poor small coins out of her hard earnings. And the Master praised them above all the shekels of the rich. Now who else but Jesus would have noticed that widow, or judged values in that unrealistic manner?

Indeed, His very first sermon gives the key to His ideas of the true values in life. For after He had taken His text from the book of Esais, He spoke of a widow who lived in Sarepta, outside the confines of

Israel, in the long-ago days of Elijah the prophet. His next reference
was to Naaman, a Syrian leper. Both of these non-Jews, He said, were
used and accepted by God to do His work through His prophets. They
were chosen, rather than Jewish widows or lepers. Thus from the outset
He began His crusade. On hearing such revolutionary and detestable
ideas, the leaders of religion threw Him out of the synagogue. They
tried to kill Him; they did not wish to be redeemed from their masculine pride and Jewish isolationism, ecclesiastic or nationalistic.

This attitude of the Master to widows, in particular, is unique among
the great thinkers of the world. True, memorial arches, often of beauty,
and finely sculptured, may be found bestriding the highways of China,
set up to widows; but these are to commemorate the faithfulness of
these women to their spouses, their refusal to marry again. It is their
relationship to some man that matters most; it is not any tribute to
their own personalities.

Jesus Christ, however, has changed the whole trend of human thought
towards women, and widows are a special test. I, a widow, living in a
land that is more Christian than it knows, can testify that its men treat
a widow with a kindness and gentleness which are infinitely healing.
'Pure religion and undefiled before God and the Father is this, To visit
the fatherless and widows in their affliction,' said S. James, the Master's
servant, and possibly brother. And the very governments in Christian
lands to-day endeavour to put this creed into action, by providing pen-
sions for them.

In return, Christian widows find themselves gradually drawn beyond
and through their personal loss and loneliness into this outer circlement
of warmth and fellowship. Many of them try to pay back some of
the consideration shown them, and give years of unselfish service to
the community. And it is from the Church of Jesus Christ that they
supremely draw their inspiration, and find their comfort.

Lady Hosie, *Jesus and Women* (London: Hodder & Stoughton, 1946), pp. 44–5

*Mary Warburton Booth's account gives us a sense of what this inspiration
and comfort might actually mean, and how desperately they were needed.*

Things spoken in whispers before were now talked out openly. Another
wedding was proposed, and preparations made, while the childless wife
suffered and waited to know what to do. She tried to think of what
her sin was, for she knew that, next to being a widow, nothing could

be worse than being a childless wife, and her tears washed her face continually.

Instead of the bright, strong young woman who had made comfort in the house, Star became a sickly person, fretting herself ill, dreading the day when another wife would take her place, knowing it would come true — and she — where would she be? She got up, walked to the well, looked down and shivered. Many had done that before her, she said to herself, but she hurried back and tried her strength over some preparation for the change yet to be.

She was pushed aside and despised. 'What good are you?' asked the mother-in-law. 'You think of all the expense you have been to my son, and howl your heart out. Think of the burden you are to me, and lie down and die. I wish you were dead.' Star wished that also.

The day of the second wedding was nearing. In desperation she watched the preparation. 'If he died I would be "Suttee",' she said to herself, and that would be the end — 'but this I cannot bear.' She went to the door again and stood there, then took a few steps and stood again. A group of people tethering their buffaloes stood near the village pond. She walked slowly towards the well, and a voice with a terrible note called her to retreat.

A very angry man came out to meet her. What he said cannot bear repeating. He was angry, she was sullen, and in desperation he knocked her down. She did not rise while he stormed, and the whole village gathered round, and that night she disappeared.

Not a word was said to anyone, but the following day someone heard a voice calling for help. Ropes were tied together and a man went down the well. She was safe, but very injured. She lay on the grass waiting for the end. Who could help her now? Her husband was prevailed upon to take her to the Government Hospital some miles away, where he left her, and there she lay week after week, feeling utterly desolate and alone. Poor Star, what had she to live for? Nothing!

There was a Christian nurse in the hospital, who noticed the hopeless expression on the face of the patient. She stopped and talked with her. 'Why don't you try to get better?' she asked.

The patient gave her a glassy, hopeless stare.

'Why don't you try to get better?' nurse repeated. And a weary voice answered, 'Why should I try? I have nowhere to go. No one cares for me.'

The nurse stood by her side and looked longingly into her face, and then, bending over her said: 'I Know Someone Who is saying, "Come unto Me, all ye that labour and are heavy laden, and I will give you rest".'

The patient opened her eyes wide, whilst nurse repeated the words again and again. 'It is quite true,' she added, 'And if you will try to get better, I will tell you where He lives.'

Day after day the words were repeated, until they were believed and received, and a change came over the patient. Her husband did not want her back, she was unlucky, she had no home, her friends believed the gods were angry with her. What was she to do? Where could she go?

Nurse repeated daily: 'If you will only try to get well, I will tell you where He lives, the One Who calls the weary and the heavy laden.' And one day Star left the hospital.

It was early evening when she arrived at our bungalow. One of the girls was busy on the veranda. She looked up, and a questioning voice asked, very timidly, 'Does Jesus Christ live here?'

'Yes,' was the prompt reply, and after a good look to take in all she could, she came straight to me with the announcement: 'Mamajee, a sister is standing outside and she wants to know if Jesus Christ lives here. Shall I bring her in?' A glad, welcoming smile radiated our child as she went to bring the stranger in.

How can I describe her! She looked miserable enough, and certainly very ill. Her sari was the usual Hindu type, with an all-over pattern of red. She stood for a moment, just inside the room, and then she fell to the ground in her eagerness to say her greeting.

'Salaam, Jesus Christ,' she said, and I jumped up.

'Oh, don't say that. I am not Jesus Christ, but He sent me here to tell you all about Him. Come and sit down.'

She listened with her heart, and her eyes scarcely left my face. Something of the holiness of the occasion gripped her, for she put her hands together, as if in prayer, and listened thus.

It was a marvellous opportunity for me, and never to be forgotten. All she had ever heard before, you will find in St. Matthew 11.28. She believed it, and came to us to prove it.

There was something about the Lord Jesus Christ that drew her right in, and she was one of those who walked into the Kingdom heart first. All her loneliness was lost in Him, and she gave herself to be His for ever.

All I could tell her in an hour was enough to make her feel loved, and I knew I could trust Him to teach her Himself, if only she gave herself to Him.

That night she set out in the way of the Cross, and she entered our family.

Mary Warburton Booth, *These Things Have I Seen*
(London: Pickering & Inglis, n.d.), pp. 72–5

This illustration makes a telling point without falling into the trap identified in 'The Missionary Address', a forthright account from the Revd Joyce Ruther-erford in a collection of writings which has an extraordinarily contemporary title: Women Talking.

Each point should be well illustrated and should lead on to the next point and so on to the conclusion. Having made this plan, stick to it. As in cake-making, you must keep to your recipe and not be led away by the sight of so many lovely sultanas that you put an extra half-pound into the cake. So in speaking, do not add all sorts of details because they seem interesting to *you*, they will probably spoil your main purpose.

THE BEGINNING AND THE END

Many missionaries' addresses are ruined because they begin at the wrong place and end without a proper conclusion. Do not begin with an obscure foreign place-name, or the geographical description of a place no one is interested in. How then could you interest a women's meeting in the missionary work done in Central Africa? If you, yourself, have been there begin by describing something that you have seen and something that has happened to you. If you have not been there you can begin with a story of ordinary everyday life and compare it with life at home. It is possible to give women's meetings a good deal of information that is often supposed to be too advanced, if you begin in the right way. Write out your ending and emphasize your main purpose again. If your story is already complete in itself do not add anything extra.

ILLUSTRATIONS

Illustrate your points wherever possible. There is a right way and a wrong way of doing this. You might produce a laugh, or a cry, or even a gasp of horror. If you have the knack of doing this, it might be harmful to your address and divert the audience from your main purpose.

On the other hand, stories may be very helpful, and, of course, missionary addresses can abound in tales of adventure, cannibalism, exploration, and stories of human degradation and unhappiness. Avoid sentimentalism like the plague. If in doubt about how to use a story, read again and again the parables in the Gospel.

Jane Sheldon (ed.), *Women Talking: A Handbook for Women's Meetings*

(London: James Clarke & Co., 1945), pp. 62–3

Lucretia Mott saw even more clearly what was at stake when a missionary 'adventure' becomes a missionary account. She asks us to look at the issues involved when the rhetoric risks becoming a naive kind of propaganda. We can only condemn what we observe in the missionary field if we are prepared to acknowledge that we are ourselves 'thus bound'.

It is not so Apostolic to make the wife subject to the husband as many have supposed. It has been done by Law, and public opinion since that time. There has been a great deal said about sending Missionaries over to the East to convert women who are immolating themselves on the funeral pile of their husbands. I know this may be a very good work, but I would ask you to look at it. How many women are there now immolated upon the shrine of superstition that man only has a right to the pulpit, and that if a woman enters it she disobeys God; making woman believe in the misdirection of her vocation, and that it is of Divine authority that she should be thus bound. Believe it or not, my sisters. In this same epistle the word 'prophesying' should be 'preaching' – 'preaching Godliness, &c.' On the occasion of the very first miracle of which it is said, 'whatsoever he biddeth you do, that do.' The woman of Samaria said, 'come and see the man who told me all the things that ever I did.'

Dana Greene (ed.), *Lucretia Mott: Her Complete Speeches and Sermons*

(New York and Toronto: The Edwin Mellen Press, 1980), p. 217

The cost of being thus bound is one which Lady Hosie herself hints at.

A widow knows that it was not flesh alone which bound her to her husband, but the delight of mind working on mind, of spirit growing into spirit; she is like a creature cut in two, when he is gone. And no doubt many a widower feels the same, and to him Jesus, too, offers hope and faith in God. For if all that marriage of mind and soul means is as perishable as the marriage of limb and body, then the whole of the loved and longed-for past has been but a fool's paradise; love is not strong as death, but weak and trailing, ephemeral as a convolvulus flower, whose glory and colour die with the setting of the sun. And the universe is in truth cruel, irrational and meaningless.

Lady Hosie, *Jesus and Women* (London: Hodder & Stoughton, 1946), p. 46

How desperate the cost when the widow in question has not even enjoyed the blessings of intimacy, because she was only three years of age.

Not only is widowhood a state of degradation and suffering, but there is no hope of relief. A child of three, widowed by the death of her aged husband, is condemned to life-long widowhood, since the remarriage of widows is absolutely abhorrent to all Hindu ideas. So fixed is this idea in the very structure of society that, after years of agitation that provoked the bitterest resentment on the part of even educated Hindus, the entire number of marriages of widows in all India is less than two hundred.

Helen Barrett Montgomery, *Western Women in Eastern Lands*
(New York: Macmillan, 1911), p. 62

What the missionary women themselves learned, though, was that, at a place by the river, where not simply waters but also women meet, a timeless interchange could take place. The waters meet and the waters break where new life is offered. The word recalled by Mary Warburton Booth echoes Jesus' questions to the two disciples of John the Baptist as they walked beside another river, the River Jordan, 'What are you looking for?' 'Whom do you seek?'

She held her hand to her heart as she looked into my face in the light of the starlight night, and Sundri began to tell them her story.

'I, too, have been there, and I know all you feel', she said; 'for years I sought salvation, I was like you, a widow on pilgrimage − only I was much sadder than you are, for I had a daughter, also a widow, and we had to suffer the penalty. I came here and joined in all they offered and all I could find, and went away with a water-washed body, but nothing had touched my soul − the burden remained, and I wended back heart-sick and weary. There was no hope for me, I said, and I met others who felt exactly the same.

'It was after a *mela* in Adjudya that I met a woman who seemed to know all about me. We stood by the river there, where the waters meet, and she said to me, "What do you want? Tell me is it really and truly salvation you seek?"

'I assured her that the longing had taken all my life and I had sought in vain. "Why did you go to Nepal?" she asked. And I answered: "I went to get a vision. I wanted to see God."

'She opened a book and read the words: "People with a pure heart shall see God."

'"Are you pure in heart?" she asked. "Can you be made pure?"

'Then she told me how she had been seeking, and Some One had found her, and oh, how I longed to have my heart emptied and made pure, so that I could get the Vision.

'"If you have a box full of dirty clothes and you throw it in the river, will that make the clothes clean? If you throw your body in the Ganges and you bathe there, will that make your heart clean?" she questioned. "There is only One Who can make you clean, He is the Giver of Salvation." And then she sang:

> "Salvation, salvation is a very great thing,
> I have got salvation."

'I felt like one who has reached the source of a river where life is found, and I wondered what to do. She talked to me until the sun was setting, and then she asked me to go home with her, and I went.

'She opened a Book and read wonderful words of life, and strange feelings came to my heart.

'I stayed with her for two days, and then I went away, but the words she read from the Book were inside me, and kept saying the Name of the Giver of Salvation as I walked along the way.'

Mary Warburton Booth, These Things Have I Seen
(London: Pickering & Inglis, n.d.), pp. 126–7

Maude Royden's account is more sophisticated, for she sees that true purity lies with God. But her concern too is the expression of freedom, where we should be 'free to use every power' — beyond any limits of personality or gender.

To escape from the limitations of personality, to think of eternity as a 'ring of pure and endless light,' to realise that even those who deny the personality of God may still reach Him and do still reach Him under other eternal aspects — this was a great service to all those who seek for God at all. If we can once realise that, then, though we think in terms of time, and though we must always do so, and speak to one another in words that imply time and space, so that our very effort to express the Eternal falters and fails upon our lips, yet we shall be able to apprehend the eternal God whom we can never wholly understand.

That would set us free to use every power to search for God, to cultivate every gift to serve God without fear or anxiety lest truth should prove to destroy God, or be too mighty for our faith, or too cruel for our hope. We should be free to serve.

Maude A. Royden, *Prayer as a Force*
(London: G. P. Putnam's Sons, 1922), pp. 142–3

Our friends the talking women cast this as a prayer; and so Elsie Chamberlain's contribution to their collection runs:

WOMEN'S PLACE IN THE WORLD

Almighty God, who dost offer to all the freedom of children; we thank Thee for the pioneering women of every age and nation who have won for us freedom from slavery, the rights of individuals, and the opportunities of education and vocation that we have to-day.

Forgive us that we have taken our privileges lightly; that we have failed to develop all the gifts Thou hast given us; that we have become too engrossed with physical life, and have neglected our mental and spiritual development. May spiritual food be more important than the food we eat; the wings of the soul more important than the clothes we wear. And as Thou hast given us the power to set the standard of life, may we lead men and women towards ever higher ideals of service and freedom, through Christ, whose service is perfect freedom.

PARTING FROM A MEMBER

All-wise and All-loving Father, when those we love are beyond our reach, we know they are not beyond Thine; when we are parted one from another, we know we are still with Thee.

So may Thy Love make all bonds of human friendship sacred, and may we be strengthened to go our separate ways richer for old friendships, and better equipped to make new ones.

Bless Thy servant, our friend, in the new sphere to which she shall go; may it prove a sphere of wider service for thee; may the beauty of

Jesus be seen in her, and the fellowship and experience of our worship
and work together equip her that she may give new sympathy and new
understanding, and respond to new demands.

The Lord bless her and keep her. The Lord make His face to shine
upon her, and be gracious unto her. The Lord lift up the light of His
Countenance upon her, and give her His peace.

Jane Sheldon (ed.), *Women Talking: A Handbook for Women's Meetings*
(London: James Clarke & Co., 1945), pp. 36–7

*Small wonder that Olive Wyon saw that those who might try to avoid any
new or wider sphere, for whatever reason, would in fact become stunted souls,
and so broken victims themselves. It is not simply the missionary women who
were to move 'onward'; journey is beholden on us all.*

God's call to move onward may come in many forms. To some it comes
in a new personal experience: in a time of great sorrow or suffering,
when life seems utterly blank, and we feel helpless and desolate; in a
new experience of human love, so joyful that life seems 're-born'; in
a time of critical decisions, when we feel our ignorance and weakness
as never before. To others, Christ's Call comes in a new and solemn
sense of vocation, at the outset of new work, or in the removal to a
new district, to a new home, to a fresh beginning in outward things. To
many young parents the new experience of motherhood and fatherhood
brings a profound sense of call to a new life for the sake of the little
child who has come into their hearts and lives. To others, the call
comes in the midst of the ordinary ways of life, possibly when we are
not thinking about God at all; suddenly, 'for no earthly reason', as we
say, a light shines into our hearts, and we know – in a deeper way
than ever before – that God is calling us to some new experience of
Himself. But in whatever way the call comes, it is felt and recognised
by us as a call to a fresh 'conversion', and happy are we if we know
the signs that mark our Day of Visitation. It is at times such as these
that we can say with deep conviction: 'Thou hast beset me behind and
before, and laid Thine Hand upon me.'

We neglect such 'calls' at our peril. If we could see beneath the surface
of many a life, we would see that thousands of people within the church
are suffering spiritually from 'arrested development'; they never reach
spiritual maturity; they never do all the good they were intended to
do: and this is due to the fact that at some point in their lives they

refused to go further; some act of self-sacrifice was required of them, and they felt they could not and would not make it; some habit had to be given up, some personal relation altered or renounced, and they would not change their ways; they refused to take the one step which would have opened up for them a new and vital development. They are 'stunted souls'.

Olive Wyon, The School of Prayer (London: SCM Press, 1943), p. 98

What, after all, was the alternative to such journeying? What do stunted souls look like? Miss French and Miss Cable came and went as they chose; they enjoyed quite extraordinary freedom. They also had a shrewd eye when it came to observing the unfreedoms of other women.

Life behind the curtain was far from ideal. At the age of forty Ma's wife was a creature for whom he had no longer any use, and she only held her place of authority by fierce determination and tenacity. Her eldest child was a boy of eighteen with a wife of the same age and an infant one year old. This young woman waited on her mother-in-law and was obliged to submit to her every whim, but there were other and younger women in the *ménage*, whose status was never defined. Their number steadily increased, and the last comer was always the favourite. They spoke of each other as sisters, but eyed each other as rivals. The work of the house, the preparation of meals, all the needlework and the grinding of wheat, devolved on them. The person with most power in the whole group at that moment was a girl of sixteen, for she completely swayed the master of the house. She enjoyed her brief hour of power to the full, but knew that any day some other young girl might come to take her place. She was therefore pitifully anxious to bear a son, as this, and only this, would assure her some kind of position when she was no longer the master's favourite.

The lord of the household came and went, issued his orders, ate the meals which were so carefully prepared for him, and gave no account of himself to any one. Several children ran about the courtyard, but, as discreet visitors, we never enquired concerning the various relationships. We moved in and out of that women's court as enigmatic and inexplicable beings who were independent and unattached, celibate yet satisfied, childless yet happy. There was no son to mourn for us when we should die, and no one to secure us continuity of existence through coming generations, yet we were serene and unafraid. All these women

watched us and marvelled. To them continuity of life was bound up with
that prolongation of existence which a son secured, one who carried on
the life which he owed to his mother, and thus, through the successive
generations of her descendants, she would live on. In answer to the many
questions which they asked me, I spoke quite otherwise. 'Life and death
is God's gift,' I told them, 'and does not depend upon a son and his
worship at my shrine. I shall never be an orphan spirit seeking shelter,
for Christ has secured me immortality and has planned all my future.'

We talked often of these things, but it was hard for them to understand what I told them, and they would turn it off with one excuse
or another. 'She is different from us,' they said, 'her life is given up
to good works and her merit will secure her an entrance to Paradise.'
Some envied, some pitied, some just stared and made no effort to understand. Others summed it up in these words: 'Eastern ways are for the
East, Western ways are for the West.' But here and there was one who
caught a gleam which lifted her for ever above the sordidness of the
life to which so strange a fate had bound her.

> Mildred Cable and Francesca French, *The Gobi Desert*
> (London: Hodder & Stoughton, 1942), pp. 74–5

*The word 'bound' creeps inexorably into the text, and in this account the binding
is attributed to fate. So how could freedom come? Who could break the pattern?
The missionary women's word of healing and liberation had to be heard and
translated into the life and experience of real people, in this case two little girls,
Matinga and Susana, honorably possessed by their parents.*

Mr. and Mrs. Su have the honour of possessing little twin girls, known
as 'Ma-ti-nga' (May) and 'Su-sa-na,' (Susanna) — the latter so called
because, as the father explained, he had only to add a 'Sa-na' to his
surname 'Su', and the Biblical name of 'Susanna' was complete!

To heathen parents, the birth of twin girls would have been considered
an extreme misfortune, to be immediately followed by infanticide; so
that little 'Ma-ti-nga' and 'Su-sa-na', unconsciously teach a lesson of
Christian behaviour, and, by their very existence, are a strong plea
against the terribly prevalent custom of infanticide. And it may safely
be stated that they are the only twin girls living to-day in the Prefecture of Kien-Ning.

> Mary E. Darley, *The Light of the Morning*
> (London: Church of England Zenana Missionary Society, 1903), p. 243

The importance of their names and their parents' pride in naming them is underlined by Helen Barrett Montgomery.

To destroy girl babies at birth was formerly exceedingly common, and not regarded as a crime by the majority. Often no name, simply a number, is given to the girl baby, and a father in counting his family mentions only sons. Girls are simply sold as bondmaids to relieve poverty; and a wife may be legally sold or rented by her husband to another man for a fixed period. The binding of the feet is but an outward and visible sign of the crippled lives and energies of one-half of the Chinese people. While, strictly speaking, there can be but one legal wife in China, the law sanctions, and custom permits, secondary wives or concubines, and forbids the first wife to object to her lord's bringing such an addition to the family. The whole force of Chinese conservatism weighs down the aspiration of women for free or self-directed life. One indication of this is the amazing frequency of suicide among Chinese girls and women.

There is no better authority in matters Chinese than Arthur H. Smith. He speaks of suicide among the Chinese wives and daughters as very common, epidemic at times, and gives as a reason the unhappy status of women in married life. He instances cases in which young girls band themselves together to commit suicide rather than consent to marriage, and says, 'The death roll of suicides is the most convincing proof of the woes endured by Chinese women.'

Helen Barrett Montgomery, *Western Women in Eastern Lands*
(New York: Macmillan, 1911), pp. 48–9

Death begets death; in the wake of cruelty further cruelty follows. The patterns of violence were analysed by Mary Slessor in the Calabar with as much accuracy as the China Inland Missionaries identified them in the East. Those who are broken or victimized break and victimize in their turn.

The evil of twin-murder had a terrible fascination for her. A woman who gave birth to twins was regarded with horror. The belief was that the father of one of the infants was an evil spirit, and that the mother had been guilty of great sin; one at least of the children was believed to be a monster, and as they were never seen by outsiders or allowed to live, no one could disprove the fact. They were seized, their backs were broken, and they were crushed into a calabash or water-pot and taken out — not by the doorway, but by a hole broken in the back wall, which was at once built up — and thrown into the bush, where they were left to be eaten by insects and wild beasts. Sometimes they would be placed alive into the pots. As for the mother, she was driven outside the bounds of decent society and compelled to live alone in the bush. In such circumstances there was only one thing for the missionaries to do. As soon as the twins were born they sought to obtain the possession of them, and gave them the security and care of the Mission House. Some of the Mission compounds were alive with babies. It was no use taking the mother along with them. She believed she must be accursed, for otherwise she would never be in such a position. First one and then the other child would die, and she would make her escape and fly to the bush.

Mary realised that the system was the outcome of superstition and fear, and she could even see how, from the native point of view, it was essential for the safety of the House, but her heart was hot against it; nothing, indeed, roused her so fiercely as the senseless cruelty of putting these innocent babes to death, and she joined in the campaign with fearless energy.

She could also understand why the natives threw away infants whose slave-mother died. No slave had time to bring up another woman's child. If she did undertake the task, it would only be hers during childhood; after that it became the property of the master. The chances of a slave-child surviving were not good enough for a free woman to try the experiment, and as life in any case was of little value, it was considered best that the infant should be put out of the way.

The need of special service in these directions made her suggest to the Foreign Mission Committee that one of the woman agents should be set apart to take care of the children that were rescued. It was impossible, she said, for one to do school or other work, and attend to them as well. 'If such a crowd of twins should come to her as I have to manage, she would require to devote her whole time to them.' More and more also she was convinced of the necessity of women's work among the women in the farming districts, and she pressed the matter upon the Committee. She was in line with the old chief who remarked that 'Them women be the best man for the Mission.'

W. P. Livingstone, *Mary Slessor, Pioneer Missionary*
(London: Hodder & Stoughton, 1915), pp. 36–7

Where no check is in place, women become the 'unhappy victims of envy, hatred and jealousy' and, as Mary Bird observed in Persia, they can be as broken by other women as by men.

Rules and regulations as regards woman are based on the assumption that she will inevitably fall into sin at the first opportunity, and that the only safeguard is to give her no possible chance of going astray. She is, therefore, hedged about with the most tiresome and humiliating restrictions and treated always like an evilly-disposed child.

Her mind is cramped and starved, she has no education — among the poorer classes only about three Persian women in 1,000 have learned to read — her only subjects of interest and conversation are her clothes, her jewels, her children — generally dreadfully mismanaged — and her quarrels and petty intrigues with her husband's other wives.

For of course she is married! The single woman, independent, respected and self-respecting, is unknown in Persia, and *girlhood*, as we know it, a non-existent state. There is the little child up to ten or twelve years old, pretty, merry, and frolicsome, with the wonderful, dark, gazelle-like eyes of the East, probably already betrothed, but not taking much heed of the fact. Then, at one bound, she is the bride, decorated for the ceremony of marriage like a lamb for the sacrifice, handed over to some fully-grown or even middle-aged man who she has possibly never seen, and carried off by him to his own home, sometimes crying piteously for her mother. Thenceforward a prisoner, a plaything and pet if her husband is kindly disposed and loves her, but too often the unhappy victim of envy, hatred, and jealousy, and ever with the terror of divorce hanging over her. For it is so easy in Persia for a man to rid himself of an aging, or bad-tempered, or childless wife, or even one that he cannot afford to keep, that most women have been divorced at least once in their lives, and the proportion of marriages annulled in this way are said to be eighty or ninety per cent. The right of a husband to inflict corporal punishment on a wife who in any way displeases him is never questioned in Persia; it was enjoined by Mohammed. But greater than the fear of being beaten or even divorced, is the Persian wife's horror of the introduction of a rival into the household. The word for 'fellow-wife' means in Arabic 'injurious,' or 'harmful.' The new wife is generally regarded as an enemy, and though for a time she may be in high favour with her lord, she needs to beware of the secret poison which may either kill her outright or leave her a raving maniac.

Jennie Chappell, *Three Brave Women: Stories of Heroism in Heathen Lands*
(London: Partridge, 1920), pp. 126–7

*Another injurious intruder was the girl-child. Mary Warburton Booth's account
comes from Nepal.*

Lola was a mother when she was just beginning her teens, but the joy
of motherhood was shrouded by a cloud, for her first child was a girl,
and the disappointment in the family was great: what good could a girl
do? How could she carry on the ancestral spirit of the father? Only a
boy could do that, and the father wanted a son. The mother-in-law
wanted one too, so did everyone else. It was a calamity instead of a
joy to have a girl for the firstborn, and sorrow filled her soul: all happiness died, and she walked as one in a dream. What had she done
that this should be her lot? Why were the gods angry with her? She
had done her best to serve her husband and the family she was married
into. Why? why? why? she questioned, and then, one day, she heard
songs that were new and strange to her, and listened to the refrain.
A band of women wearing white saris had come to their village to
tell the people of a remedy for sin: they told of One Who had said
and was still saying: 'Come unto Me, all ye that are weary and heavy
laden, and I will give you rest.' She had never heard of Him before,
and she listened with a mind that did not believe. It was something
new, and wonderful to hear of One Who called the weary, and she was
fascinated as she listened. The women sang on and then they separated,
and after a while one of them came where she was squatting by the
village pool, and they began to talk. Lola listened as one in a dream,
and then she went into the house to her child and to think.

It was a strange and wonderful story, and that was the only time she
ever heard it in her village.

Those women never came back again and the memory of what she
heard dimmed almost to extinction as time went on, but not quite,
for it all came back to her long after when she was far away from the
early scenes and her life was a real battle to her. Then she remembered the women and the news they had brought to her village, and
she wondered where those women were and what they were doing and
if anyone else knew the story they told. She was 16 years old and still
no son had been given, and the mother-in-law began to be impatient

and her temper was expressed in stinging words! What sort of a wife was she? What had she done that the gods refused to give her a son, an heir to carry on the family traditions? Who was going to appease the family gods? They were angry, else why no son?

Mary Warburton Booth, My Testimony
(London: Pickering & Inglis, 1947), pp. 134–5

But time and again, as the Misses French and Miss Cable noted, the very tenets of these women's faith led to the oppression and brokenness to which the missionaries sought to minister.

The poor little patient sat nursing a foot devoured by a terrible sore. She was the first of many to seek help, and the rapid improvement in her condition has opened to us the doors of otherwise fastbarred harems. Many of the patients are girls who have been married four or five years and have not yet borne the desired child. Fear of the fate of a repudiated wife haunts them, with its miseries, disgrace, poverty and dependence on the whim of some man to admit them to his household. In other cases a woman has already borne ten or more children, not one of whom has survived, and her terror is lest she should have reached the limit of her productiveness. According to Moslem moral code: 'You may make of your wife anything you like except a corpse,' and the childless woman may any day hear the dread words:

'The door is not shut. I leave the bridle loose on your neck. You can go away.'

Kind words and a sympathetic touch have healing power for such broken hearts.

Mildred Cable, Evangeline French and Francesca French, A Desert Journal
(London: Hodder & Stoughton, 1934), p. 108

Amy Carmichael's account of child prostitution is more hazy. After all, how could such broken victims be set free? What makes this account especially chilling is the fact that it could still be written today.

The child told us things that darkened the sunlight. It was impossible to forget those things. Wherever we went after that day we were constrained to gather facts about what appeared a great secret traffic in the souls and bodies of young children, and we searched for some way to save them, and could find no way. The helpless little things seemed to slip between our fingers as we stretched out our hands to grasp them, or it was as though a great wave of swept up and carried them out to sea. In a kind of desperation, we sought for a way. But we found that we must know more before we could hope to find it. To graze upon the tips (of herbage) is the Tamil synonym for superficial knowledge. If we were to do anything for these children it was vain to graze on the tips of facts; it took years to do more than that.

Amy Carmichael, Gold Cord (London: SPCK, 1932), p. 22

Gladys Aylward's version of her work with children sounds totally playful and disguises the anguish of unbinding mutilated and maimed feet.

'That's it. Come on now. Hurry up! If God intended little girls to have horrible stubby little feet, He'd have made them like that in the first place, wouldn't He? Feet are to walk with, not to shuffle up and down with, aren't they? I don't care if the husbands say you should do it or not. They should try it sometime, and see if they like hobbling about on little club feet. Any other man who tells you to do it goes to prison at once; that's the law now . . .'

The last bandages dropped, revealing tiny white feet with toes bent downwards and up into the soles.

'Look at those feet!' exclaimed Gladys. 'Disgraceful, absolutely disgraceful! How d'you expect the poor child to walk properly with those feet?'

She almost pushed the women away, and, kneeling down, gently prised the toes up and away from the sole. The child regarded her with wide, timid eyes.

'There,' said Gladys softly. 'Five little piggies all ready to go to market.'

She massaged the foot tenderly. Suddenly there was a quick liquid giggle of sound from the child, who wriggled with delight.

The spell was broken. The women came closer, chattering happily. In the years that followed Gladys was to realise what an independent, courageous group these mountain women were. Even now they were friendly. 'Yes, it is a good law,' they said. Everyone now wanted to help in the foot massage; everyone wanted to tell of the pain and the trouble their own feet had given them for the past ten years. One of the neighbours rushed off to the next house to explain what had been done, and the news went round the village before Gladys had finished her first examination. As she proceeded she soon found housewives dutifully exhibiting all their little girls with unbound feet.

Alan Burgess, *The Small Woman* (London: The Reprint Society, 1959), p. 84

Such freedom was slower in coming in the experience of Mary Warburton Booth.

It was a wonderful experience to be taken, and I was gripped by the appalling apathy. No one seemed to say, 'Come and help us'. The women were curious and asked very personal questions as if nothing were private in life, and I answered as many as I could, but held to my purpose that if I listened to them, they must listen to me. And their reading books were opened and the Bible-woman with me gave the lesson which was the slowest thing I had ever seen, and there was always the Scripture lesson with questions and answers and all the time a prayer in my heart: 'Lord what wilt Thou have me do?' It all felt barren, so lifeless, and the atmosphere thick with superstition, and in some houses Satanic forces seemed to rule supreme. We went into windowless rooms, where light only came in through the door, sat on the edge of their beds where there were no chairs, and gave lessons to women who had never been to school and wanted to learn to read. We made friends with them, learned from them, and tried to picture what it must be never to go out for a walk, never to step out into the street, always, all the days, every day, to live in seclusion and never once to go out to a meeting. I asked, 'Why?' and the answer was one word, 'Custom'. I asked other questions and most of them had the same answer: 'It is not our custom' − and they settle down in it and never attempt to move out of it, for they are bound by custom, and customs do not easily change in the East. But − we can and do go to them, and sometimes lethargy is stirred and a glimmer of light beyond their dwelling-place reaches them, and something awakens in them and the scene is changed.

The interest grew as I got to know more, and my heart opened to the women who suffer in seclusion. I began to think how I could tell these people what Jesus could do for them, and I went deeper into the language. Oh! to be simple enough to be able to tell these people so clearly that they would not think about me, but see and hear Him.

Mary Warburton Booth, *My Testimony*
(London: Pickering & Inglis, 1947), pp. 70–1

French and Cable felt less incapacitated than this when they found that the whole onus for gospel work did not lie with them. The benefit of good example cannot be underestimated, as two women from Kashgar demonstrate. The Gobi desert missionaries were somehow reluctant to use words like 'Satanic forces', and could attack a good dish of boiled lamb along with the best of them.

Among our first visitors were two women from Kashgar. They were remarkably picturesque, and with splendid physique and deportment. They wore long, straight gowns of brilliant-coloured cloth, and a finely-woven veil falling below the waist, which softened the strong, handsome features, and gave them a most attractive appearance. They immediately mounted the *kang* barefoot, and it was a sight to see the face of Mrs. Liu — a model of Chinese propriety — as they slipped off their shoes, and the shapely feet were exposed. However, as they spoke Chinese fluently, she was soon in happy conversation with them. These ladies insisted that we should come that very afternoon to return their visit in their own home, and in an hour's time sent two charming children, wearing miniature Wellington boots, to escort us there. They led us safely past several ferocious dogs, through a spacious courtyard, to a living-room, where the whole family was assembled, the patriarch of the group being an Ahung, which corresponds to a Levite among the Israelites. After we had been seated for about half-an-hour, during which time they all listened attentively to the Gospel Story, a woman-servant appeared bearing a large dish of boiled lamb, the joints of which, being of the minutest size, were easily handled. The hostess, with unimpeachable manners, lifted the joints by the knuckle-bone, and gave us each one, saying, 'You know that it is not our custom to use chopsticks.'

Mildred Cable and Francesca French, Through Jade Gate and Central Asia
(London: Hodder & Stoughton, 1927), p. 141

Other customs would exclude not simply chopsticks but onions, garlic, vinegar and red pepper as well. A familiar backdrop is provided by the card-playing men in the background with their cups of tea.

The most rigorous asceticism rules the lives of many Kanchow women. Not content with being under a vegetarian vow, as is usually understood, they so fear any subtle indulgence of the appetite, that even onions, garlic, vinegar and red pepper, the necessary condiments to flavour the insipid dough-string diet, are eschewed. During the spring months almost every day sees the recurrence of some festival, which draws the crowds alternately to each temple in the neighbourhood. Theatrical troops move from fair to fair, repeating their performances to the never-failing concourse of village people, whose bullock-carts are parked in a wide semi-circle facing the stage, and in which the women sit the whole day long exposed to the heat of the sun. Most of the younger women and girls adorn themselves for the occasion with paint and powder, until the face is converted into an expressionless mask. Their hair is beautifully dressed and decorated with artificial flowers. Most of the small children are stamped on the forehead, nose and chin with minute geometrical patterns, traced in red circles.

Just out of earshot of the stage, the food-vendors pitch their stalls, where cooked eatables of all descriptions are on sale. Pork fried and stewed in a thick gravy, is served up on small saucers and eaten with chopsticks, as also fried meat-dumplings, garnished with vinegar and red pepper. A large mould of steamed rice containing the fruit of the jujube tree is popular, and dried apricots, macerated in water, are in demand as a cooling drink. Not far off are long tables sheltered by an awning, where men will sit for hours sipping tea and playing cards.

Mildred Cable and Francesca French, Through Jade Gate and Central Asia
(London: Hodder & Stoughton, 1927), pp. 56–7

Ma Slessor, meanwhile, was not adverse to a cup of tea herself as she sat in judgement over miscreants in the Calabar.

So Ma became again the only woman judge in the Empire. The Court was held in a thatched building at Ikotobong. Ma sat at a small table, and around her were the chiefs getting their first lessons in acting justly and mercifully towards wrongdoers. Often she had to keep them in order. They were very fond of talking, and if they did not hold their tongues she just rose and boxed their ears.

She sat long days trying cases, her only food a cup of tea and a biscuit and a tin of sweets. She needed all her courage to get through, for the stories of sin and cruelty and shame poured into her ears were terrible for a white woman to hear. 'We do not know how she does it,' the other missionaries said. She could not have done it had it not been that she wanted to save her black sisters and the little children from the misery they suffered. She was like no other judge in the world, because she had no books to guide her in dealing with the cases, nothing but her knowledge of the laws and customs of the people and her own good sense.

W. P. Livingstone, *The White Queen of Okoyong*
(London: Hodder & Stoughton, n.d.), p. 148

No wonder Olive Wyon could associate the missionary movement with a development both for the women in question and for the Church as a whole.

The basic motive for the establishment of the women's communities was the desire to lead a consecrated life. But this fundamental desire was reinforced by various other factors which made active communities of women to be seen as an advantage both to the women and to the Church as a whole.

Partly due to the influence of Florence Nightingale, and the experiences of the Crimean War, by 1863 various women's communities had been founded and were slowly beginning to be recognised as useful and valuable, although there was still a great deal of prejudice and hostility to be overcome. By this time several men also began to feel that the desire for a consecrated life was as strong for them as for the women. Being in the ministry already, they had plenty of outlet for their energies. They seemed to need some additional reason for founding a community. What brought this about was the need for foreign missionary work.

Olive Wyon, *Living Springs* (London: SCM Press, 1963), p. 44.

No wonder, either, the high profile Lucretia Mott assigned to women in the project of evangelism.

In the phrase in which 'Phebe, the servant of the church,' is mentioned, those who are familiar with the original have found, that the same word, which is, in her case, translated *servant*, is, in the case of men, translated *minister*. And has not conscious evidence been afforded by this translation, of the priest-craft and monopoly of the pulpit, which have so long held women bound?

I long for the time when my sisters will rise, and occupy the sphere to which they are called by their high nature and destiny. What a change would then appear in the character of woman! We should no longer find her the mere plaything of man, and a frivolous appendage of society. We should not find her so easily satisfied with a little domestic duty — with embroidering the light device on muslin and lace, or with reading the sentimental novel. When I look at the 'Ladies Department' in our newspapers and magazines, I blush for my sex, and for the low sphere of action they are content with. I believe that if woman would but look seriously at herself, she would learn how great an evil her nature suffers in being prevented from the exercise of her highest faculties. What a different race would be brought forth — what a different and nobler generation should we behold in the next, from that which preceded it, if the high duties of women were all fulfilled! I believe the tendency of truth, on this subject, is to equalize the sexes; and that, when truth directs us, there will be no longer assumed authority on one side or admitted inferiority on the other; but that as we advance in the cultivation of all our powers, physical as well as intellectual and moral, we shall see that our independence is equal, our dependence mutual, and our obligations reciprocal.

It is this perception, my friends, that I long for. I feel bound, when in company with my sisters who have thought it improper or sinful to exercise their highest powers of mind on the most important subjects, to beseech them to think so no longer, and to come forth into that noble and becoming freedom which they, in common with man, have received: — so useful will they then be in their own day, and so happy will be their influence upon generations yet to come.

Dana Greene (ed.), Lucretia Mott: Her Complete Speeches and Sermons
(New York and Toronto: The Edwin Mellen Press, 1980), pp. 28–9

*   *   *

Lucretia Mott's defence of a 'noble and becoming' freedom for women had especial relevance for crusading women who found a specific rather than a generalized cause. They became pioneers of something altogether new in the Church's self-perception. Not surprisingly the impetus came from the Society of Friends.

By the end of the nineteenth century, the women's rights movement, with its large Quaker component, had come of age. Seneca Falls, when the women felt it necessary to ask a man to chair their meeting, was far behind. The devotion to reform movement on the part of most of the women crusading for women's rights had won them the support of the black woman, the working class woman, the single working woman. The pioneers who set out on the lecture trail in the 1840s, because they had a Divine leading to speak out against slavery, could never have dreamed what results would flow from their single, simple act of courage.

> Margaret Hope Bacon, *As the Way Opens: The Story of Quaker Women in America* (Richmond, Indiana: Friends United Press, 1980), p. 99

Mrs Johnston cannot have been the only missionary wife to offer instruction to enslaved women and their children, even when ordinances such as those of the Kingston Common Council were in place.

These hindrances to Gospel work were sources of great trouble to both Mr. and Mrs. Johnston. For several months they removed from the station, where missionary effort was permitted under certain restrictions. Many bitter tears were shed in secret by Mrs. Johnston, during the dark and gloomy period of suspense, while very earnest petitions were constantly made that all hindrances might be removed, and the way opened for unfettered promulgation of the Gospel. In the meantime, she embraced every opportunity of instructing the poor female slaves and their children, privately. Gathering them around her by stealth, in her own home, she taught them of Christ — and not in vain. These secret labours were blessed to the salvation of many souls.

> Mrs E. R. Pitman, *Lady Missionaries in Foreign Lands* (London: S. W. Partridge, n.d.), p. 69

Her biographer, Mrs Pitman, is clear. Mrs Johnson had something unique to bring to the women whom she helped. She strove to 'raise, civilise, christianise, and refine them'. And in the process — because this is the wonderful irony of missionary work — she too was raised, civilised, christianised and refined in her turn.

Settled once more, Mrs. Johnston commenced earnest labour among the female slaves and their children. All the surroundings of her life were depressing, and, to a sensitive mind, the circumstances amid which the slaves lived, were calculated to still further depress the spirits and sadden the hearts of those who ministered to them. The wonder is that in those days of cruelty, outrage, and bondage, any of the negroes should have embraced the Gospel, or have cared to risk the severe punishment which at that time followed attendance upon the means of grace. It was only by stealth that Mrs. Johnston could instruct any, and these mostly came to hear the 'wonderful words of life', in the evenings, after their day's labour in the plantations was over.

The daily life of a slave was so full of hardship, toil, and suffering, that it seemed well-nigh impossible to make an impression on ears dulled by fatigue, and hearts dark and ignorant for lack of the simplest knowledge.

They had grown from childhood to adult age destitute of the commonest cultivation. The associations of their daily life were all on the side of immorality and evil. Their allowance of clothing was so small that the slaves worked nearly naked in the fields, and their children under ten years of age went entirely naked. Hard toil from morning till night was the rule in all weathers; while Sundays and holidays — these latter very rare — presented the only opportunities for cultivating their own patches of ground. Infants were carried to the fields by their mothers, and were secured to their backs during their work; or, if able to walk, the children played about till the mothers were permitted to return at nightfall to their huts. On large estates, these little children were, however, taken care of by some old negress past active labour, and as they grew up, were put to weeding and other light employments, until fit for fieldwork.

The punishments dealt out to slaves were brutal in the extreme. An old historian says: 'They be whipped by the overseer with lancewood switches till they be bloody, and several of the switches broken. After they be whipped till they be raw, some put on their skins pepper and salt, to make them smart; at other times their masters will drop melted wax on their skins, and use exquisite tortures. For attempting to escape from their masters, they put iron rings of great weight upon their ankles, or pot hooks about their necks, or a spur in their mouths; or at other times half the foot was cut off by an axe. Rebellion was punished by burning to death. At other times such offenders were hung up in iron cages and starved to death. This lingering mode of dying took eight or nine days to accomplish.'

It was but little that one woman could do for people so brutalised and down-trodden as these West Indian slaves. But what one could do, that Mrs. Johnston did. Leaving to her husband the more public work of the mission, she went in and out unceasingly among the female population, striving to raise, civilise, christianise, and refine them, by teaching, 'in season and out of season', the Gospel of Christ, and its kindred lessons. And though her time for labour in Prince Rupert's was very short — only about twelvemonth — she sowed seed which sprang up and bore fruit to God's glory, long after she had passed away.

Mrs E. R. Pitman, *Lady Missionaries in Foreign Lands*

(London: S. W. Partridge, n.d.), pp. 74–5

As fruit to God's glory, or as a child of sudden glory, Mary Fisher — a former 'slave' herself as a servant-girl in Yorkshire — features as a romantic figure in this drama.

If romance, like laughter, is the child of sudden glory, the figure of Mary Fisher is the most romantic in the early Quaker annals. First known as a servant-girl in Yorkshire, she died in Carolina, in her own house, bequeathing real and personal estate and a black slave to her heirs. Unmarried at thirty-nine, she died at seventy-five, a widow for the second time, leaving two daughters and a son behind. She was the first Quaker apostle to the colleges, and headed the long list of heroic sufferers who were publicly flogged in England for their religion. She, too, with an older woman, was the pioneer who brought the Friends' doctrine to New England in 1656, and tasted the first-fruits of the persecution which was meted out to her fellow-believers, even to the extremes of mutilation and death, by those who were themselves the survivors of the Mayflower. Then, carrying the Gospel into Turkey, she spoke face to face with the Sultan, and was treated by him and his subjects with every refinement of courtesy and kindness.

　　Mary Fisher was one of many servants who were 'convinced' in company with their master and mistress, the conversion of an entire household being a common feature of early Quakerism.

Mabel Richmond Brailsford, *Quaker Women 1650–1690*

(London: Duckworth & Co., 1915), p. 94

While Mrs Johnson and Mary Fisher kept slaves, according to the next account Hester Lane — 'whom we should delight to clasp by the hand, and call by the . . . holy name of sister' — actively collaborated with the liberation of eleven other human beings. The language is quaint, even offensive, but the analysis is sound. Freedom in Christ is about freedom indeed, not about further contempt or reproach.

Hester Lane — and we note the fact, because it is assumed by some men of intelligence and superior culture that the negro race is a *lower* race — was a negress; if the position or assumption be correct — and we stay not now to argue the matter, as our readers, without any aid but that of common sense, have long since for themselves settled the question — then in the performance of the highest duties of the Christian life the greater honour is due to Hester Lane. This good woman, whom we should delight to clasp by the hand, and call by the reverent and holy name of sister, when visited by a friend of the negro, Mr. Abdy, was between fifty and sixty. He describes her reception of him as being open and without affectation; just such a reception as any sensible cultured woman, of whatever colour, would have given him. By her own hard earnings in Philadelphia, which, as a member of the despised coloured race, would indeed be hardly earned, she managed during a long course of years, with the utmost resolution, never for an instant relaxed, to accomplish an almost incredible amount of good. She had at different times, by her own unaided efforts, purchased from slavery *eleven human beings*. The first slave redeemed by her was a girl of eleven years of age; the price was a hundred dollars. She had been present when she was born, she afterwards assisted at her marriage, at the birth of her four children; and then, when she died, had the mournful satisfaction of assisting at her funeral. Her next purchase was a boy of fourteen, for whom she paid two hundred dollars. She then bought a man thirty years of age for two hundred and eighty dollars. Her next purchase was a man, his wife, and child. As the parents were old and sickly, she was permitted to purchase the three for one hundred and forty dollars. Owing to their incapacity for labour, however, their subsequent maintenance largely devolved upon her. The fifth case was that of a woman and three children, whom she bought by auction in Maryland: subsequently she purchased the husband for two hundred dollars, not without great difficulty, as the owner insisted upon having three hundred dollars. She was not content with redeeming the children from slavery, but considered that her duty consisted in caring for their morals and paying for their education. When Mr. Abdy called upon her, she was teaching herself French; she had also succeeded in discovering a new method of colouring walls, from which source, and the proceeds of a small shop, she had been enabled to maintain herself, and make the important purchases we have intimated. This woman belonged to a *lower* race of beings! What may the higher actions of the highest race be?

Hester, with that indignation which became her, spoke of the treatment which she and her race received from the hands of the whites, who, in their self-assumption, treated them as only upon a level with the dirt under their feet. She could not do other than consider the dispensations of Providence as wise and good; yet it was mysterious to know that the African should be subjected to unmitigated and unmerited bondage; and when freed from the yoke, still be subject to contempt and reproach.

Joseph Johnson, *Brave Women and Their Deeds of Heroism*
(London: Gall & Inglis, n.d.), pp. 226–7

The most famous of the missionary writers such as Miss French and Miss Cable perhaps do us a disservice when they avoid political questions such as these (though anyone interested in food will find the following account quite lyrical). They wrote so persuasively and evocatively that we are easily swept into something akin to the mythical 'Woman's Land' they attributed to Turki ladies.

After the talk we drew up to a low table where a delicious meal was served. First we nibbled melon seeds, then we tasted fresh fruits from their own gardens, mulberries, early apricots, the stalkless cherry which they call *ginesta*, sun-dried melon strips, and a variety of sweetmeats. After this we started on the *pièce de résistance*, which was the *pilau*. The Turki people make this dish from savory rice cooked with all kinds of flavourings — spices, cloves, garlic, onion, sultanas, nuts — on top of which is laid fried chicken cut into small pieces. It was very good indeed, for it had been prepared by a first-class cook.

The ladies knew that we were on the eve of leaving for their country home, and that they were eager to tell us all about it:

'There are eighty fruit gardens,' they said, 'and you will arrive in the height of the mulberry season. This is the time when we ourselves leave town every summer, but the old king is too ill to take the journey this year. We do not let the people know how weak he is, but now they have dismissed the doctor who was looking after him and brought another one. Perhaps he will get well under new treatment, and then we will move the whole household up to the hills for the grape and walnut harvests. If you can stay so long we will have a jolly time together. We will make a feast every day and you will tell us of all the countries you have seen. You must some time have travelled through Woman's Land where there are no men at all but only women, and also through the country where people are round and have a hole through their bodies like copper cash so that they can be strung together. You have been to so many places and seen so much, but we never move from home,' this they said with a deep sigh.

Mildred Cable and Francesca French, *Wall of Spears*
(London: Lutterworth Press, 1951), pp. 134–5

So where does true freedom lie? What is the landscape which lies beyond any brokenness or victimization, beyond any persecution or social and cultural restraint? Mary Ward saw it as a state of justice, and one which women — whether members of her religious Institute or not — were well qualified to pursue.

I would exceedingly gladly, both for my better satisfaction and greater security, acquaint you with what hath occurred in these two days, especially that which yesterday I wrote to your Reverence about, and going now to set it down, the better I discern it, the less able I find myself to declare it. I seem to love it, and yet dare not embrace it for truly good till it be approved.

It seems a clear and perfect estate to be had in this life, and such a one as is altogether needful for those that should well discharge the duties of this Institute.

It is not like the state of the saints, whose holiness chiefly appears in that union with God, which maketh them out of themselves. The felicity of this estate, for as much as I can express, was a singular freedom from all that could make one adhere to earthly things, with an entire application and apt disposition to all good works. Something happened also discovering that freedom that such a soul should have had to refer all to God . . .

I seemed in my understanding to see a soul thus composed but far more fair than I can express it. Yet then occurred, and so still continues in my mind, that those in Paradise before the first fall were in this estate, it seemed to me then, that hope remains still, that our Lord let me see it to invite me that way and because he would give me grace in time to arrive to such an estate, at least in some degree.

That word of 'Justice', and those in former times that were called just persons, works of justice, done in innocence, and that we be such as we appear, and appear such as we are: these things often since occurred to my mind with a liking for them. I have thought moreover on this occasion, that perhaps this course of ours would continue to the end of the world, because it came to that in which we first began. Once I found a questioning in myself why this state of justice, and the virtue of sincerity should appear to me so especially requisite as a ground of all other virtues necessary to be exercised by those of this Institute . . .

M. Emmanuel Orchard, IBVM (ed.), *Till God Will: Mary Ward Through Her Writings*
(London: Darton, Longman & Todd, 1985), pp. 40–1

To go back to the beginning, to the state of justice that preceded the fall, is to take an immense theological leap. It is to lay claim to a new understanding of the creation stories, one that interprets them in a way that re-enfranchises Eve. In a state of justice Eve cannot be blamed for all human woes; women cannot be persecuted or victimized for something they never did. The very roots of discrimination are challenged in a way that invites us all to make community — as women and men obviously, but as nations too. The state of justice, ultimately, is what the missionary women were working for. Only they would have called it the coming of the kingdom.

CHAPTER 8

———

MINE THE MIGHTY
ORDINATION OF THE
PIERCED HANDS

'To set at liberty those who are oppressed' (Luke 4.18)

To cast out devils is an extraordinary ministry. In the mission fields, women discovered that they were called to do just that. Their calling gave them the authority to make a stand against the ultimate expressions of evil. At its most graphic this gives us accounts such as this, from Miss French and Miss Cable.

One morning, two young Chinese girls crossed the stream at our tent door, and as they did so one fell to the ground in a condition of demon-possession. A voice, which was not her own, spoke through her lips, commanding that a vow be made on her behalf and certain rites performed. We did our best to control her and to help her terrified companion; the bystanders, meanwhile, brought yellow paper charms and burnt them over her head, watching to see if the charred fragments would fly upwards or fall ineffectively to the ground. The young woman was a victim of the demons whom her family had come here expressly to worship, but there was opportunity for us to warn them of the danger to which they were exposing her, and to tell them of the only possible way of release.

Mildred Cable, Evangeline French and Francesca French, A *Desert Journal*
(London: Hodder & Stoughton, 1934), p. 53

At its most charged, this gives a story which reveals the source of this authority as well as the love which Mary Warburton Booth brought to her work. In the power of the pierced hands of Jesus, she was ordained to a ministry of exorcism.

How can I describe her? She was about four and half years of age, a little old person, hair cropped close to her head, a very cunning expression in her eyes, her little body rather hunched, and her hands ever on the wave as her tongue wagged. There was nothing young about her except her back. She looked exactly like a little old woman who had forgotten to grow, and her face bore marks of much suffering. 'Yes I have been married,' she was saying; 'I was married to an old man, the helpless one, he died like that' — she gave a swift dash forward with her hands — 'and I, well, I am here.' She held herself as if she were forty instead of four and half, and I called her to me, asking 'How old are you?' A deep sigh and a look all around and her feet moved towards me — 'I', she pursed her lips, 'I, ah — it is many days since I knew' — and she chatted on about the things around her. She noticed the bread on the table, and, pointing with her chin, blurted out, 'Ek-Ekane,' meaning — that bread is one anne? She knew, she was no child, she was old and a widow, and I accepted her from the God of the widow to keep for Him. 'Tell me where you were born?' I asked her. Again her little face puckered up, and looking like some old, old creature, she ventured: 'Who knows? It is very many days since I was born!' and all I can say is — she looked it.

She walked round me talking all the time, and then sudden quietness — she was asleep at my feet. I lifted her up and put her gently to bed. She slept for twenty-four hours, and that was her beginning with us.

She spent all her time playing around me between meals. She seemed to have no desire to be with the children. She talked to herself and to me incessantly, and I tried to know her. Who was this little girl? Why did she look so old? What had brought that cunning expression on her face? I asked these questions again and again as I watched the child

settle down in our hearts and become a part of us. She had suffered
unspeakable things, fear dodged her, and when the lamp was carried
from one room to another she was close to it. Darkness held some dark
moments for her; she breathed quickly in short gasps if any lighted the
lamp — why?

I kept her with me. She seemed to want that. She followed me from
room to room although, when I was busy, she was apparently oblivious of
me, but if I moved she was there; she seemed to feel safe that way, and I
was glad to have her, for I wanted to know and understand this old child
so miraculously brought to us. For how could I help if I did not know?
It is the close-up that compels into action that counts, and, day by day,
week by week, the child hovered round me, fearful, yet bold, cunning
yet open, old yet young. What made this mixture? She was baffling,
sometimes repelling, and yet drawing. The appeal in her was the utter
contradiction to anything a little girl four and a half should be, and
my heart and arms opened wide to her. She seemed afraid of love, and
yet she nestled in my arms for a while, then pulled herself up and out
and stood back to question what it all meant. I do not think she had
ever had affection before. She knew torture, she knew pain, she knew
what no little girl should know and certainly never suffer. She drew
back and showed me her body, and I winced under her searching gaze,
for it cried out to me the one word: 'Help — help — help.' How could
I help one who knew such depths at her age? Her little head nodded
slowly. 'They did that, he did that,' she said slowly. 'You don't know,'
she continued, 'I know, I know,' and I watched her walk round and
round the room as she repeated: 'I know, I know, I know.'

When she had been with us for a few weeks she was still playing round
me and beginning to look a little younger. She never laughed, nothing
amused her; she was too old to make merry; joy seemed to have missed
her, but I loved to have her near. The longer she stayed, the more I
was mystified.

She would rush up to me, lean hard, compel me to stop whatever
I was doing to attend to her, and then with a strange and sometimes
weird expression, stand still and just gaze at me. Some days she was
listless and nothing seemed to arouse her; it was one of the latter days
that opened my eyes to the reality of evil possession. For hours she
sat unmoved. I called her, she turned slowly and stood. I said 'Come,'
and very slowly and reluctantly she came and very swiftly went back to
where she had been. I prayed to know what to do. 'Lord, what would

Thou have me do?' I prayed as I continued at the writing table, looking yet not looking, watching yet waiting. She had moved, she was out of the room and onto the verandah. I heard her humming to herself, and I looked out to see her little body swaying backwards and forwards – and then there was silence for a long time. I spoke several times, and she looked half dazed, and I thought perhaps she was sleeping, so bade her lie down and go to sleep. I heard singing in a monotone, and looked out to see, she was up on her feet and turning round and round and repeating some words that sounded liked blasphemy, but thought I must be mistaken. I watched her, riveted by the little totem body revolving; first the movement was slow, and the circle wide, but it narrowed down as the child increased her speed, words just tumbling out of her mouth until, like a suddenly shot thing she dropped. I thought she was dizzy, and went to see her and help her up, and the little body stiffened, her chest heaved as if a mountain of feeling was inside, her eyes were dilated, froth oozed from her mouth; I bent over her, and she cursed me. I touched her, and she poured out the most awful words I have ever heard from a child. I called Bua and asked what we had better do. 'She is ill,' I said, 'poor little darling,' and Bua, with the sternest of expressions, replied 'Ill? Ill? ah, this is no illness, this is the devil, it is an evil spirit in possession.'

I stared at the woman. 'Help the child, help me to help the child,' I cried, and Bua, in the sternest of voices said, 'Don't touch the child, cast out the evil spirit.'

If I ever felt helpless in my life, it was then. Here was I, a missionary, a messenger of the Cross, entrusted with the glorious News of Salvation, sent in love by Him who died to save. I could truly say,

> Christ the Son of God, hath sent me
> To the midnight lands;
> Mine the mighty ordination,
> Of the Pierced Hands.

And yet, there I was with the little Indian girl, possessed by evil spirits, and an Indian woman, saved, to serve, and I did not know what to do except pray. I dropped on my knees praying.

Bua put her hand on mine. 'Don't pray,' she said, 'cast them out.'

I faltered, 'How? What can I do?' And she answered swiftly, 'As it is written in the Book, so do. Have you forgotten? Oh Mamiji, did not

Jesus say, "I give unto thee power over all the power of the enemy."
Cast out in the Name of Jesus.'

There she stood like a sentinel pointing the way. That dear Indian
fellow-worker, and I, scarcely realising anything except that it was time
for action or for ever lose the field. I did as I was told, and we found
it as He said, according to His Word.

The cursing stopped, the eyes closed, the little body quivered and
then quieted down; she was asleep, but the agony had left its mark,
and I lifted the child in my arms and then carried her in. 'Poor little
widow, only a child and what a curse.' I wept sorely.

For days she lay like one awakening from a terrible dream; we spent
all our time with her. Then she asked to get up, and she went straight
into the corner and crouched there like a little frightened animal. I
gathered her in my arms; she nestled like a weary child, too weary to
fight any more, and a sigh of content was the comfort I had.

From that time the change began, and only once since have I seen
anything of the kind in her, and that was over almost immediately,
but I always feel that the young life with such experience has a scar
that only the Pierced Hands of Jesus can take away.

In three months' time she was in the school under the trees, learning
as fast as, or faster than, anyone else.

Mary Warburton Booth, 'Whosoever Shall Receive'
(London: Marshall, Morgan & Scott, 1929), pp. 11–15

*A confrontation such as that is a naked confrontation with evil, and the
gospel itself sanctioned Mary Warburton Booth's response. In the mission
field — the midnight lands — uniquely, a woman could face evil, name it,
and cast it out.*

*   *   *

*There are other encounters, however, where what was met was simply oth-
erness, what was experienced was simply fear, and the only vocabulary
available to describe this encounter was still the traditional language of sin
and evil. In point of fact, if there was sin around, one could be forgiven for
assuming it was in the minds of white colonizers, bent on exploitation, profit
and greed. Because often the name of this sin was racism and the women col-
luded with it as much as the men, the missionaries as much as the traders and
trappers. At its most unredeemed, as in this story of Mr and Mrs Burleigh's*

arrival at Keppel Island in the Falklands, the very adjectives the author uses
give her game away. After all, what they met was simply a different land-
scape and climate, as well as different people. How easy, though, to use
a vocabulary and metaphors which reveal that what was normative for the
Burleighs was a white European person; everyone else was deviant.

The natives of the mainland were as unattractive as their place of habi-
tation. The Yangans, among whom the Burleighs especially desired to
work, were a copper coloured race, so singularly disproportionate, to
our European ideas, as to form, that one writer has said they looked
as if made up of odd limbs from various individuals. Their heads and
chests were huge, and it is difficult to understand how their puny legs
could carry them. Their faces were flat and wide, their small, black eyes
bleared and full of cunning, their coarse black hair, uncut and untended,
hung wildly about their faces and shoulders, giving them the look of
'furies, rather than human beings'. Their sole garment was a piece of
skin or blanket, slung round their shoulders, but they endeavoured to
make up for this deficiency by a profusion of paint, particularly on the
face, where their natural uncomeliness was augmented to the hideous,
by lines traversing the face from the eyes to the chin. Some wore shell
necklaces, and braces made of strips of sealskin.

   They are a nomadic people, seldom remaining more than a few days
at a time in one place; these wanderings are necessitated by the difficulty of finding food, and their dwellings, rude wigwams formed of the
interlaced branches of trees, were like untidy birds' nests turned upside
down, having far less fare and skill expended on their construction,
and certainly affording inferior shelter to those designed by most of
our feathered fellow-creatures.

   The food of these poor degraded beings was mainly shell-fish, seals
and water-birds, which they would pursue in frail canoes covered with
beech-bark, sewn together with threads made of hide, or with reeds. The
carcase of a whale cast up by the sea was the occasion of a great feast,
no matter how far gone in decomposition. 'All the people within reach
flock to the spot, while fleets of canoes surround the stranded monster,
and its body is covered with little copper-covered men, carving away at
the blubber with their shell-knives. Each cuts as much as he can, and
when he has torn and carved off a large piece of blubber, he makes a
hole in the middle, puts his head through the aperture, and this leaves
his hands free to carry more of the dainty food.' The men were in the

habit of marrying as many wives as they pleased, and as usual among savage and non-Christian races, the women were looked upon as drudges and slaves, and expected to do all the hardest and heaviest work, while their lords sat at ease.

Jennie Chappell, *Three Brave Women: Stories of Heroism in Heaven Lands*
(London: Partridge, 1920), pp. 89–90

Students of social anthropology, let alone biologists and naturalists, would give a great deal to see sights such as these, or even to read about them in a temperate, moderate way. In accounts such as Jennie Chappell's, the author is so bent on demonstrating the heroism of her brave women that her narrative sweeps her along. To the late twentieth-century reader she herself becomes just as much of a curiosity as the Keppel Islanders of whom she writes.

Interestingly though, when the women missionaries themselves met with cultural conflict, they were inclined to translate it across into another medium, and so many of the stories which they tell are about washing and cleaning. Not only did they meet copper-coloured bodies, they began to wash them. Not only did they wash them or teach washing as a good Christian practice, but they developed a way of thinking in which the words 'white' and 'clean' came dangerously close to being interchangeable.

After a while Mrs Ward started a regular school and commenced with two boys. Another joined. All these spoke different dialects. Next week a class was formed for girls. They were as difficult as young goats these bush maidens. After a month's schooling Mrs Ward thought that she might begin to teach them some housework, so she asked one of the girls to commence by washing her hands and face. The girl did not understand that this could be necessary, and when Mrs Ward tried to show her how to wash herself, she was seized with sudden panic and fled at top speed to the native's camp. This was repeated more than once. At last the lesson was learned, and the root idea of cleanliness was implanted.

E. C. Dawson, *Missionary Heroines in Many Lands*
(London: Seeley, Service & Co., 1912), p. 157

So much for any root ideas about the gospel of the Lord Jesus. Small wonder that the sick Mary Slessor's young companion, Janie, picked up mixed messages when she travelled home with her on furlough.

Even she, however, gave in at last. She became so ill that she was taken to Duke Town a wreck and carried on board the steamer and sent home. Janie again went with her, a woolly-headed lassie with velvet skin and eyes that were always ready to laugh. She was beginning to think that it would be a fine thing to be a white girl. One night, in a house in Glasgow, when she was being bathed, she took the sponge and began to scrub the soles of her feet, which were whiter than the rest of her body. 'Why are you doing that, Janie?' she was asked. 'Oh, because the white place is getting bigger, and if I scrub perhaps I'll be all white some day!'

> W. P. Livingstone, *The White Queen of Okoyong*
> (London: Hodder & Stoughton, n.d.), p. 83

What is disconcerting is that this episode is related as though it were rather sweet or funny. Mind you, to congregations reared on the racism of some of Miss Havergal's less worthy lines, this reaction was inevitable.

> There are little ones among them,
> Child-ministers of prayer,
> White robes of intercession
> Those tiny servants wear.
> First for the near and dear ones
> Is that fair ministry,
> Then for the poor black children,
> So far beyond the sea.
> The busy hands are folded,
> As the little heart uplifts
> In simple love, to God above,
> Its prayer for all good gifts.

> Frances Ridley Havergal, *The Poetical Works*
> (London: James Nisbet & Co., n.d.), p. 785

It stands to Christina Forsyth's credit that the black women with whom she worked in fact had the last say.

It was pitiful to see her during the final days. Several times she murmured with a quivering face, 'It's not the place, it's the people I can't bear to part with.' To them the parting was equally sore. 'Smoyana,' said a deputation of women who came to see her, 'you are not white, you are black. Your heart is black, you are just one of ourselves.' It was the highest compliment they could pay; it meant that she understood their real nature, and so was able to sympathise with and help them in their peculiar needs.

W. P. Livingstone, Christina Forsyth of Fingoland
(London: Hodder & Stoughton, n.d), p. 216

*   *   *

The theme of cleanliness and its relationship to godliness is one which it is all too easy to dismiss or trivialize, either out of embarrassment at its evident racism or because we have too sanitized a view of missionary life. Among the Mizos, images of dirt haunted Gladwys Evans' dreams as well as her daytime living.

Then the health centre was all but finished and we could use it. Leaves and bamboo were put upon the roof until such time as we could have the corrugated iron from Aizawl. It had to be carried for about thirty five miles along the jungle paths.

The health centre was sixteen feet by thirty four feet, divided into three rooms. One was my sitting room cum bedroom cum office, with a separate little hut for a cook house. It was a real treat to have proper windows and doors and to be able to make it comfortable. I had local craftsmen to make wicker chairs which were really comfortable.

The middle room was for examination and treatment of patients with a cupboard for medicines, stools and collapsible tables for treatment, and a long table for examination of patients which served as an operating table and labour bed if necessary. The third room had three small beds for patients from different villages needing special care. When we had patients staying in, my nights were not very restful, because relatives stayed with the patients and they were not quiet.

Rats were my constant companions and even my cats could not cope with all of them. One night I dreamt of stroking a lovely white rabbit, I woke to find a huge rat on my bed.

May Bounds and Gladwys M. Evans, Medical Mission to Mizoram
(Chester: Handbridge, 1986), p. 63

Small wonder that, in the Fingoland, Christina Forsyth eventually succumbed to the lure of a comfortable bath.

But now and then they endeavoured, almost surreptitiously, to send out little articles that might conduce to her well-being. When Mrs Stewart was home she suggested a table-lamp, and this she herself conveyed out, though with more and more misgiving as she approached Kafraria. They also consulted Miss Auld when she was in Scotland, and on her recommendation resolved to despatch a bath and easy-chair to Xolobe. On Miss Auld's return to Paterson she dropped a casual hint as to what was coming, whereupon Mrs Forsyth reached hastily for pen and paper and wrote to Miss Macfarlane. 'We have excellent bathing facilities here, and an easy-chair would be a cumbersome thing to get here, as there is no traffic by wagon, so if you would not be offended I would rather not receive them. We have an excellent water-supply within five minutes walk of the house.'

Later, however, when she grew feebler, and was unable to go the river, she proposed to buy a bath.

W. P. Livingstone, *Christina Forsyth of Fingoland*
(London: Hodder & Stoughton, n.d), p. 206

French and Cable's next account reminds us that the theme of cleanliness is even more hazardous in the case of women, and that all women, whatever their skin colour, can be persecuted in the name of purity rituals.

It is well known that no unclean food is used in our kitchen and we rigorously exclude all products of the pig (except our hair brushes) from the house. All the meat we eat comes from a Moslem butcher, and the beast has been slaughtered with its face towards Mecca, so the Ahungs have, so far, raised no objection to free intercourse with their women folk, and at any time we can slip into the harems, certain of a welcome. Infidels of course we are, but they make a distinction between us − 'infidels of the Book' and the Chinese who are 'infidels of the pig and idol.'

The women are troubled by no such sophistry. They merely recognize that for the first time in their lives somebody cares for their welfare, loves to sit with them and proclaim to them the good news that God is no respecter of sex, that they too are immortal, that they may have salvation and enter heaven as ransomed souls, not as the *houris* of the male paradise.

'We are not like you,' they will say, 'you are pure in God's sight, but look at me. I have a small child, my dress is not clean, and the Ahung will not allow a women to even pray when she has small children, for cleansings are impossible to her.'

Conversation with these truly lovable women is interspersed on their part with sighs so deep, so tender yet so desponding, as do more to reveal the tragedy of their lives than any spoken word.

Mildred Cable, Evangeline French and Francesca French, A *Desert Journal* (London: Hodder & Stoughton, 1943), p. 226

Dorothy L. Sayers is not alone in speaking out against the entire mindset which creates rituals where there should be none.

Setting aside the scandal caused by His Messianic claims and His reputation as a political firebrand, only two accusations of personal depravity seem to have been brought against Jesus of Nazareth. First, that He was a Sabbath-breaker. Secondly, that He was 'a gluttonous man and a wine bibber, a friend of publicans and sinners' — or (to draw aside the veil of Elizabethan English which makes it all sound so much more respectable) that He ate too heartily, drank too freely, and kept very disreputable company, including grafters of the lowest type and ladies who were no better than they should be.

For nineteen and a half centuries, the Christian Churches have laboured, not without success, to remove this unfortunate impression made by their Lord and Master. They have hustled the Magdalenes from the Communion-table, founded Total Abstinence Societies in the name of Him who made the water wine, and added improvements of their own, such as various bans and anathemas upon dancing and theatre-going. They have transferred the Sabbath from Saturday to Sunday, and feeling that the original commandment 'thou shalt not work' was rather half-hearted, have added to it a new commandment 'thou shalt not play.'

Whether these activities are altogether in the spirit of Christ we need not argue. One thing is certain; that they have produced some very curious effects upon our language. They have, for example, succeeded in placing a strangely restricted interpretation on such words as 'virtue', 'purity' and 'morality.' There are a great many people now living in the world who firmly believe that 'Christian morals,' as distinct from purely secular morality, consist in three things and three things only: Sunday observance, not getting intoxicated and not practising — well, in fact, not practising 'immorality.' I do not say the Churches themselves would agree with this definition; I say only that this is the impression they have contrived to give to the world, and that the remarkable thing about it is its extreme unlikeness to the impression produced by Christ.

Dorothy L. Sayers, *Unpopular Opinions* (London: Victor Gollancz, 1946), p. 9

So much for Mary Warburton Booth and her bar of Sunlight soap.

She was a little fury, and stood to tell every one what she thought of them. It must have been something very vile; the expression of horror on the faces told me that much, but I did not understand. I took her in, and asked her to tell me where she learnt it. She looked triumphant as she turned towards the crowd she had poured out to, and her proud little face turned to me with a grin.

'Tell me where you learnt that language?' I repeated.

'I learnt it there,' she turned her body, and with her chin, signed towards the little village far away.

'Your tongue must be very dirty,' I said. 'I think you had better wash it. Go to my bathroom, and you may use plenty of soap. Sunlight, if you like. It will need a good scrubbing to make it clean.'

She was gone some time, and then I heard a voice and looked round. There she stood, soapsuds covering all the lower part of her face.

'See Marmajee,' her tongue hung out its full length as she came nearer, 'I have cleaned it.'

I looked at it and examined her mouth.

'Now use plenty of clean water to wash it all away, and then come back to me,' I said, and the child washed her mouth clean and I prayed that my words might be in the Spirit while I talked with the child.

Something had to be done. Punishment would not convict her of sin, beside, she did not know what sin is. It was not her fault that she had learnt obscene language. She wondered why it caused so much consternation in the family, and I think she excelled in bravado, for her words were torrential, and, in the gasps between, her little body bent forward, gloating over the consternation she raised.

Something had to be done, something must be thought out; what?

The child was washing her mouth and scrubbing her tongue with Sunlight soap and water to clean the filth away.

She came back to me, and I looked into her bright eyes and examined her clean mouth, while her tongue was hung out for special inspection again.

'What are we to do?' I asked. 'We cannot go on like this; your tongue looks clean now, but these words would never get on your tongue if they were not in your heart. How can we get that clean?'

She looked at me, and I looked at her, and we looked at each other to see if there was any possibility of getting to the heart.

No — she could not see mine, I could not see hers. But I said, 'I know *Some One* Who can make your heart clean, and He will, if you ask Him.' Her eyes shone with glad appreciation, and her hand slipped into mine, and then I told her how it could be done. Then she learnt the verse: 'If we confess our sins, He is faithful and just to forgive us and to cleanse us from all unrighteousness,' and then we knelt together.

'Oh, clean us up,' she prayed. 'Lord, take those bad words away that no one likes; make my heart clean, don't let there be any dirt there, I want to be clean, and please will You wash me in the Blood of the Lamb, and I shall be white.' She prayed on, forgetting all else for the moment, her eager voice pleading the prayer the Saviour loves to answer.

She was not convicted of sin, but she was convinced of her unpopularity and glad to know of a way out of her difficulty, and the Saviour Who loves her understood and answered her prayer.

She was a little bit awed by the transaction, and there was less turmoil for a bit, and I was expecting to see a bud open to the Light.

The ordinary routine of life is full of interest, there are plenty of God's own extras to enrich us, the danger of contamination was passing, and the fledgling was beginning to fly, all desire to cage her in to save her was losing its power.

She was growing into a natural, carefree girl. Anxiety over her was fast waning and we walked about the Compound in freedom.

'The danger is passing away,' we said to each other with a sigh of relief, and my room was filled with all she wanted for the time being. Others were there with her, talking, laughing, playing, when something happened to upset her, and then, like a pent-in flood, something removed the boulder and the torrent poured forth.

I was on the spot in a moment, but everyone else fled. She threw herself at me, 'I didn't think the words first. I didn't know they would come. I opened my mouth and they all came out, and I didn't know they fell out of my mouth,' she cried.

And then realising the dismay I felt, disappointment swept over her, and she crumbled down on the floor, a little forlorn creature, with dishevelled hair hanging over her face. She was the picture of utter despair. Poor child, what was she to do with such a handicap? She was silent in her grief and disappointment for the joy of being kept had been hers and now ...? I sat down with her, I wanted her to feel that I cared and understood her disappointment, and together we would find the way of deliverance.

As I sat there, I seemed to hear a voice saying: 'Come and let us reason together, saith the Lord,' and then I thought with wonder of how God comes to us and takes us into His confidence, saying, 'Come, come, come and let us talk it out together.' And I prayed to be like Him as I settled to talk it all out with the child He had entrusted to me.

I was silent in the presence of such disappointment and sorrow. 'The words came and I don't know how.' Great tears rolled down her face, 'I thought they were all gone,' she cried, and she was concerned over her plight.

'If I were you,' I said, 'I would ask Jesus Lord to give you a new heart.'

She lifted her tear-stained face to mine.

'You see,' I began, 'if He gives you a new heart it will be clean and pure, none of those words will ever have been there.'

I reached for 'The Book' and opened it. 'Listen,' I said, 'listen to what God Says,' and I read: 'A new heart also will I give you, and a new spirit will I put within you, and I will take away the stony heart.'

Her tears were dried, a new hope came into her eyes as I repeated the words.

'A new heart,' she repeated with a sigh of relief, while I realised how troubled a little girl could be over an evil habit that had overcome her, and there and then she asked and received what she longed for.

Old things passed out of her life, a new and living way opened to her, and I, who have known her through the years, testify that she has grown in grace and graciousness, and her life is an eloquent sermon of what God can do with a little girl who will take what He offers.

Mary Warburton Booth, *These Things Have I Seen*
(London: Pickering & Inglis, n.d.), pp. 61–5

Behind the weird practice there lies an insight as old as any testament or covenant we know, the covenant which requires a new heart. In this testimony from Florence Allshorn the starting-place is very different from the missionary compound and the stream of dirty language; but the ending place is the same. And she too is concerned about 'the devil's own playground', even if she defines it as post-war inertia.

The world has lost vigour and the sustaining power to *do*; it can think, but it cannot bring its thinking into being, and perhaps that is the most terrifying of all our post-war neuroses, because inertia of any kind is the devil's own playground. Average men and women are magnificent when their backs are against the wall; they lapse into triviality and slackness immediately danger is over, because they have no inward dynamo to keep them going. The most stimulating literature is poured out these days, it is read more widely than it has ever been read before, yet so little happens! But here again is another miss, because to meet that we have a power — regenerative, reactive, redirective, refreshing and sustaining. Good news indeed. It was this power proceeding from God through Jesus Christ, residing in the Christian 'Koinonia' and falling upon many on their first contact with Christianity that transformed St Paul, a divided and distracted man indeed, into one with clear-cut purpose, enormous vigour, and an inexhaustible inward sense of peace and joy.

But when the world looks at some churches and some Christians they see the withered sapless branches of what those very same Christians are telling them should be a fruitful vine.

The Holy Spirit quickeneth. But a supernatural treasure is not got by anything tainted with slackness, and here we can only be faithful, often coldly, drearily, faithful, before that hot miracle comes to save us. And how can we expect a fitful, furtive patchy praying to be of any use? Here truly is perpetual decision; here is the very core of dying and resurrection because here, in praying, we must die to our comfortable slackness and casualness.

It would be good to soak ourselves in the Psalmist's high vigorous contempt for all that was not positively vital in faith. 'The fool hath said in his heart: "There is no God."' *No* — 'He made darkness His secret place; at the brightness that was before Him thick clouds passed. It is God that girdeth me with my strength, He maketh my feet like hind's feet, He teacheth my hands to war so that a bow of steel is broken by mine arms. Those things that were set against me, them did I beat small as the dust before the wind, I did cast them out as the dirt in the streets.'

A vigour of belief so far removed from the miserable little petulant living of so much of our life in these days. And how strange that this positive vitality and future vigour should only be attainable by those whose new beginning is a broken and contrite heart over the past and the present.

A member of St Julian's Community, *The Notebooks of Florence Allshorn*
(London: SCM Press, 1957), pp. 20–1

Helen Barrett Montgomery matches the eloquence of this writing with her own defence of the Bible. Interestingly, she uses the words 'white glory', and makes extraordinary claims for it.

The deepest affront to womanhood is the levity and impurity with which the facts of sex have been approached in life and literature. If the Bible be contrasted with any of the ethnic faiths, with the myths of Greece and Egypt, with thought as recorded in carving and temple and hieroglyph, the white glory of the Book shines out. Frankness there is in the Bible; the frank plainness of speech in regard to facts and vices which belongs to a primitive time and people; but of evil suggestion, of obscenity, of immoral beautifying of ugly sin under fine names, not a trace. All other bibles tried by this test fail; by this test the Bible stands without even the smell of fire about its garments. Where in all literature will one find such terrible, searching denunciation against impurity of life and thought, such faithful holding up of the consequences of evil?

Helen Barrett Montgomery, *Western Women in Eastern Lands*
(New York: Macmillan, 1911), p. 70

The only problem is that she was not prepared to ask the question Kathleen Bliss identified: whose Bible are we talking about?

How often the Church has stood in its own light! The hold that the Church claimed, and to a large extend achieved, on all expressions of thought in the later Middle Ages meant that new ideas had to struggle not only against common human apathy and suspicion of new ways of thinking and living but against the Church. If the Church had not had such a hold on intellectual life (and indeed the whole of culture) would such a bitter struggle have been necessary? Why has the coming of science and technology to other countries and cultures outside the

West precipitated no comparable conflict? Perhaps because these new forces did not grow up within those cultures and therefore could not appear as a threat in the same way. But that cannot be the whole reason; one is driven to the conclusion that an unusual degree of domination by religion over culture made it *inescapable* that a change in culture such as was brought about by scientific thinking and discovery was seen as a threat to the authority of religion.

Within the New Testament itself Christian faith is balanced on a knife-edge between its other-worldly and this-worldly elements. On the one hand is the Jesus who declares that his kingdom is not of this world; on the other the Jesus whose parables speak trenchantly of the obligation to serve one's neighbour, whose teaching and life alike speak of a love that goes beyond duty, and has its indestructible source in God. Christianity is rightly spoken of as 'world-affirming'. Yet once given power by the succession of events following the conversion of Emperor Constantine how rarely and how feebly did the authoritative representatives of the Church resist the temptation to world-domination. The conviction that the Church *had* to be right justified in the eyes of many not only the defence of Europe against the Moors, but the aggressive enterprises against Islam, against Eastern Christians and against heretics.

Christianity has been the religion of Europe and of white men. Some of the incontrovertible facts about Jesus are that he was not white and not a European. He was a Semite, of the same racial stock as Jews and Arabs. He did not belong to a princely caste or an imperial country: he was a poor man who worked with his hands and a citizen of a small, shamefully treated colony.

Kathleen Bliss, *The Future of Religion* (London: C. A. Watts & Co., 1969), pp. 136–7

This is why Lady Hosie's Jesus and Women *is such a seminal book. Not only did she write as a woman, but she also wrote as a missionary woman, as someone who knew what the good news could look like in another culture. Indeed the illustrations in her text show a much more Chinese-looking Jesus than would ordinarily be the case, even in present-day books for children, for example.*

Soon after that again, S. Luke gives us what is perhaps the most beautiful of all the stories of Jesus and Woman. Now Jesus must have been a man in full vigour of manhood, strong and healthy, able to walk long distances, climbing mountains, giving out of His energy day after day, as He healed and preached. S. Luke has already told us how, in a synagogue on the Sabbath day, the Master healed a man with a withered hand: and now, He says, it is another Sabbath day, and He is in a synagogue, but this time the sufferer is a woman. As her spine had been bowed down for eighteen years, it is not likely she was young, or fair of face. But to Jesus, the lines and wrinkles and pain in her face only meant that she needed His help. Her beseeching eyes caught His, as she sat, caged in body and spirit, on the woman's side of the building. He had to beckon her to come forward. Drawn by His command she came hobbling forward. And He stepped out, laid His strong living hands upon her, looked into her face, upturned with difficulty, and said:

'Woman, thou art loosed from thy infirmity.'

Never has another teacher acted like this to a bowed old woman. She straightened herself up, says S. Luke the doctor, quite simply, and stood up freed. Then she burst into praise aloud, to God who had endowed this Man not only with power, but with compassion and desire to liberate a fettered old woman.

The ruler of the synagogue, however, said in much vexation that this was all very irregular, and that there were six other days when the populace could come expecting healing, and not on a Sabbath. He uttered never a word of gladness that the woman's long eighteen years of bondage and hopelessness were ended. Whereupon Jesus turned upon him, called him a hypocrite and proved it in a way all present could understand. In the Orient, a countryman may weigh the advantages of marrying a wife, or buying an ox to draw his plough, or an ass to pull round the heavy roller of the grinding-stone on his threshing floor. To us, permeated more than we ever realise with the values of Jesus, such ideas are unworthy of humanity. But on the plains about Peking, not so many years ago, before Christian ideas changed men's minds, there was a bitter saying current in the mouths of women: 'A man can buy a wife for five dollars, but has to give ten for a good donkey.'

The Chinese serving woman, who repeated that phrase, burst into tears as she said it, because she saw an American husband kiss his wife good-bye, when he was going out for a short walk. He was an unconscious follower of Jesus, who said that human beings were worth infinitely more than sparrows, and who let a whole herd of swine be destroyed to save a human spirit.

The Master, moreover, called this useless woman a 'daughter of Abraham' – just as He was presently to call Zacchaeus, the publican, 'a son of Abraham.' He reminded the rulers that they were of the same stock and race as themselves. Then suddenly we realise that it is these rulers who are in bondage in spirit, more so even than was the old woman in muscle. They needed, and did not know it, a truer liberation than she: and it is good to read that they were 'ashamed', for in that shame lay their hope. The people meanwhile were filled with joy. To them also had come a deliverance, and they knew it, from harsh domination, from an evil way of thinking of God and His worship.

Lady Hosie, *Jesus and Women* (London: Hodder & Stoughton, 1946), pp. 198–9

* * *

In the event the actual business of casting out devils is better recalled by an aside such as Richenda Scott's from the 1964 Society of Friends' Swarthmore lecture.

Then, at once, concern for others is awakened, and we find the patience and the power to discern the inner truth of our fellow human beings, beneath those things which irritate and divide us, so that knowing them in that which is eternal, we can come to know and appreciate them in the things which are temporal, in the rub of daily encounters, in the sorrows and disappointments, the jokes and laughter and little absurdities that are the enduring stuff of friendship.

In such live meeting points we learn that good deeds do not necessarily make a good man or woman, as Fox well knew. Goodness is the state or condition of living in the light of God, of choosing the good because the will is keyed to the eternal harmony sounding below the discords of the universe.

Richenda Scott, *Tradition and Experience: Swarthmore Lecture 1964*
(London: George Allen & Unwin, 1964), p. 50

Something of what this eternal harmony might mean is hinted at in Olive Wyon's analysis of the nature of worship.

Worship is a universal practice. The prayer flags of Tibet, the great temples of Hinduism, the mosques of Islam, and the spirit-huts in the

great African forests, all bear witness to the fact that all over the world
men and women are reaching out to a Being greater than themselves,
a Being or a Spirit to whom they feel they must offer something – or
someone – often at great cost to themselves. In whatever form this
worship may be offered, and however far it may be from the truth
of the Christian revelation, it is always a response to an objective
reality, a reality which either fascinates or repels the worshipper, filling
him either with longing or with fear and awe. Thus when we try to
worship as Christians, we are not doing something as an 'extra'; it is
an instinctive practice carried on all over the world, which has been
a marked feature of man's life from the very earliest days. In the words
of Evelyn Underhill, worship extends from 'the puzzled upward glance
of the primitive to the delighted self-oblation of the saint.'

Olive Wyon, *The Altar Fire* (London: Cargate Press, 1954), p. 25

*How is one to equate such benign and enlightened writing with the experience
of Mrs Bishop, for example?*

Every one in the mountains was in terror of tigers. Mrs Bishop saw none,
but they persuaded her to put up with the heat and sleep with closed
windows lest she should be snatched from her bed by some man-eater
during the night. She found the whole population in bondage to the
fear of evil demons. Demons are supposed to infest every tree, ravine,
spring and hill and to hide away in roofs, chimneys, and jars.

E. C. Dawson, *Missionary Heroines in Many Lands*
(London: Seeley, Service & Co., 1912), p. 77

*Perspectives change when you are there in among the tigers, and even store
jars represent hidden dangers. Maybe that is why some of the missionaries'
accounts of the sheer otherness of the culture they found is both mocking in
tone and tinged with fear. How else are we to explain the note of parody
struck in this description of the temple gods in Kanchow?*

Do you realize what a grotesque figure an idol is? When a carpenter
wants to make a very large one he drags the trunk of a great tree down
from the mountains and chips it with an adze until he has made it more
or less into the shape of a man. When he has trimmed up the woodwork
he calls in a painter who paints in the features, eyes, nose, and mouth
and after this he sends for the tailor who makes its clothes. Then he

stands it upright and the temple priests all bow down and burn incense before it. Many of the people who come to the temple are very clever in business, yet they are so stupid in regard to idols that they cannot realize that one piece of the log out of which it is made is burning in the fire, and another piece will be used to make chairs and tables.

They bring offerings of food to this false god, and baskets of silver paper twisted up to look like money. If they used their wits they would understand that though it has eyes it cannot see, and ears it cannot hear; though it has a mouth it cannot speak, and though it has arms and legs it is unable to move. When the prophet Isaiah watched men doing this kind of thing he said, 'None of them has sense and wit enough to say to himself, "Half of it I burned in the fire . . . and am I to make the other half a horrid idol?"' Ashes will satisfy a man who is so duped by a delusion that he cannot pull himself up by asking 'Am I not holding to something false and vain?'

Not only are the temples and shrines in Kanchow packed with gods, but every mother in the home will tell you of three hundred and sixty-five of them, one for each day of the year. In her kitchen there is a kitchen god which is pasted up on the wall over the cooking-stove; she is afraid of him because she has been told that once a year he goes back to heaven and it is his business to report everything he has heard in that kitchen throughout the year, so before she sends him back, which she does by burning the paper he is made of, she always buys some sticky sweet and glues up his mouth so that he cannot report anything at all. There is also the little needlework god that makes her clever with her needle; and in the stable outside there is the god who looks after the cattle. The god of wealth has his place over the scales on which the head of the family weighs out his silver, for that is his particular god. Outside each farmhouse is the tiny god of heaven and earth.

Mildred Cable and Francesca French, Wall of Spears
(London: Lutterworth Press, 1951), pp. 38–9

Mary Darley should really not have been so baffled. Where suspicion and culture meet, conflict is inevitable.

Soon after my arrival in 1897, the annual dragon festival was celebrated, when hundreds of men walked past our house, carrying trays of food to the river-side, as an offering to some being, whose anger had to be appeased.

'Tell the foreigners,' they said, 'not to sing their hymns and not to play their music for three days, lest the dragon be attracted back to us.'

And this was after a period of ten years, in which the God of love had been preached daily in the place.

Mary E. Darley, *The Light of the Morning*
(London: Church of England Zenana Missionary Society, 1903), p. 25

Nor was this suspicion limited to those of other faiths; it certainly extended into the very soul of Mary Slessor.

When in February she heard that the Roman Catholics were intending to settle at Bende her heart was heavy. 'The thought that all that is holiest in the Church should have been shed to create an opening for that corrupt body makes me ill. And not even a station opened or the hope of one! Oh if I were able to go or send even a few of my bairns just to take hold. The country is far from being at rest, but if the Roman Catholics can go so can I ... There is a great future for Nigeria; if only I were young again and had money!'

W. P. Livingstone, *Mary Slessor, Pioneer Missionary*
(London: Hodder & Stoughton, 1915), p. 196

In an ecumenical age it is hard to remember that it clearly astonished Mary Warburton Booth that 'those of the R.C. persuasion' could draw nigh to God and that she should be able to minister to them as they did so.

There was the city, there were the villages, and there were the far distant places where we could only go in the cold weather; and last but not least, there were the English-speaking peoples who could gather for a meeting. So every Tuesday afternoon about forty ladies met in the Church to study the Word and talk about Him.

Some are scattered all over the world, and some have gone to the Land that is fairer than day. One was called to give her life to God for definite work in a Mission, and we had our own valedictory service and started her out in a distant Province. She is still working and winning. I sit back and think of those early beginnings and wonder what the harvest will be.

We represented every grade of society, and we were European, Anglo-Indian and Indian. Class and colour denomination were 'nil'. Denominational difficulties never came near us, yet our members were from Anglican, Methodist, Episcopal, Presbyterian, United Free Church, Baptist, Brethren, Seventh-Day Adventist, Pentecostal, Salvation Army and Roman Catholics.

No distinctions were made and none felt. We were there to study the Bible and to talk about Jesus. Some of these ladies had lived in India for years, but they had never met the Indian except those in their services. Some of the Indians had never met on equal footing those who were from across the seas, how could they ever know each other? Then there were those people who are neither one or the other, and whose hearts yearn for friendship and who give a response that is wonderful in its enriching.

Week by week we gathered, and we had real Bible study. The Book of Job gripped them, and if for any reason one could not be present, a little note was put into my hand with the question 'Which friend of Job is the subject today?' There was real interest, and we learned much from the oldest Book in the Bible. Job and his friends became real to us, and we learned our lessons. One was that our dearest may not be able to help us know and trust the Lord.

Someone asked for more of the Old Testament, and so we started off with the Exodus and even now I feel the thrill as I discovered with them how up-to-date the Bible is. The human heart is just the same and we began to see the way that was marked out for those who would know God. Prayer had a new meaning for many, and very definite requests were brought that needed and got very definite answers.

It was just such a revelation to those of the R.C. persuasion that they could draw nigh to God and in the Name of Jesus ask for things that appear temporal to some but are very vital to the life of a wife and mother.

Mary Warburton Booth, 'They That Sow'
(London: Pickering & Inglis, n.d.), pp. 161–3

Things that appear temporal are meat and drink to Helen Barrett Montgomery. In grand style she retrieves herself from any howlers about the white glory of the Bible when she makes the one connection which eluded so many missionaries in the field.

We see the century opening with women in the cribbed, cabined, and confined sphere to which the natural prejudices of a man-monopolized world had assigned them. In such a world there could be no broad national organization of women for the benefit of women and children in the non-Christian lands. Certain great liberalizing and unifying forces had first to prepare the way. The movement for education culminated in the free admission of girls in increasing thousands to the highest educational opportunities; the anti-slavery agitation swept into it the most generous and gifted women of the nation, broke down their isolation, expanded their horizon, liberated their spirit.

The agitation against the vested wrong of slavery was also an emancipation proclamation for the womanhood of the North. With passionate intensity, untrained and unprepared they threw themselves into the movement. By its sweep they were dragged out of their isolation, forced to think, to read, to find their voices, and lose their ever numbing consciousness of sex, to brave opposition and contempt in defence of something higher and holier than the proprieties. When the Grimke sisters in 1837 braved actual persecution because they dared to speak in public in behalf of the slaves, they helped more than they knew to strike off the fetters that bound the minds of women.

Helen Barrett Montgomery, *Western Women in Eastern Lands*
(New York: Macmillan, 1911), pp. 8–9

In the final analysis, any fetters that bind the minds of women are to be cast out and cast off with equal vigour. The missionary women could not develop a totally new morality. What they did do was to apply the morality and ethics that were available to them with as much integrity as they could, within the context of their own circumstances. What they learned on the missions was what they liked and what they did not like. They learned to exercise judgement and to apply principles. Present-day Christian women — whether we claim that ours is the 'mighty ordination of the pierced hands' or not — are the spiritual heirs of the missionary women. In our times it is as imperative as it was in theirs to be fearless in our naming and casting out of evil, and to claim the authority of a gospel call for what we do.

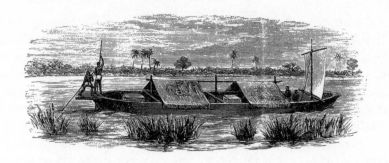

CHAPTER 9

THAT AMAZING BEAUTY

'Enlarge the place of thy tents' (Isaiah 54.2)

The missionary women's work took them to the very ends of the earth. They gazed on sights which no white woman had ever seen before; they were exposed to a wealth of experiences, tastes, scents and sounds. At her most reflective Mary Warburton Booth gives us a snapshot impression of what this could mean.

The monsoon had broken and left a little lake in the garden, and all the Heavens were reflected in it — a flock of green parrots chattered their way overhead. I stood there in that amazing beauty, perspiration standing in great drops on my arms and hands, for the rains turn the climate into a Turkish bath, every garment must be changed at least three times a day. Who can stand in such an atmosphere, let alone live in it? Damp and wet and hot and steamy — everything that is exposed is covered with mildew in a night, insects abound in millions, frogs come to live and fill the air with their croakings. They love corners and crevices, and hiding under little things, but their special home is in the pair of shoes you want to put on in the morning. Half-awake, very tired, you struggle to get your foot into your shoe, and wondering what the block is, you give a shake, and a big fat frog drops on the floor, and

then you are alive and astir, for the little things of life have awakened
for the day's duties. Mice and rats come out from their hiding, and it
is the time for snakes to appear. There is nothing still, and no one will
walk along the narrow paths at nightfall without a lantern to give light
for the feet. It is a dangerous and marvellous country, and it demands
all that a man or woman hath to live the life there. He or she whom
God calls must make sure of endowment from on High to live the life.
God is no respecter of persons, and He will fit and equip anyone who
will only let Him, but it takes time. He does not throw His equipment
at us or on us. We need to prepare ourselves, and be prepared to be
clothed with power from on High, and yet all the time, He waiteth
to be gracious.

Mary Warburton Booth, These Things Have I Seen
(London: Pickering & Inglis, n.d.), p. 153

*Along with this literal journey there goes a philosophical one. Maude Royden's
mental leap has an astonishingly contemporary ring to it. She is quite clear: theology preached by men only is incomplete, just as a one-dimensional Western
conception of Christian faith is incomplete. The missionary endeavour enriches
those who undertake it in immeasurable ways. The 'place of their tents' is
inevitably enlarged.*

It has been said by missionaries that no Christian will ever know all
that Christ meant until all nations have received him. The West has
brought its triumphant practical sense, its desire for victory, into its
conception of the Christian faith. It needs yet the deeper spirituality
of the East. It needs the wonderful capacity of the Chinese to hold
the spiritual and the practical together. It needs indeed the genius of
every nation ... Shall we not require the help of both sexes? Would
it not be strange indeed if only one sex had anything to bring to the
better understanding of the teaching of Christ? It would be as strange
and unnatural as though India were to be able to teach us nothing or
China to contribute no wealth of her own to our conception of God
and his Christ.

As long as women are shut out from preaching, and largely from
teaching, theology will be deemed to be outside their province. It is
true that they can even now study it, read it; they are even permitted
to write it, although as yet they are rarely permitted to speak it. But
it remains as a great presupposition against them that theology is not

for them, and our whole theological system has been build up almost entirely by the minds of men.

When the vocation to the ministry, whether of prophet or of priest, is expected of women as well as men, and by women as well as men, the whole situation will be changed. Women will begin to feel that they also have something to contribute to our theology. They will begin to contribute it. We shall begin to understand better him whom we worship.

'Upon this came his disciples, and they marvelled that he was speaking with a woman: yet no man said, What seekest thou? or, Why speakest thou with her? . . . So the woman left her water-pot, and went away into the city, and saith to the men, Come, see a man, which told me all things that ever I did: can this be the Christ? . . . And from that city many of the Samaritans believed on him because of the word of the woman.'

Dale A. Johnson, *Women in English Religion 1700–1925*
(New York and Toronto: Edwin Mellen Press, 1983), pp. 322–3

Does this explain Mrs Gobat's resolution to wrestle and pray and not faint as she works out her vocation to be 'a priestess in Thy house'?

Mrs Gobat was accustomed to pray in German, as a rule, that being her mother-tongue, but among her papers were found some beautiful prayers in English. The following one is a sample: 'O Lord, long-suffering and gracious, how many years hast thou added to my life, and yet I am still an unfruitful fig-tree; although thou, O Heavenly Gardener, hast not failed to dig, to prune, and to do all that ought to have made me fruit-bearing to thine honour and glory. Oh! spare me yet, and continue Thy working in me till I have wholly yielded to Thy constraining love. O Lord Jesus, Lamb of God, make me feel assured that Thou hast taken my sins on Thee so that I am now free from condemnation. Oh! give me grace to be taught by Thy Holy Spirit, to be led by Him, and not to resist His admonitions – His warnings. This is one of the causes, I am afraid, of my not enjoying more the gracious promises of Thy Holy Word, and possessing that peace which passeth all understanding. Let me wrestle and pray and not faint till I have *fully* found *Thee*, and with Thee and in Thee, everlasting life. Let me be a mother in Israel, a priestess in Thy house and in my family.'

Mrs E. R. Pitman, *Lady Missionaries in Foreign Lands*
(London: S. W. Partridge, n.d.), p. 121

For Li Tim Oi the journey into priesthood was about fidelity and the strength-
ening of her belief.

Li Tim Oi's destination was the home of the old pastor in Xingxing,
the Rev. Lai Kei Chong. She and Bishop Hall arrived there, both
after long and arduous journeys from opposite directions, within half
an hour of each other. 'I arrived in the evening, got out of the sedan
chair and found Bishop Hall who had just arrived. We knelt down
immediately, in Pastor Lai's sitting room, to thank God. It was so
peaceful to meet again. For the next few days Bishop Hall and I talked
and prayed together. He asked me many questions about my work and
my calling.

'One very important thing he said. The priesthood was a vocation
for life. It was not like an ordinary job. You have to be faithful to
your vows to the end. It was a life which could require great sacrifice
as it was dedicated to the service of others. We did not talk about my
being the first woman to become a priest. He did not mention it, or
if he did, I don't remember, I took no notice of that.

'Then on the day of my ordination we left Pastor Lai's house in
Xingxing and travelled a short distance to Zhaoqing, where there was
a small, old Anglican church. It was a very beautiful place, called the
lake of the seven stars.

'God had brought me through many dangers to the place, it
strengthened my belief that it was his will that I become a
priest. Here was I, a simple girl wishing to devote my life to
his service. The wider issues of the ordination of women were far
from my mind as I entered the little church. I was being obedient
to God's call. The notion that this step I was taking would be
controversial and have worldwide repercussions was something that
never occurred to me until after I had returned to Macao and the
war was over.'

Florence Tim Oi Li with Ted Harrison, *Much Beloved Daughter*
(London: Darton, Longman & Todd, 1985), pp. 44–5

Thérèse of Lisieux, a sick woman by 30 July 1896 when she wrote this
letter to Père Roulland on his departure for the mission, enlarged the space
of her tent within the confines of her convent cell. Her own call to the
priesthood was checked, as was her desire to go to the Carmelite mission
in Hanoi, but nevertheless the Scriptures continued to nourish her dreams,

and to supply her with a missionary zeal that required daughters to rise up as well as sons.

To PÈRE ROULLAND

On the point of leaving for the Mission

Lisieux, 30 July 1896

Jesus †

My Brother,

I hope you will allow me from now on to call you by no other name, seeing Jesus has deigned to unite us in the bonds of the apostolate. It is very sweet to think that from all eternity our Lord formed this union, which is to save Him souls, and He created me to be your sister ... Yesterday we got your letters; it was with joy our good Mother brought *you* into the cloister. She has allowed me to keep *my brother's photograph*, it is a *very special* privilege, a Carmelite has not even the portraits of her nearest relations; but Our Mother realised that yours, far from reminding me of the world and earthly affections, will raise my heart to regions far above, will make it forget self for the glory of God and the salvation of souls. So, Brother, while I shall cross the sea with you, you will remain with me, hidden in our poor cell ...

I am surrounded by things that remind me of you. I have pinned the map of Su-Chuen on the wall of the room in which I work, and the picture you gave me lies always on my heart in the book of the Gospels which never leaves me. I thrust it in haphazard and this is the passage it came to: 'Whoever has left all to follow me, shall receive a hundredfold in this world, and in the world to come eternal life.' Jesus' words are already fulfilled in you, for you tell me: 'I start out happy.'

I realise that this joy must be wholly spiritual. It is impossible to leave father, mother, native land without feeling all the rending of separation ... O my brother! I suffer with you. I offer your great sacrifices with you, and beg Jesus to pour His abundant consolations upon your dear family, until the union in heaven where we shall see them rejoicing in your glory, a glory which will dry their tears forever, and fill them with joy overflowing for a blissful eternity.

This evening at prayer, I meditated on passages of Isaiah which seemed to me to be so appropriate to you that I felt I simply must copy them out for you:

'Enlarge the place of thy tents. Thou shalt spread out to the right hand and to the left and thy seed shall inherit the Gentiles and shall inhabit the desolate cities ... Lift up thy eyes, round about and see: all these are gathered together, they are come to thee, thy sons shall come from afar and thy daughters will rise up at thy side. Then shalt thou see and abound, and thy heart shall wonder and be enlarged when the multitude of the sea shall be converted to thee, the strength of the Gentiles will come to thee.'

St Thérèse of Lisieux, *Collected Letters of Saint Thérèse of Lisieux* (London: Sheed & Ward, 1949), pp. 244–5

Back in India, a million miles away from the experience of the Carmelite cell in Lisieux and Thérèse's late nineteenth-century Catholic piety, Mary Warburton Booth was sustained by her access to exactly the same book. The Bible alone could bring together the dying nun and the foot-sore evangelist.

Blue mist began to hover over the villages. The cattle strolled past in lazy gait, women and children with waterpots were going and coming to the wells, the sun was on the bend, and the sky was a panoply of gold when we reached our first resting-place for the night. Weary? Yes, and foot-sore. But there was the thrill of having done something we had never done before, and at least seen the country and a people very few Europeans had. With songs of praise, we settled into our little camp and slept.

Dogs yelped, jackels screamed, but they didn't keep us awake. We simply turned in our camp beds, for had we not read the very last thing before we turned in, 'here shall no evil befall thee, neither shall any plague come nigh thy dwelling!' And I knew that it was true.

Mary Warburton Booth, '*They That Sow*' (London: Pickering & Inglis, n.d.), pp. 51–2

*   *   *

If missionary work involved literal journeys and implied a philosophical one as well, the idea or symbol of the journey has always been a metaphor for human life. The threefold nature of this final kind of journeying is set out by Olive Wyon.

Symbols express the aspirations and desires of men and women in every country and in every age; they constitute a kind of universal language. In poems, folk-lore and fairy-tales, the ordinary man or woman, the thinking, feeling human being, expresses his deep conviction that there is a reality behind the changeful kaleidoscope of human life, and behind the wonderful universe in which he lives. This inarticulate conviction or awareness expresses his desire for unity, for wholeness. Symbols give him a sense of the fundamental meaning of the universe, though he can only express this feeling in poetry or story form. The 'meaning' is never clearly apprehended; it is elusive and mysterious; yet the man at work in the depths of the silent forest, or out on the wide sea, is aware of a desire for the unknown which seems to promise satisfaction, to give a clue to the meaning of the whole.

It is significant that people who have lost touch with nature, or with the common life of humanity — either through a practical materialism or a one-sided intellectualism — are not aware of this mysterious and elusive intuition of reality and this desire for the unknown. To such people symbols are simply conventional images, springing from the sub-jective realm of the human imagination. But real symbols are not 'mere conventions'. They are full of meaning; they point towards a trans-cendent reality. The symbol was not *invented*; it is born, not made. It does not merely *signify* reality; it *embodies* reality.

When we study the symbols which occur again and again in poems and fairy-tales, we notice that some of these recurring symbols, appearing in very various forms, seem to fall into a kind of universal pattern; and this pattern suggests an underlying unity of mankind. This uni-versal pattern is so simple and familiar that it is very easy to overlook its significance. This pattern has three parts: departure, journey (and encounter) and arrival. Usually it takes the form of a pilgrimage, or a long journey, or a quest. It moves from the known to the unknown, and the chief symbol in this first part of the design is that of a house. The second part of the pattern uses various symbols, e.g. a well, a lamp, a fountain, or even a monster. This 'journey' includes the element of encounter — whether pleasant or unpleasant — and its central meaning is one of challenge. The third part of the pattern consists of arrival at the end of the journey and the entrance into the house or palace, or haven, and denotes peace and satisfaction. The desired end has been achieved. The pilgrim has come home.

Olive Wyon, *On the Way* (London: SCM Press, 1958), pp. 16–18

*With the advent of Christian missionary women came a whole new set of
aspirations. What does it mean to talk about departure, journey and arrival
when it is women who do the travelling? It is no coincidence that Helen
Barrett Montgomery wrote her book at the time when the suffrage was being
extended to women.*

The solidarity of the world is strikingly shown by the fact that this
reaching out of women for fuller freedom and juster opportunities is
confined to no race nor country. With the evidences of the movement
in Europe and America we cannot deal, but we believe that this and
the movement in the Orient have a common source. They spring
from the gradual penetration into the common consciousness of
certain principles which Christ enunciated and of which the New
Testament is full.

> Helen Barrett Montgomery, *Western Women in Eastern Lands*
> (New York: Macmillan, 1911), p. 206

*This journey into an understanding of the 'common consciousness' brings
religion and culture into dialogue and invites us to 'trample down the
barbed-wire fences of the world', a theme which Caroline Graveson of
the Religious Society of Friends would explore in her Swarthmore Lecture
of 1937.*

As a confessed society of peacemakers, we cannot afford to forget
that nothing is so international as culture, and no body of people
so little troubled by frontiers of race and country as scholars and
musicians and artists. Universities have no international quarrels.
The evil of war may be overcome by resolute practice of peace. By
a great extension of the practice of student-exchange, international
conferences, travel parties and holiday courses, of every facility for
the interchange of the intellectual and aesthetic possessions of the
nations, we may do much to trample down the barbed-wire fences of
the world. But this sharing of the fruits of culture must, I believe, be
made in a universe of Christian values, widely interpreted, if it is to
be truly effective.

> Caroline C. Graveson, *Religion and Culture: Swarthmore Lecture 1937*
> (London: George Allen & Unwin, 1937), pp. 48–9

Another woman, Kathleen Bliss, strove to put this vision of wholeness and inclusivity into words.

If this or that company of Christians is spoken of as 'the Church' in that place it is so not because its members have contracted together to form a church but because it stands there worshipping, serving the Lord of the Church as part of the one Church of the One Lord, in all places, in all centuries of time and in eternity. Nothing less than this vision is a vision of the Church, and every congregation in it partakes of the nature of the whole.

Kathleen Bliss, We the People (London: SCM Press, 1963), p. 79

This is heady stuff, so what did it look like in the field? 'A smattering of danger' is proper to life there as well as in the mind. Whether sitting at a desk writing about it, or wrestling with the leeches, or raising their petticoats to ford running streams with their bare legs, women were pushing forward the boundaries which designated ways of thinking and feeling to them — and enjoying it like the Salvationist Mrs Booth-Tucker.

Mrs Commissioner Booth-Tucker had her first bullock-brandy ride from Potuhera to Talampitiya, and first experience of crossing the paddy fields in bare feet, plunging through mud puddles, crossing bridges comprised of a branch of a tree, at other times jumping across running streams. All this, done by the uncertain flickering light of torches, giving a smattering of danger to the adventure, made the whole thing quite enjoyable.

The visit to our Swamiwattee Estate followed the next morning. Rains of the previous day, and heavy dew during the night, left the path muddy and slippery. Bare feet being the quickest and easiest means of locomotion, the Commissioner led the way, and apart from two or three blood-sucking leeches fastening upon them, everything went off well. The meetings were full of interest and glorious spiritual results.

It would be seem that Mrs Booth-Tucker was thrown in at the deep end by this experience, but she was a woman of high spirits, adventurous and with great personal resources and would have enjoyed it immensely.

Solveig Smith, By Love Compelled: The Story of the Salvation Army in India and Adjacent Countries (London: Salvationist Publishing, 1981), p. 85

And if anyone thought it appropriate to be sentimental or patronizing about this, let Mother Mabel Digby's words ring in their ears: 'Weren't they fools!'

So far the passage is not good; there is a strong head wind, so we are losing time. Our Mother feels it very much, but thanks to all the prayers has stood it better than I should have dared to hope ... Aug 17 [the anniversary of Mother Digby's first arrival at Roehampton] Posts have been active since this was written. She had a great surprise; she liked so much what you sent, and said 'Poor old Roehampton, fancy their remembering this!' then she read out, 'Her children rose up and called her blessed.' 'Weren't they fools!' she added. It was dreadful; but so characteristic that I have to tell you!

Anne Pollen, Mother Mabel Digby (London: John Murray, 1914), pp. 252–3

But if boundaries in thinking were being renegotiated, so too were relationships between women and men. That is why the designated place of women (as 'gay and enchanting girls', 'purchased ... for the ancient and honourable delights of love') contrasts so oddly with the extraordinary freedom of Gladys Aylward. For her the missionary journey was one which took her into both worlds, as an emissary between the two.

The friendship between the Mandarin of Yangcheng and the tiny ex-parlourmaid from Belgrave Square is probably one of the oddest in the entire history of Eastern and Western relationships. Although she spoke the language as fluently as a native it was years before she managed to dig down through the layers of his mind. He was enigmatic. He regarded her urbanely, his thin face, with its high cheekbones and thin, dark almond eyes, always impassive. A glossy pigtail dropped from under the round silk cap; the gowns he wore were embroidered in wide scrolls of many colours, inevitably beautiful: scarlet, blue, green, gold. To Gladys he always looked as if, by some miracle of time, he had just stepped down from an antique Chinese scroll. His was a feudal society. From his *yamen*, civic authority was administered in much the same manner as it had been dispensed in the time of Confucius. His aides and counsellors bore ancient and honourable titles which defined their interest in transport, sanitation, roads, water and household duties.

In one of the inner courts was the place of the women. They were not wives, or even concubines, but slave-girls, young and lovely creatures purchased with *yamen* funds for the ancient and honourable delights of love. Gladys was not shocked when she understood the implications of the women's court. It was a custom which dated back many hundreds of years; everything was very proper. They were watched over by the older women, most of whom had themselves been *yamen* maidens, and whose daughters would grow up and continue in the same service. They were gay and enchanting girls, singing songs, playing instruments and learning dances; not secluded like harem women of the East, but able to trip through the bazaars fingering the soft bales of silk, and buying the combs and cheap jewelled ornaments they adored. Gladys had many friends amongst them, and often, when she was visiting the Mandarin, she would walk through to the women's court to chat and drink tea with them. There is little doubt that at first, to the Mandarin of Yangcheng, Gladys Aylward was as alien a species as a creature from the moon. She was a female, which meant that in the eyes of man she was socially and intellectually less than dust. Nevertheless, as news of her exploits reached him, and as, over the months, she continually bombarded him with applications, supplications, admonitions and near-threats, she loomed as astonishingly as a new planet thrust into his orbit. Indeed, as their contacts and acquaintanceship increased, the Mandarin of Yangcheng found, to his growing astonishment that not only was she becoming an adviser of sorts, but also a friend. By immemorial Chinese standards, he was a highly intelligent man, but his background was circumscribed by the contemplative scholarship of a formal education.

Gladys blew into his *yamen* with the winds of the world around her ears. To him, she was worldly and foreign. She never forgot his first gentle admonition after she had delivered herself of a particularly impassioned piece of Christian propaganda. 'Ai-weh-deh,' he said softly, 'you send your missionaries into our land, which is older by far in civilisation than yours. You see us as a nation of heathens and barbarians, do you not?'

She tilted her head, looked up at him with inquiring eyes. She was rapidly becoming aware that this intellectual sparring in flowery and formal language was as integral a part of Chinese social relations as taking tea together. 'Not by any means,' she said.

Alan Burgess, *The Small Woman* (London: The Reprint Society, 1959), pp. 110–11

*Irene Petrie's glorious account — in a chapter she entitles 'The Last Journey' —
of a foray through Kashmir, hints at something quite new. If ideology and
relationships were to be renegotiated in the wake of the journeys of missionary women, so too was the delicate balance of nature. The metaphor
of the broken glacier, trickling and growing into a tumultuous river, could
not fail to imprint itself on the imagination of Miss Petrie and her companions. If nature is subject to process and change in this way, then so
is everything else. The perpendicular cliffs look sheer now, but it was not
always so. Nature is an agent of change, a mirror into which, if we gaze
long enough, the workings of the divine will become clear. Ecological questions now join the agenda for change.*

July 14th — By 5 a.m. our procession is starting, and the four ladies,
dandy, two ponies, six servants, ten baggage ponies and ten coolies, wind
across the first glacier of the Zoji-La in a thin line. After a long pull of
2000 feet up the steep zig-zag path, we give the green and wooded land
of Kashmir a last look, and turn into the long valley between peaks
14,000 feet high and upwards, which is the summit of the Pass. Here
for many hours we tramp along the snow. At first no water is seen in
the hollow, then at its bottom the glacier is broken, and the streamlet
of the Dras River appears, trickling between vast blue cliffs of ice, to
the north-east, for we have crossed the water-shed. Our horses look
remonstrance for being brought into such places; the little terrier from
Peshawar is trembling with fright and cold in the bearer's arms. It is
like nothing we have seen before, except pictures of Greenland. The
river grows bigger and more tumultuous, and the horses are led through
the water breast high to the path beyond. An oasis where the snow
is melted, and pretty yellow and white anemones have come hurrying
out, enables us to sit down for lunch; but the water we boil for cocoa
seems curiously cold, till we realise the effect of 11,500 feet of altitude
upon boiling point. At last we reach spongy meadows, with only occa-
sional glaciers. One or two of these are a test for the giddily disposed as
the path is only a foot wide, and below the ice slopes with tremendous
steepness to the perpendicular cliffs.

Mrs Ashley Carus-Wilson, Irene Petrie: Missionary to Kashmir
(London: Hodder & Stoughton, 1900), p. 313

*In the Gobi desert Miss French and Miss Cable learned this lesson well.
They knew that women could learn to live through their eyes, without*

*being subject to mechanisms of interpretation already elaborated for them
by men.*

If you want to be a really good traveller you must learn how to be quite
happy while cut off from all the occupations which normally make up
your daily life. For the time being you must live through your eyes, for
the world lies before you somewhat like a great picture-book. Reading,
writing and anything occupational is put far away, and you just sit and
look around you. This seems to be easy and natural when the journey
only occupies a few hours, and sitting in a railway-carriage, you look
through the windows of an express train and see fields and houses shoot
by at a terrible pace; but when you think in terms of Gobi travel the
journey may stretch out into weeks and months during which you will
only cover thirty miles a day. Yet those thirty miles will have taught
you more than much rapid travel could do ... You will have had time
to observe the vegetation, and you may have seen large patches of the
liquorice plant, or the pale earth of the desert suddenly covered by
masses of the dwarf iris flowering in lovely shades of blue. You have
noticed clumps of camel-thorn, and you have wondered what kind of
a thick lining that beast can have to its mouth that it cares to eat such
a prickly plant.

Mildred Cable and Francesca French, Wall of Spears
(London: Lutterworth Press, 1951), p. 163

*This emphasis on the value of a journey that takes weeks or months is under-
lined by Mary Warburton Booth. When time, too, is renegotiated, prayer, of
its essence, changes things. When the missionary women prayed, they entered
into a dynamic of change which effected things, people, all of life.*

When I got up He was there to meet me, and He taught me how to
pray, and how to wait before Him. The Scriptures opened out priceless
treasures, and I soon learned that real prayer is vital in its working,
and it wasn't long before I discovered that it takes time to know God.
'Be still and know' became a reality. I could not live on the past, I
must go ahead but I needed guidance, and how could He guide me if
I would not wait for it? Very soon I could say with the Psalmist: 'He
waketh me morning by morning,' and I acquired the habit of rising at
4 o'clock to watch and pray and to hear what He would say to me in

His Word. It was then that prayer became fundamental and the power in work. Prayer changes things, and it changes people too, and all my life has been transfigured by the habit of prayer cultivated, preserved and pursued. It is a wonderful way of getting to know God: real prayer leads to real communion and a growing fellowship with Him with Whom we have to do. The place of prayer increases in holiness and the Shekinah Glory is there and an understanding of the words to Moses: 'Take off thy shoes from off thy feet, for the place whereon thou standest is holy ground.' It is there He calms my mind and makes quiet my heart, and then He speaks to me and my soul doth magnify the Lord for He has done great things for me.

Mary Warburton Booth, My Testimony (London: Pickering & Inglis, 1947), p. 84

* * *

The words of the Magnificat which nourished this twentieth-century missionary Mary are recalled by Caryll Houselander in her account of the Way of the Cross, the final journey of Jesus.

'Behold, from this day forward all generations will count me blessed.'

Christ goes on his way; no word is spoken now; Mary follows him in the crowd. Another woman has anointed his feet for burial; another will meet him on the way and wipe the blood and dirt from his face; others will weep aloud for him.

Mary remains silent; she does not lift a hand; only when he is suffering no more will she anoint his body. She simply accepts this supreme gift of his love, his suffering given to her.

It is a complete communion with him. They are as completely one now as they were when he was the child in her womb, and her heart-beat was the beating of his heart.

Caryll Houselander, *The Stations of the Cross*
(London: Sheed & Ward, 1955), pp. 46–7

Union with Christ, whether as the heart-beat recalled from the womb or as the regal figure in red garments, is tied inextricably with a sense of being near 'some mighty secret'. Dora Greenwell links this with 'a sense of greatness' and tells out her own Magnificat.

Then suddenly, there fell upon my soul a sense of greatness, telling me to be no more sorrowful, for that I was not really alone, but part of a Whole in which I should find all things — those that I had left behind, those that I had failed to reach to, yea my own life also. If it be indeed so, I thought, then I refuse not to die; to lose that which is in part, in the coming in of that which is perfect. But how may my spirit attain unto this baptism? Oftentimes I seemed near some mighty secret, to lie on the very threshold of Truth; *but to be chained there*: a spell was upon that threshold that never allowed me to overpass it. On the flower, the shell, the wing of the butterfly, were traces of a writing whose counterpart was in my own soul; as when a page has been torn down the midst, I found I had only to join these characters to make their meaning plain. The winds, the leaves, my own voice, and that of the birds, were harmony; I strove to master it; to pierce to its deep fundamental structure. Then the rocks began to give forth music at sunrise and sunset; not like that alluring bewildering music of the forest and ruined temple, but solemn and chastened. That sweetness dissolved the spirit; this built it up within its mighty chord. Each scattered drop, each bright spark of melody that had fallen here and there, making some stray blade or blossom lovely, shone there, gathered up into a lofty arch of sound that might grow, I thought, to one of Triumph, spanning earth and heaven. It was ever pure, ever prophetic; yet now, as I listened, it seemed to me that there were but two who spake within it, exchanging, as in some old, simple song, the *I* and *Thou* of an unalterable constancy; then it would grow to the voice of a great multitude, to the sound of many waters. I heard harpers harping on their harps, compassing me about with songs of deliverance; and yet the music did not change.

For hours I would lie listening to the birds; for hours I would toil amongst the flowers and fossils I had collected; once more I read at morn and even in my book. Then as I lay at midday, a light above the brightness of noon would sometimes be cast around me, and a well-known Form would pass me, as one in haste. His step was still regal; His garments red, from the battle or the vintage, I knew not which; but His eye was calm as that of one who follows out some vast long-deliberated plan. He did not stay to speak with me, but in passing me His step was slower, and once he turned and looked upon me for a moment. I understood that silent appeal.

Dora Greenwell, *Two Friends* (London: Epworth Press, 1952), pp. 22–3

Frances Ridley Havergal looked at an image of this mighty secret, the trans-
figuration and glorification of herself, her niece Constance Crane and her
friends whom she lists as Elizabeth, Margaret and Bessie.

Imagine yourself midway between heaven and earth, the sharp point of
rock on which we stood hardly seeming more of earth than if we had
been in a balloon, the whole space around, above, and below filled with
wild, weird, spectral clouds, driving and whirling in incessant change
and with tremendous rapidity; horizon *none*, but every part of where
horizon should be, crowded with unimaginable shapes of unimagined
colours, with rifts of every shade of blue, from indigo to pearl, and
burning with every tint of fire, from gold to intensest red; shafts of
keen light shot down into abysses of purple thousands of feet below,
enormous surging masses of grey hurled up from beneath, and changing
in an instant to glorified brightness of fire as they seemed on the point of
swallowing up the shining masses above them; then, all in an instant, a
wild grey shroud flung over us, as swiftly passing and leaving us in a
blaze of sunshine; then a bursting open of the very heavens, and a
vision of what might be celestial heights, pure and still and shining
high above it all; then, an instantaneous cleft in another wild cloud,
and a revelation of a perfect paradise of golden and rosy slopes and
summits; then quick gleams of white peaks through veilings and un-
veilings of flying semi-transparent clouds; then, as quickly as the eye
could follow, a rim of dazzling light running round the edges of a
black castle of cloud, and flaming windows suddenly pierced in it; oh,
mother dear, I might go on for sheets, for it was never twice the
same, not any single minute the same, in any one direction. At one
juncture a cloud stood still apparently about 200 yards off, and we
each saw our own shadows gigantically reflected on it surrounded by
a complete rainbow arch, but a full circle of bright prismatic colours,
a transfiguration of our shadows almost startling, each moreover seeing
only their own glorification! When the whole pageant, lasting nearly
an hour, was past, we sang 'Abide with me,' and the dear old joyous
'Glory to Thee, my God'.

Maria V. G. Havergal, *Memorials of Frances Ridley Havergal*

(New York: Anson D. F. Randolph & Co., 1880), pp. 142–3

Helen Waddell's translation of a Chinese lyric has a much more elusive theme
than dear old 'Abide with Me'. But she too looks upwards and outwards and

beyond to discover where the journey should go now, when the stars which previously constellated on it and for it no longer do their work.

780 BC

I see on high the Milky Way,
But here's a rougher road.
The Sacred Oxen shining stand;
They do not draw our load.

The Sieve is sparkling in the South,
But good and ill come through.
The Ladle opens wide its mouth,
And pours out naught for you.

At dawn the Weaving Sisters sleep,
At dusk they rise again;
But though their Shining Shuttle flies,
They weave no robe for men.

Helen Waddell, *Lyrics from the Chinese* (London: Constable & Co., 1938), p. 29

Sarah Grubb, the Quaker, tells the same story of movement towards a God whose holiness is set on top of the mountains, and 'above all the hills'.

From time to time my spirit is brought into a deep sense of my own nothingness, even in a peculiar manner; and oh! frequently before meeting breaks up, my heart is made glad that the Lord alone is exalted. What a solemn sense of His goodness is mostly afforded in awful silence, toward the latter end of a meeting crowded with people sitting and standing; the bodily feelings are lost in a sense of the Divine influence. For ever magnified and praised be Israel's God; He is more and more bringing the people to the experience of true spiritual worship, even in the silence of all flesh. Whether we, as a Society, will become more spiritually minded or not, I cannot say, but God will be glorified, and truth and its testimonies exalted in the earth, even until all nations shall flow unto the mountain of His holiness, which is set on the top of the mountains, and above all the hills.

Sarah Grubb, *A Selection From the Letters of the Late Sarah Grubb* (Sudbury: J. Wright, 1848), p. 192

* * *

The final nothingness and the final journey are those we call death. So what happened to missionary women when they died, and what happened to death itself and the ways we understand and attempt to interpret it?

On the one hand there are the accolades which avoided the topic of death but served as epitaphs instead. Madame Coillard, according to Canon Dawson, fulfilled all the right norms.

She was cut out for a missionary's wife. She had the keenest admiration for her husband, whom she followed without hesitation and without a thought for her own safety or convenience. M. Coillard tells a very characteristic story of her when he and she had agreed to meet at a place named Leribe to keep the anniversary of their wedding day. She was at Harrysmith negotiating for wood for the Mission buildings, he was on a missionary tour; between them ran the River Caledon. When she reached the stream the waters were in high flood. It was reported to her that her husband had been swept away and drowned in trying to cross to her. This sounded quite probable, since drownings were of frequent occurrence in those days, but when she discovered this was a false tale she determined herself to cross the water to him. Two powerful Zulus took her, one by each arm, and swam across with her, other men swimming before and behind. The procession of swimmers fought the strong current resolutely and silently. From the opposite bank her husband watched this adventurous crossing. Only the head and shoulders of his wife appeared above the flood. At last they reached the shallows and Mme. Coillard came out, drenched and exhausted but triumphant, to change into a habit and ride with her husband to their little turf hut at Leribe.

Nothing ever daunted her from doing what she thought she ought to do. M. Coillard says: 'No one will ever know what she was to me *as a missionary*. You know her tastes. She loved society, and she loved her home ... Like the bee, she took her honey from every flower ... But when the call of God made itself clearly heard, immediately, without hesitation ... she sacrificed everything ... and did it cheerfully.'

Her courage was often put to the proof, for she went through the war of 1866 between the Boers and the Basutos, and was the witness of many scenes of shocking barbarity. She spent most of her life among peoples with whom human life counted as nothing. But she never flinched. When an opportunity was offered to her husband to adopt a safer and less arduous sphere of work in Mauritius, and he asked her opinion, she refused to even consider it. God had sent them both to heathen Africa. They had taken the vow of poverty and self-forgetfulness, and they must at all costs be true to their mission. To which he replied: 'Thank God, we are of the same mind, and, since that is so, we will never discuss it again.'

Mme. Coillard will always be a convincing argument in the mouths of those who advocate the marriage of missionaries, granting that the right women can be found. She was the centre of the women, the admiration of the men, the mother of all. At the same time they all came to know that she was not made to be taken advantage of. The rudest got his answer, and the roughest learned to respect her. She soon came to understand perfectly the tedious custom of bargaining over every trifle, and would patiently continue, giving and demanding justice for all, till she had won their confidence and trust.

E. C. Dawson, *Missionary Heroines of the Cross*
(London: Seeley, Service & Co., 1930), pp. 212–13

The missionary wife's husband probably makes a better witness.

The large room in which she lay was covered with the kneeling forms of Indians, all silently praying. In the meanwhile the prayer-meeting at the chapel never for one moment stayed its course. During three days and nights her spiritual children prayed for her in relays, one following the other, and the chapel and the adjoining rooms being always full. Every ten minutes tidings of her state were passed from the sickroom to the chapel. When they learnt it was the will of the Lord of life and death that she should not recover, they changed the tenor of their petitions, and prayed that she might pass happily and peacefully into the world of spirits.

The Bishop says that 'Many found the light during the death struggle. In her death she, by her beautiful and tender words and patient endurance ... drew more souls' to the Saviour of the world than ever.

When all was over her husband committed her body to the Indians, that they might honour it as seemed best to them.

E. C. Dawson, *Missionary Heroines in Many Lands*
(London: Seeley, Service & Co., 1912), p. 129

It would be interesting to know what deep instinct led her husband, the Bishop, to consign Mary Ridley's body to the Metlakahtla Indians, where it would be beyond platitudes — however well meant.

The testimony of words seems inevitably to fall flat or sound out of place, even when these words come from other women. In a chapter entitled 'Visitors from Scotland' Christina Forsyth is observed and assessed. The problem, of course, is that standards and categories which work in one context cannot possibly be applied in another.

As Mrs M'Laren edited the *Women's Missionary Magazine* of the Church she was specially sympathetic to the women's side of the work, and was anxious, while in South Africa to see Xolobe and Mrs Forsyth. Both visitors came away impressed by the saintliness of her character, her absolute trust upon God, and her devotion to the work. Here is Mrs M'Laren's own account of her experience.

'Mrs Forsyth had come over the mountains from Xolobe to meet us at Paterson. We thought it best after a short rest to accompany her on her return home. The first hill we had to surmount was like a stony staircase. The road leading over it was so steep, so bad, so impossible for horses, that Mr Davidson kindly gave us four oxen to draw our cart and us up. After a time our horses were inspanned, and by walking up the hills we managed to drive the greater part of the way. Eventually we left our cart at a kraal, and walked, amid grand and wild surroundings, to the little Mission-house, perched on a ridge, with a rocky drift in front and a deep dark canon behind.

'For long Mrs Forsyth lived in a Kafir hut, but owing to the strong wishes of her friends she consented to the little Mission-house being built. It had only one good room, the other two, which opened off this middle one at each end, being very small. True to her constant practice that God and his work must come first, Mrs Forsyth had given up her one bright room entirely as a class-room, the mud-and-wattle schoolroom close by being quite inadequate to contain the children who come to be taught. The two little rooms she had for herself were bare and destitute even of very ordinary comforts, but her six little native maidens, who lived with her, and whom she was training for God, kept them scrupulously clean and tidy.'

W. P. Livingstone, *Christina Forsyth of Fingoland*
(London: Hodder & Stoughton, n.d.), pp. 140–1

If only the 'little native maidens' had been able to tell their side of the story!

*   *   *

Probably the most eloquent statement of all comes not in words but in the evidence of the facts. This account closes the life of Mary Livingstone.

On February 1, 1862, she reached the Zambezi. The long detention on the coast in the fever season proved fatal. On April 21 she became ill; six days later she was gone. It was a dreadful blow to her husband. He wrote in his Journal: 'I loved her when I married her, and the longer I lived with her I loved her the more. A good wife and a good brave kind-hearted mother was she. God pity the poor children who were all tenderly attached to her; and I am left alone in the world by one whom I felt to be a part of myself.' A little prayer was found among her papers: 'Accept me, Lord, as I am, and make such as Thou wouldst have me to be.'

They laid Mary Livingstone to rest near the great baobab tree at Shupanga. Professor Drummond says that he found the place where she lies buried an utter wilderness, matted with jungle grass, and trodden by the beasts of the forest but, as he looked at the forsaken mound and contrasted it with her husband's tomb in Westminster Abbey, he thought that perhaps the woman's love, which had brought her to a spot like this, might not be less worthy of immortality.

'A right straightforward woman, no crooked way was ever hers; and she could act with decision and energy when required.' Such was her husband's testimony. Livingstone was spared to labour for eleven years longer as the apostle of Christianity and civilisation in the Dark Continent. The end came at midnight, in a rude hut at Ilala, whence he passed to join his much-loved wife, who had sung seventeen years before —

> 'You'll never part me darling, there's a promise in your eye;
> I may tend you while I'm living, who will watch me when I die?
> And if death but kindly lead me to the blessed home on high,
> What a hundred thousand welcomes will await you in the sky!'

John Telford, *Women in the Mission Field* (London: Charles H. Kelly, 1895), pp. 36-7

This account closes the life of Mrs Forsyth:

In one sense the contrast between Mrs Forsyth and other missionaries in the South African field was very great. She had the smallest sphere of any of us — just one station, and even that was under the care of her minister. We missionaries have many stations — fifteen, twenty, even thirty or over. We are superintendents. We ride about like bishops, ordaining, ordering, giving charges, working late and early. No one can call it easy work — and in a sense we are great men in our districts. She was different, a humble figure without charge or function or office in any ecclesiastical sense, ranking as an honorary lay missionary. She had no house to speak of, only a but and a ben, no horse or trap. She simply walked on foot and visited the heathen in their houses close by, and spoke to them of the way of salvation. How different from the missionaries with their large dioceses and much organisation and much travelling and heavy correspondence. Yet, no doubt, she was the most apostolic figure amongst us carrying on a more apostolic work.

She lived in a remote corner of Fingoland far from the railway and the road and the beaten track. There are tracks to her house, as there are tracks to everywhere in South Africa, made by the feet of savages and by their flocks and herds searching for food, but Xolobe is a dull and lonely spot for a white woman. To live there alone among a few black folk, in a house not much better than theirs, and sharing largely their simple life and simple fare — it was an eccentric thing, perhaps, like that of the new Bush Brotherhood in Australia, but in her case there was no sense of spiritual pride because of ascetic distinction or connection with a great contemplative or historic Order in the Church. She was simply a lone women, separated by no special function or training or qualification or churchly ritual, merely a decided and sincere Christian with a great love of souls in her heart, and a deep yearning for the salvation of the heathen. They were in hundreds around her. Heathen men and women and children, likable, even lovable, in many ways, but grossly ignorant of the best things in life and without hope for the next life. To her this was a great chance — to be free to live amongst them, and day in, day out, strive to teach them the better way.

Few can endure such loneliness as hers for very long. Even the most isolated of our unmarried missionaries has a certain and unfailing social

solace and variety, his itinerations, his constant dealing with churches
and schools and mission agents, and persons in trouble, or needing
advice, who visit him daily from one part or another of his district.
The missionary's life is really not dull or lacking in intercourse with
his fellows by any means.

But Mrs Forsyth had none of these social opportunities. She lived at
Xolobe for thirty years, month after month and year after year, and
daily set her face gladly to the same hard work. She did not throw it
up disappointed after five years; she endured it until age and health
compelled her to retire. It is unique in our South African mission-field.
It is a unique case of the triumph of the soul over a comfortless and
heathen existence.

W. P. Livingstone, *Christina Forsyth of Fingoland*
(London: Hodder & Stoughton, n.d.), pp. 228–31

*   *   *

*The best epitaph for all the missionary women comes from the pen of Helen
Barrett Montgomery.*

In this rapid survey only the principal activities of women's work for
women in non-Christian lands have been touched upon. Their mission
stations are, as has been said already, great social settlements suffused
with the religious motive. Following the need of each community, they
are bound to blossom into manifold ministries. For the growth of personality under the stimulus of the Gospel is like the modern evolution
of buildings. The savage lives in a hut, primitive civilisation in a cottage,
but modern life demands many stories and diversified structure. These
schools, hospitals, clubs, libraries, are developing a new woman in the
East, with wants her mother never knew. To meet these expanding
desires an expanding ministry will be required. The nurse, the business
woman, the musician, the journalist, the dietician, the naturalist, may
all find that their contribution is needed to round out this amazing
undertaking.

Helen Barrett Montgomery, *Western Women in Eastern Lands*
(New York: Macmillan, 1911), p. 148

*The inference is clear. Where the place of the divine tent is expanded, some-
thing quite new begins to happen for women. We stand at the interface of*

the divine/human encounter with the same authority as Mary, the Mother of Jesus, who first bore him into the world and as Mary Magdalene, who first told the news of his rebirth in the events of the resurrection. We stand firmly at the place where God is in dialogue with the world, where revelation happens, at the place where God and our deepest desires meet.

BIOGRAPHICAL NOTES

Florence Allshorn (1887–1950). She sailed to Uganda with the Church Missionary Society in 1920 and worked in Busoga. On her return to England she became warden of St Andrew's Hostel, one of the CMS's two training colleges for women. She went on to found the St Julian's Community for returned missionaries.

Ethel Ambrose (1874–1934). Born in Australia of Scottish descent, she qualified as a doctor in Adelaide and was the first woman to be appointed to Perth Public Hospital in 1902. In 1905 she went to India to serve in Nashrapur.

Gladys Aylward (1902–70). She left school at fourteen to become a parlour-maid and was then called to serve on the China mission. She saved her own fare and left for Tiensin in 1930. At first she served with Miss Jeannie Lawson, who had the inspiration to start an inn for muleteers where Christian teaching would accompany the hospitality. She harangued the muleteers while Gladys minded the mules. After Miss Lawson's death the local mandarin employed her to go round the villages unbinding feet. She went on to rescue over one hundred Chinese children from the advancing Japanese during the Second World War, and eventually set up an orphanage in Taiwan in 1953.

Florence L. Barclay. A notable Edwardian speaker and writer, her novel *The Rosary* sold over one million copies and was translated into French, German, Norwegian, Swedish, Polish, Finnish and Dutch.

Mary Bird (1859–1914). A Church Missionary Society missioner, she went to Persia in 1891 with Miss Laura Stubbs as the first unmarried women to be sent to work there. The journey to Joffa took a month and was followed by a five hundred mile camel-ride into the interior.

Isabella Bishop, née Bird (1831–1904). Widowed in 1886, she took off to India, Persia, Kashmir, Tibet, Korea, Japan, China, Turkey and Morocco.

Known as the friend and mother of missions, she was elected the first woman fellow of the Royal Geographical Society in 1892.

Kathleen Bliss (1908–89). One time General Secretary of the Church of England's Board of Education and lecturer in Religious Studies at Sussex University, she was also a well-known broadcaster.

Sarah Boardman Judson (1803–40). She became a Baptist in 1820 and sailed to India five years later with her husband George. She combined scholarship with motherhood in her missionary work and died in Mauritius when journeying home.

Victoria Booth-Demarest (1890–1982). The second daughter of the Maréchale, she was named Victoire Marguerite and proved to be another outstanding Booth woman. She was made an Honorary Doctor of Divinity in Florida in 1977 at the age of eighty-seven.

Emma Booth-Tucker (1860–1903). The second daughter of Catherine and William Booth, she became principal of the first training home for women of the Salvation Army and had up to 300 women in her care. She married Commissioner Frederick Tucker in 1888. Seats at their wedding, to which 5000 people came, were available at five shillings – all the money going to India.

May Bounds. A medical missionary to the people of Mizoram, which lies to the east of Bangladesh. A Welsh Presbyterian nurse, she was called to serve at Durtland Hospital in the middle years of this century.

Angela Georgina, Baroness Burdett-Coutts (1814–1906). She inherited £2 million from her grandfather's second wife and spent the money on good works. For instance, she founded the National Society for the Prevention of Cruelty to Children and the British Goat Society. She also erected the Greyfriars Bobby statue in Edinburgh as well as endowing churches and bishoprics in the colonies, notably in Adelaide, Cape Town and British Columbia.

Ellen (or Nellie) Burleigh. Born in Malta née Gilbert. In 1879 she went to Tierra del Fuego. Married Henry Burleigh of the South American Mission and went with him to the Keppel Islands off the Falklands and from there to Baily Island in the Wollaston Group.

Josephine Butler, née Gray (1828–1906). A lifelong campaigner for women's rights and suffrage, this prominent Anglican laywoman worked for the repeal of the Contagious Diseases Acts which forced medical examinations upon women in seaports and military towns. A pioneer for women's education, she campaigned on behalf of prostitutes, especially in Liverpool.

Mildred Cable (1878–1952). With Francesca and Evangeline French, she crossed the Gobi desert five times and penetrated into deepest Chinese Turkestan. They travelled mainly by night with two specially devised carts which they nicknamed 'The Gobi Express' and 'The Flying Turki'. They continued to travel together after retirement from the China Inland Mission and completed their final journey — to South America — when they were aged 72, 79 and 81 respectively.

Gladys Calliss. Born in 1913 in Australia, she became a soldier in the Salvation Army in her native Australia in 1928 and served as a corps cadet, company guard, cradle roll sergeant, primary sergeant, sunbeam leader and young people's sergeant major before she was twenty. After training in Melbourne, she was a missionary in Indonesia and in Colombo.

Amy Carmichael (1867–1951). She was born into an Irish family of Anti-Burgher Seceders, a group which had separated from the Church of Scotland. She went as a missionary to Japan, China, Ceylon and India, where she spent fifty-three years and established the Dohnavur Fellowship and home for children.

Elsie Chamberlain. A Congregational minister, she became the first woman chaplain of the British Women's Royal Air Force and National President of the Women's Council of the Free Churches. She broadcast regularly with the BBC from 1950 to 1967, and was a director of the London Missionary Society.

Eleanor Chesnut. She went to China as a Presbyterian medical missionary after training at the Women's Medical College in Chicago. She worked in primitive conditions at a hospital in Lien-chou, survived the Boxer Rebellion, but was later murdered during a religious festival in 1905.

Charity Cook (1745–1822). Born in Maryland to Quaker parents, she married her husband Isaac in 1762, had eleven children, became a preacher and travelled through England, Germany and Ireland with two women friends, Sarah Harrison and Mary Swett.

Edith Couche (1878–1960). By her own admission a 'cheerful missionary', she went to China with the Church of England's Zenana Missionary Society. She died in Ireland on her return.

Martha B. Croll. A member of the United Free Church of Scotland in Jamaica, she was born in Aberdeen, went to India in 1891, and thence to Jamaica in 1898. She died in 1906.

Mary E. Darley (1869–1934). Born in Dublin, she was sent as a missionary to China with the Church of England's Zenana Missionary Society. She went to the Kien-ning Prefecture of the Fuh-Kien province in 1897.

Mabel Digby (1835–1910). Born in a strongly Protestant home near Staines and raised in France, she converted to Catholicism and became a nun in 1857. She returned to England and worked at the Sacred Heart convent in Roehampton until called to serve at the Generalate. She eventually became General Superior for sixteen years.

Philippine Duchesne (1769—1852). A Visitation sister in Grenoble before the Revolution, she subsequently founded her own order which amalgamated with the Religious of the Sacred Heart after she met Madeleine-Sophie Barat in 1804. Then in 1818 she set off for America where Louisiana became her mission field.

Janet Erskine Stuart (1857—1914). Born in the Anglican rectory at Cottesmore in Rutland, the youngest of thirteen children, she became a Roman Catholic in 1879 and a Religious of the Sacred Heart two years later. For three years she served as Superior General of her congregation and travelled widely at this time.

Etheria. The first woman travel writer, she retraced the wanderings of the Israelites recorded in the Book of Exodus, including climbing Mount Sinai. Her account of these adventures was copied in the seventh century by a monk called Valerius, and twelve pages of it have been preserved. Her pilgrimage took place between 381 and 384.

Gladwys M. Evans. From 1936, a nurse at Mizo District Mission Hospital in Assam, India, an area the size of her native Wales. A Presbyterian who established health centres in the wake of the Welsh evangelists sent there by her Church.

Mary Fisher. A seventeenth-century Friend who travelled to Barbados and to North Carolina as well as suffering imprisonment in her own country. She was accompanied by Anne Austin, 'a woman well stricken in years' and the mother of five children.

Fidelia Fiske (1816—64). Born in Massachusetts, she travelled to Trebizond in 1842, where the American Mission in Persia had been founded in 1834 among the Nestorians. She wrote *Woman and Her Saviour* in Persia.

Christina Forsyth. Born in 1844, she was widowed after a short marriage. She was sent to Emgwali in East Africa and worked alone for thirty years in an isolated mission station in Fingoland. The Greenock Ladies' Association for Promoting Female Education in Kafaria (founded in 1841) sponsored her work.

Elizabeth Fry (1780—1845). The great Quaker prison reformer was born near Norwich, one of the seven daughters of John Gurney of Earlham. While her work among prisoners in the UK is well known, it should not be forgotten that she also sought to improve the conditions of convicts being sent to the colonies, and notably women sent to Parramatta in Australia.

Marie Gobat (1813—79). Born at Zofingen in Switzerland, she married Samuel Gobat and went with him to Abyssinia with the Church Missionary Society. Samuel became Bishop of Jerusalem in 1849. They worked together there for thirty-three years and died within three months of each other.

Caroline C. Graveson (1874–1958). This Quaker woman gave the Swarthmore lecture on 'Religion and Culture' in 1937. For thirty years she was vice-principal for the women's side at Goldsmith's College, London University, and wrote educational books and children's stories.

Dora Greenwell (1821–82). Born into a prosperous Lancashire family which fell upon hard times, she lived with her mother and wrote extensively. A friend of Josephine Butler, she tackled subjects as varied as the treatment of the insane, single women, Lacordaire, and the Quaker John Woolman, as well as writing spirited theological reflections.

Sarah Grubb (1773–1842). This Quaker woman preacher was born in London, lived in Ireland and died in East Anglia after extensive travels. She preached in markets and in the streets for fifty-two years.

Frances Ridley Havergal (1836–79). The youngest of six children, she was reading the Bible at four, and subsequently learned French, German, Welsh, Hebrew and New Testament Greek. She published over thirty collections of hymns, all characterized by strong scriptural and evangelical influences. She was the daughter of the vicar of Astley in Worcester and, as well as writing her own hymns, edited all his music in 1871.

Hildegard of Bingen (1098–1179). This German woman possessed the gift of prophecy even before entering the convent at the age of eight. Here she saw visions and wrote extensively until her death at the age of eighty.

E. Hope-Bell. Went to China in 1911 with the London Missionary Society where she served for twenty years in the pioneer days of nursing there. For three years she was executive and travelling secretary of the Nurses' Association of China and travelled extensively there and in Japan.

Lady Dorothy Hosie. Born in 1885, the only daughter of the Revd W. E. Scothill, MA, professor of Chinese at Oxford University. Educated at Newnham College, Cambridge, she married in 1913, as his second wife, Sir Alexander Hosie, cultural attaché in Peking. She was a member of the Royal Asiatic Society and a prolific writer and lecturer on Chinese subjects.

Caryll Houselander (1901–54). A prolific Roman Catholic spiritual writer of prose and poetry, this laywoman had profound mystical experiences while still in her teens and an acute sense of the presence of Christ in others.

Mrs Johnston (d. 1811). She married George Johnston of the Wesleyan Missionary Society in 1807 and went with him to Jamaica, where missionaries were not made welcome. They moved on to Dominica, where both died only four years after leaving home.

Dorothy Jones (1802–59). She sailed for Antigua as a Methodist missionary with her husband Thomas in 1824. Their mail boat, the *Maria*, sank and

Thomas died in the shipwreck. She survived and returned home, remarried and worked in the home mission.

Sybil Jones (d. 1873). Her foreign service began when she visited Liberia in 1851. After that, with her husband Eli, she travelled regularly on behalf of the Society of Friends and became the Elizabeth Fry of her day, comforting dying soldiers of the Union Army in the Civil War, and Mrs Lincoln after the President's assassination.

Ann Hasseltine Judson (1789–1826). Born in Bradford, Massachusetts, she joined the Congregationalist Church there in 1806. In 1812 she sailed for Calcutta with her husband, to labour in Burma. They became Baptists and went on to Rangoon, where she died at the age of thirty-six.

Hannah Kilham (1774–1832). Born in Sheffield, she joined the Society of Friends in her late teens and went on to found schools in Britain and Ireland as well as to travel extensively in West Africa. In the words of her biographer, she improved the 'condition, social, moral and spiritual of the Negroes in their own country'.

Isobel Kuhn. The author of eight books of missionary writings, she set up the Rainy Season Bible School which was adjusted to the climate of China where she laboured from 1928 until 1950. Then she moved on to Thailand with her husband, where she died in 1957.

Mary Livingstone (1821–62). Arguably the most famous and the most neglected of missionary wives, she was born to Mary and Robert Moffat in Africa and met David Livingstone, whom she subsequently married, when he came out to work in the mission there. She married him in 1845 and they worked together in Africa until her death in 1862.

Alice Meynell, née Thompson (1847–1922). Born in London, she was reared on the Continent and converted to the Roman Catholic Church. She published volumes of essays such as *Hearts of Controversy* as well as the poetry for which she is better known.

Mary Moffat (1795–1870). Née Smith, she married Robert Moffat and went to Africa with him in 1819, where they laboured together in Kurlimand until 1870 when they returned home and she promptly died.

Helen Barrett Montgomery (1861–1934). A North American Baptist minister and translator of the Bible.

Lucretia Mott (1793–1880). Born to Quaker parents and married to a New York friend called James, she had six children by the time she was thirty-five. They both campaigned against slavery, and Lucretia became a passionate advocate of the rights of women. She was a noted preacher and public speaker.

Florence Nightingale (1820–1910). The English hospital reformer began training as a nurse at Kaiserwerth in 1851. She served as superintendent of a hospital for women in London before taking thirty-eight other nurses off to the Crimea with her in 1854. On her return from Scutari she founded the nursing school at St Thomas's Hospital, London.

Grace Ovenden (1915–55). A Methodist missionary in West Africa, her principal concern was with teacher training.

Jessie Payne. A twentieth-century China missionary who worked with her husband north of Peking.

Irene Petrie. An Anglican who served initially in the home missions, addressing the women at the West Kensington laundry, she went to Kashmir with the Church Missionary Service and laboured in the zenanas there until she died in 1897.

Pandita Ramabai (1858–1920). A Brahmin widow who converted to the Church of England and opened a school for Indian women, initially based in Bombay and then in Poona. She travelled extensively throughout India and translated the Bible into her own language as well as setting up famine relief projects at the Mukti mission. In 1882 she founded a home for widows, most of whom were aged between nine and twelve.

Mary Ridley. She married the first Bishop of Caledonia and worked with him as a Church Missionary Society missionary in the so-called Redskin field of Metlakahtla until her death in 1896.

Maude Royden (1876–1956). Educated at Cheltenham Ladies College and Lady Margaret Hall, she lectured in the Oxford University extension delegacy and devoted her energies to campaigning for women's suffrage and religious and ethical rights. Unable to preach in the Church of England, she was assistant preacher at the City Temple from 1917 to 1920. During the twenties and thirties she travelled in Britain, America, Australia, New Zealand, India and China, campaigning for women and addressing the religious and ethical issues raised by the women's movement.

Joyce Rutherford. The Woman Secretary of the London Missionary Society – which she joined in 1931 – and Secretary of the Candidates Department, she read science at Liverpool University and served as Travelling Secretary of the Student Christian Movement before studying at Mansfield College for ordination.

Dorothy L. Sayers (1893–1957). She read modern languages at Somerville College, Oxford, and went on to write detective stories and translate Dante. Her most celebrated work as a Christian apologist was *A Man Born to Be King*, the radio play which was broadcast by the BBC from 1941 to 1942.

Richenda Scott. Born in 1903, this Quaker woman was chosen to give the Swarthmore lecture on 'Tradition and Experience' in 1964. She worked on the drafting committee for *Advices and Queries* from 1961 to 1967, and wrote extensively about Quaker history, completing a biography of Elizabeth M. Cadbury in 1955.

Ida Sophia Scudder (1870–1960). Born in South India of a Reformed Church medical missionary, she trained as a doctor in the United States and set up a women's hospital at Vellore on her return. She served there for fifty years and saw it become a medical teaching hospital and eventually part of Madras University.

Mary Slessor (1848–1915). From the age of eleven she worked in a weaving factory, hence her reputation as a Dundee mill-girl. In 1876 she went to Calabar in West Africa with the United Presbyterian Church of Scotland. She chose to work in an isolated missionary station with the Okoyong. So great was her influence, especially when she tackled twin killing, human sacrifice and drunkenness, that she was made a local government officer or magistrate by the British Colonial Service.

Betty Stead, MBE. A former mill-girl, she worked with the Methodists as a missioner in Eastern Nigeria after qualifying as a nurse and midwife. She was presented with the MBE by the Governor of Nigeria in Calabar.

Monica Storrs (1888–1967). A Church of England laywoman who went to Peace River in British Columbia. In the words of her biographer, 'her upbringing was clerical and gentle'. In the event she road all over British Columbia, working at the Sunday School by Post scheme developed by Mrs Gwynnes in Saskatchewan in 1905 and also as an active Guider.

Mary Sumner, née Heywood (1829–1921). While studying music in Rome she met George Sumner, married and had three children. He became Vicar of Old Alresford in 1851, and she taught the Sunday school and a men's Bible study group. She founded the Mothers' Union and became its first Diocesan and then Central President when it went world-wide. Her vision was that all classes of women could unite in prayer and do God's will by working for their husbands, children, home and country.

Annie Taylor (b. 1855). Born into a Congregationalist family in Cheshire, she was converted as a young woman and in 1884 she went to China with the China Inland Mission. She became the first European woman ever to enter Tibet, where she worked on her own until her death. The 1,300 mile journey there, in 1892, took seven months and ten days to complete.

Thérèse of Lisieux (1873–97). The French Carmelite nun who wrote her autobiography at the command of her prioress, and whose spiritual teaching is known as the 'Little Way'.

Isabella Thoburn. In the words of Helen Barrett Montgomery, 'she lived and loved and toiled to the women of India for thirty-one years, and here she died'. Isabella was a North American Methodist pioneer in education who had been educated herself at Wheeling Female Seminary and the Art School of Cincinnati.

Elizabeth Marion Thompson. She married Dr James Bowen Thompson and laboured in Syria until she died in 1869.

Tim Oi Li (1907–91). Born in Hong Kong, she became the first woman priest in the Anglican Church when she was ordained in 1944.

Joy Turner (Mrs Alfred E.) Tuggy. Born to missionary parents in Venezuela, she graduated from the Columbia Bible College and its Graduate School of Mission before going off to serve with her husband in 1943. She raised nine children and taught in the Las Delicias Bible Institute in Caripe.

Evelyn Underhill (1875–1941). An Anglican laywoman, spiritual director and retreat conductor, she wrote extensively about mysticism and the spiritual life and appears in the liturgical calender of the Episcopal Church as 'mystic and theologian'.

Helen Waddell (1889–1965). Born in Tokyo to Irish Presbyterian missionary parents, she became a famous scholar and translated many medieval Latin texts as well as the Chinese one given here. She taught at Somerville College and Lady Margaret Hall in Oxford and, briefly, at Bedford College, London. *Lyrics from the Chinese* was her first book, published in 1913. Others included *The Wandering Scholars, Beasts and Saints, The Desert Fathers* and, in 1933, *Peter Abelard*.

Mary Warburton Booth. A member of the Zenana Bible and Medical Mission to India, she ministered extensively to women by offering education and the distribution of Bibles, and also by writing about her work.

Mary Ward (1585–1645). The Yorkshirewoman who founded the Institute of the Blessed Virgin Mary, the first unenclosed order for active apostolic women religious in the Roman Catholic Church. In 1616 she noted that 'women, in time to come, will do much'.

Agnes Weston. With Sophia Wintz she opened the Royal Sailors' Rests at Davenport and Portsmouth. She was known as the 'Sailors' Friend' because of her widespread ministry of letter-writing among them.

Olive Wyon. A laywoman who was directed by Evelyn Underhill during the middle years of this century. She wrote extensively about prayer and the spiritual life and was principal at St Colm's, the Church of Scotland's training college for missionaries, deaconesses and youth workers.

Florence Young. Born at Motueka near Nelson in New Zealand in 1856 and raised in Australia, she worked in the Queensland Kanaka mission in 1886 and then set off for China in 1890, the year of the Boxer Rising. Four years later she was labouring in the Solomon Islands which then remained her mission field.

BIBLIOGRAPHY

A Member of St Julian's Community, *The Notebooks of Florence Allshorn* (London: SCM Press, 1957)

Albright, M. Catharine, *Letters from India* (Birmingham: Cornish Brothers, 1902)

Bacon, Margaret Hope, *As the Way Opens: The Story of Quaker Women in America* (Richmond, Indiana: Friends United Press, 1980)

Bacon, Margaret Hope, *Mothers of Feminism: The Story of Quaker Women in America* (San Francisco: Harper & Row, 1986)

Baker, Sarah S., *Truth and its Triumph* (London: T. Nelson & Sons, 1889)

Balfour, Mrs Clara L., *Women Worth Emulating* (London: Sunday School Union, n.d.)

Barat, Madeleine-Sophie and Philippine Duchesne, *Correspondence: Second Part – I, North America (1818–1821)*, compiled by Jeanne de Charry, RSCJ, translated by Barbara Hogg, RSCJ (Rome: RSCJ, 1989)

Barclay, Florence, *The Following of the Star* (London: G. P. Putnam's Sons, n.d.)

Barclay, Florence, *The Wheels of Time* (London: G. P. Putnam's Sons, 1912)

Barclay, one of her daughters, *The Life of Florence L. Barclay* (London: Putnam & Co., 1921)

Barnett Smith, G., *Eminent Christian Workers of the Nineteenth Century* (London: SPCK, 1893)

Beaver, R. Pierce, *All Loves Excelling: American Protestant Women in World Mission* (Grand Rapids, Michigan: Wm B. Eerdmans Publishing Co., 1968)

Beck, Mary E., *Fresh Diggings from an Old Mine* (London: The Religious Tract Society, n.d.)

Bett, Henry, *Dora Greenwell* (London: Epworth Press, 1950)

Biller, Sarah, (ed.), *Memoir of the Late Hannah Kilham* (London: Darton & Harvey, 1837)

Bishop, Isabella L., *Among the Tibetans* (London: The Religious Tract Society, 1894)

Bliss, Kathleen, *The Future of Religion* (London: C. A. Watts & Co., 1969)

Bliss, Kathleen, *The Service and Status of Women in the Churches* (London: SCM Press, 1952)

Bliss, Kathleen, *We the People* (London: SCM Press, 1963)

Bounds, May and Gladwys M. Evans, *Medical Mission to Mizoram* (Chester: Handbridge, 1986)

Brailsford, Mabel Richmond, *Quaker Women 1650–1690* (London: Duckworth & Co., 1915).

Brock, Mrs Carey, *Sunday Echoes in Weekday Hours* (London: Seeley, Jackson & Halliday, 1878)

Burgess, Alan, *The Small Woman* (London: The Reprint Society, 1959)

Cable, A. Mildred, *The Fulfilment of a Dream* (London: Morgan & Scott, 1917)

Cable, Mildred and Francesca French, *Something Happened* (London: Hodder & Stoughton, 1933)

Cable, Mildred and Francesca French, *The Book Which Demands a Verdict* (London: SCM Press, 1946)

Cable, Mildred and Francesca French, *The Gobi Desert* (London: Hodder & Stoughton, 1942)

Cable, Mildred and Francesca French, *The Making of a Pioneer* (London: Hodder & Stoughton, 1935)

Cable, Mildred and Francesca French, *Through Jade Gate and Central Asia* (London: Hodder & Stoughton, 1927)

Cable, Mildred and Francesca French, *Towards Spiritual Maturity* (London: Hodder & Stoughton, 1939)

Cable, Mildred and Francesca French, *Wall of Spears* (London: Lutterworth Press, 1951)

Cable, Mildred, Evangeline French and Francesca French, *A Desert Journal* (London: Hodder & Stoughton, 1934)

Carmichael, Amy, *Gold Cord* (London: SPCK, 1932)

Carus-Wilson, Mrs Ashley, *Irene Petrie: Missionary to Kashmir* (London: Hodder & Stoughton, 1900)

Cattell, Catherine D., *From Bamboo to Mango* (Oregon: Barclay Press, 1976)

Chantal, Sister F. de, SND, *Julie Billiart and Her Institute* (London: Longmans, Green & Co., 1938)

Chapman, Mrs Paul, *The Life of Our Lord and Saviour Jesus Christ, Simply Told for Children* (London: Henry Frowde, 1904)

Chappell, Jennie, *Agnes Weston, the Sailors' Friend* (London: Pickering & Inglis, n.d.)

Chappell, Jennie, *Three Brave Women: Stories of Heroism in Heathen Lands* (London: Partridge, 1920)

Community of St Mary the Virgin, *A Memoir of Mother Annie Louise* (Wantage: Convent of St Mary the Virgin, 1953)

Couche, Edith, *Lighting Chinese Lanterns* (London: Church of England Zenana Missionary Society, n.d.)

Coutts, Frederick, *More Than One Homeland: The Story of Gladys Calliss* (London: Salvationist Publishing, 1981)

Darley, Mary E., *The Light of the Morning* (London: Church of England Zenana Missionary Society, 1903)

Dawson, E. C., *Missionary Heroines in Many Lands* (London: Seeley, Service & Co., 1912)

Dawson, E. C., *Missionary Heroines of the Cross* (London: Seeley, Service & Co., 1930)

Deen, Edith, *Great Women of Faith* (London: Independent Press, 1959)

Dennison, Dorothy, *The First Wantoknow Omnibus for Girls* (London: Paternoster Press, 1946)

Douglas Cochrane, Jeanie, *Peerless Women: A Book for Girls* (London: Collins, n.d.)

Dover, Irene, *Stories from India* (London: Poona & Indian Village Mission, n.d.)

Dyer, Helen S., *Pandita Ramubai: A Great Life in Indian Missions* (London: Pickering & Inglis, 1929)

Eckenstein, Lina, *The Women of Early Christianity* (London: Faith Press, 1935)

Enock, Esther E., *The Missionary Heroine of Calabar: A Story of Mary Slessor* (London: Pickering & Inglis, n.d.)

Exchange, Journal of Missiology and Ecumenical Research, vol. 21, 1992.

Fawcett, Millicent G. and E. M. Turner, *Josephine Butler* (London: The Association for Moral & Social Hygiene, 1927)

Friends Foreign Mission Association, *Biographies* (London: Friends Foreign Mission Association, 1916)

Graveson, Caroline C., *Religion and Culture: Swarthmore Lecture 1937* (London: George Allen & Unwin, 1937)

Greene, Dana, (ed.), *Lucretia Mott: Her Complete Speeches and Sermons* (New York & Toronto: Edwin Mellen Press, 1980)

Greenwell, Dora, *Two Friends* (London: Epworth Press, 1952)

Greenwood, John Ormerod, *Quaker Encounters*, vol. 1: *Vines on the Mountains* (York: William Sessions, 1977)

Greenwood, John Ormerod, *Quaker Encounters*, vol. 2: *Whispers of Truth* (York: William Sessions Limited, 1978)

Grubb, Sarah, *A Selection from the Letters of the Late Sarah Grubb* (Sudbury: J. Wright, 1848)

Gurney, Elizabeth, *Elizabeth Fry's Journeys 1840–1841* (London: The Bodley Head, 1931)

Hare, Lloyd C. M., *The Greatest American Woman: Lucretia Mott* (New York: The American Historical Society, 1937)

Harton, Sibyl, *Stars Appearing: Lives of Sixty-Eight Saints of the Anglican Calendar* (London: Hodder & Stoughton, 1954)

Havergal, Frances Ridley, *The Poetical Works* (London: James Nisbet & Co., n.d.)

Havergal, Frances Ridley, *Under His Shadow* (London: James Nisbet & Co., 1885)

Havergal, Maria V. G., *Memorials of Frances Ridley Havergal* (New York: Anson D. F. Randolph & Co., 1880)

Hinton, Mrs W. H., *Ethel Ambrose: Pioneer Medical Missionary* (London: Marshall, Morgan & Scott, n.d.)

Hosie, Lady, *Jesus and Women* (London: Hodder & Stoughton, 1946)

Houselander, Caryll, *The Stations of the Cross* (London: Sheed & Ward, 1955)

Howard, Elizabeth Fox, (ed.), *Friends Fellowship Papers 1921* (London: Religious Society of Friends, 1921)

Johnson, Dale A., *Women in English Religion 1700–1925* (New York & Toronto: Edwin Mellen Press, 1983)

Johnson, Joseph, *Brave Women and Their Deeds of Heroism* (London: Gall & Inglis, n.d.)

Johnson, Joseph, *Noble Women of Our Time* (London: T. Nelson, 1886)

Koehler, Lyle, *A Search for Power: The Weaker Sex in Seventeenth-Century New England* (Urbana: University of Illinois Press, 1980)

Kuhn, Isobel, *Nests Above the Abyss* (London: China Inland Mission, 1949)

Larsson, Flora, *My Best Men are Women* (London: Hodder & Stoughton, 1974)

Lisieux, St Thérèse of, *Collected Letters of Saint Thérèse of Lisieux* (London: Sheed & Ward, 1949)

Livingstone, W. P., *Christina Forsyth of Fingoland* (London: Hodder & Stoughton, n.d.)

Livingstone, W. P., *Mary Slessor, Pioneer Missionary* (London: Hodder & Stoughton, 1915)

Livingstone, W. P. *The White Queen of Okoyong* (London: Hodder & Stoughton, n.d.)

Lloyd, J. Meirion, *Nine Missionary Pioneers* (Caenarfon: Mission Board, 1989)

Maleissye, Marie-Therese de, FMM, *Femmes en Mission: Actes de la XIe Session du CREDIC à Saint Flour* (Lyons: Editions Lyonnaises d'Art et d'Histoire, 1991)

Malmgreen, Gail, (ed.), *Religion in the Lives of English Women 1760–1930* (London & Sydney: Croom Helm, 1986)

Menzies, Lucy, *Collected Papers of Evelyn Underhill* (London: Longmans, Green & Co. 1946)

Meynell, Alice, *Poems* (London: Burns & Oates, 1913)

Monahan, Maud, *The Life and Letters of Janet Erskine Stuart* (London: Longmans, 1922)

Montgomery, Helen Barrett, *Western Women in Eastern Lands* (New York: Macmillan, 1911)

Morton, W. L., *God's Galloping Girl: The Peace River Diaries of Monica Storrs, 1929–1931* (Vancouver: University of British Columbia Press, 1979)

Neill, Stephen, A History of Christian Missions (London: Hodder & Stoughton, 1964)

Newlin, Algie I., Charity Cook: A Liberated Woman (Richmond, Indiana: Friends United Press, 1981)

O'Connor, Sister M. Clare, FCJ, The Sisters Faithful Companions of Jesus in Australia (Victoria: Faithful Companions of Jesus, 1982)

Oldham, J. H., Florence Allshorn and the Story of St Julian's (London: SCM Press, 1951)

One of her Daughters, The Life of Florence L. Barclay (London: Putnam & Co., 1921)

Orchard, M. Emmanuel, IBVM, (ed.), Till God Will: Mary Ward Through Her Writings (London: Darton, Longman & Todd, 1985)

Parbury, Kathleen, Women of Grace: A Biographical Dictionary and Gazetteer (Stocksfield: Oriel Press, 1985)

Payne, Jessie, The Very Heart of China (London: The Carey Press, n.d.)

Penstone, Miss M. M., and Mrs M. V. Hughes, The Story of Christ's First Missioners (London: National Society's Depository, n.d.)

Phillips, Catherine, Memoirs of the Life of Catherine Phillips to which are added some of her Epistles (London: James Phillips & Son, 1797)

Pitman, Mrs E. R., Lady Missionaries in Foreign Lands (London: S. W. Partridge, n.d.)

Platt, W. J., Three Women (London: Hodder & Stoughton, 1964)

Pollen, Anne, Mother Mabel Digby (London: John Murray, 1914)

Robinson, Jane, Wayward Women (Oxford: Oxford University Press, 1990)

Robson, Isabel S., Two Lady Missionaries in Tibet (London: S. W. Partridge, n.d.)

Ross, Isabel, Margaret Fell: Mother of Quakerism (London: Longmans, Green & Co., 1949)

Royden, Maude A., Prayer as a Force (London: G. P. Putnam's Sons, 1922)

Sayers, Dorothy L., Creed or Chaos? (London: Methuen & Co., 1947)

Sayers, Dorothy L., Unpopular Opinions (London: Victor Gollancz, 1946)

Scott, Richenda, Tradition and Experience: Swarthmore Lecture 1964 (London: George Allen & Unwin, 1964)

Selleck, George, Quakers in Boston 1656–1964 (Cambridge, Mass.: Friends Meeting, 1976)

Sheldon, Jane, (ed.), Women Talking: A Handbook for Women's Meetings (London: James Clarke & Co., 1945)

Singmaster, Elsie, A Cloud of Witnesses (Cambridge, Mass., The Central Committee of the United Study of Foreign Missions, 1930)

Smith, Hilda L., and Susan Cardinale, Women and the Literature of the Seventeenth Century (New York: Greenwood Press, 1990)

Smith, Solveig, By Love Compelled: The Story of the Salvation Army in India and Adjacent Countries (London: Salvationist Publishing, 1981)

Stock, Sarah Geraldine, *Missionary Heroes of Africa* (London: London Missionary Society, 1897)

Strachey, Ray, *A Quaker Grandmother: Hannah Whitall Smith* (London: Fleming H. Revell Co., 1914)

Telford, John, *Women in the Mission Field* (London: Charles H. Kelly, 1895)

Thomson, D. P., *Women of the Scottish Church* (Printed by Munro & Scott, Perth, 1975)

Tim Oi Li, Florence, with Ted Harrison, *Much Beloved Daughter* (London: Darton, Longman & Todd, 1985)

Todd, Janet, *Dictionary of British Women Writers* (London: Routledge, 1991)

Tucker, Ruth A., *Guardians of the Great Commission* (Grand Rapids, Michigan: Academie Books, 1988)

Turner Tuggy, Joy, *The Missionary Wife and Her Work* (Chicago: Moody Press, 1966)

Uglow, Jennifer, *The Macmillan Dictionary of Women's Biography*, 2nd edition (London: Macmillan Press, 1992)

Underhill, Evelyn, *The Mystics of the Church* (London: James Clarke, 1930)

Utuk, Efiong, *From New York to Ibadan* (New York: Peter Lang, 1991)

Waddell, Helen, *Lyrics from the Chinese* (London: Constable & Co., 1938)

Warburton Booth, Mary, *My Testimony* (London: Pickering & Inglis, 1947)

Warburton Booth, Mary, *'Them Also'* (London: Pickering & Inglis, 1934)

Warburton Booth, Mary, *These Things Have I Seen* (London: Pickering & Inglis, n.d.)

Warburton Booth, Mary, *'They That Sow'* (London: Pickering & Inglis, n.d.)

Warburton Booth, Mary, *'Whosoever Shall Receive'* (London: Marshall Morgan & Scott, 1929)

Webb, Pauline M., *Women of Our Company* (London: Cargate Press, 1958)

Webb, Pauline M., *Women of Our Time* (London: Cargate Press, 1963)

Wilson-Carmichael, Amy, *Lotus Buds* (London: Morgan & Scott, 1909)

Wyon, Olive, *Desire for God* (London: Collins, 1963)

Wyon, Olive, *Living Springs* (London: SCM Press, 1963)

Wyon, Olive, *On the Way* (London: SCM Press, 1958)

Wyon, Olive, *Prayer* (London: Collins, 1962)

Wyon, Olive, *The Altar Fire* (London: SCM Press, 1954).

Wyon, Olive, *The School of Prayer* (London: SCM Press, 1943)

Young, Florence S. H., *Pearls From the Pacific* (London: Marshall Brothers, n.d.)

INDEX